Analyzing Language in Restricted Domains:

Sublanguage Description and Processing

Analyzing Language in Restricted Domains:

Sublanguage Description and Processing

edited by

Ralph Grishman
New York University

Richard Kittredge
University of Montreal

LAWRENCE ERLBAUM ASSOCIATES, PUBLISHERS
1986   Hillsdale, New Jersey   London

Lawrence Erlbaum Associates, Inc., Publishers
365 Broadway
Hillsdale, New Jersey 07642

Library of Congress Cataloging-in-Publication Data
Main entry under title:

Analyzing language in restricted domains.

   Bibliography: p.
   Includes index.
   1. Sublanguage — Data processing — Addresses, essays,
lectures. I. Grishman, Ralph. II. Kittredge, Richard,
1941–
P120.S9A53 1986   001.53′5   85-12850
ISBN 0-89859-620-3

Printed in the United States of America
10   9   8   7   6   5   4   3   2   1

Contents

List of Contributors

Ralph Grishman
Courant Institute of Mathematical
  Sciences
New York University
251 Mercer Street
New York, NY 10012

Richard Kittredge
Département de Linguistique
Université de Montréal
C. P. 6128
Montréal
Quebec, Canada H3C 3J7

• • •

Robert A. Amsler
Bell Communications Research
445 South Street
Morristown, NJ 07960

Joan Bachenko
AT&T Bell Laboratories
600 Mountain Avenue
Murray Hill, NJ 07974

George Dunham
Laboratory of Statistical and
  Mathematical Methodology
Division of Computer Research
  and Technology
National Institutes of Health
Bethesda, MD 20205

Timothy W. Finin
Dept. Computer and
  Information Science
School of Engineering and
  Applied Science
University of Pennsylvania
Philadelphia, PA 19104

Eileen Fitzpatrick
695 Washington Street
New York, NY 10014

Carol Friedman
Courant Institute of Mathematical
  Sciences
New York University
251 Mercer Street
New York, NY 10012

Bonnie Glover
Logicon, Inc., Operating Systems
  Division
6300 Variel Avenue
Woodland Hills, CA 91367

Don Hindle
AT&T Bell Laboratories
600 Mountain Avenue
Murray Hill, NJ 07974

Lynette Hirschman
System Development Corporation,
  A Burroughs Company
Research and Development Division
PO Box 517
Paoli, PA 19301

Jerry R. Hobbs
SRI International
333 Ravenswood Ave.
Menlo Park, CA 94025

John Lehrberger
56 89th Avenue
Chomedy, Laval
Quebec, Canada H7W-3G8

Elaine Marsh
Navy Center for Applied Research in
  Artificial Intelligence
Code 7510, Naval Research Laboratory
Washington, DC 20375

Christine Montgomery
Logicon, Inc., Operating Systems
  Division
6300 Variel Avenue
Woodland Hills, CA 91367

Naomi Sager
Courant Institute of Mathematical
  Sciences
New York University
251 Mercer Street
New York, NY 10012

Jonathan Slocum
Microelectronics and Computer
  Technology Corporation
9430 Research Blvd.
Echelon Building #1, Suite 200
Austin, Texas 78759

Donald Walker
Bell Communications Research
445 South Street
Morristown, NJ 07960

Preface

Successful computer processing of natural language requires detailed knowledge of the language at many levels: lexicon, syntax, semantics, discourse, etc. Providing the linguistic knowledge for an entire language is truly a staggering task. In fact, no single human language has yet been fully described in a form usable by computers. Fortunately, many language processing problems are effectively restricted to the language used in a particular domain, where all this knowledge can be more readily obtained. The variety of language used in a given science or technology not only is much smaller than the whole language, but is also more clearly systematic in structure and meaning. These considerations have motivated linguists and computer scientists to collaborate in studying the properties of such specialized languages, which have come to be called *sublanguages*.

The term sublanguage has gained widespread acceptance among computational linguists only recently, and a lively debate is now underway concerning its proper definition. For most of the authors represented in this collection, the term suggests a subsystem of language that behaves essentially like the whole language, while being limited in reference to a specific subject domain. In particular, each sublanguage has a distinctive grammar, which can profitably be described and used to solve specific language-processing problems.

It is the overriding concern with grammatical subsystems and their use in language processing that distinguishes current sublanguage research from earlier investigations of domain-restricted language. Most of the work reported here was done by computational linguists faced with the need to write grammars that accurately and efficiently describe the language of science and technology in such fields as aeronautics, electronics, pharmacology and medicine.

Although the authors have all worked extensively in applied natural language processing, they approach sublanguage from the varied perspectives of artificial intelligence, information science and linguistics. Within artificial intelligence, sublanguage study offers a linguistic basis for describing many kinds of domain-dependent knowledge, such as type hierarchies. Furthermore, sublanguage grammars encode the kinds of domain-dependent semantic distinctions needed for sentence disambiguation, lexical transfer for machine translation, and many other tasks within applied systems. In the particular case of expert systems that communicate with specialists, sublanguage grammars are needed to guide the analysis of queries and the synthesis of explanations with the appropriate linguistic usage.

Within information science, sublanguage techniques have proven effective for the analysis, formatting, dissemination and retrieval of textual information. And it is within sublanguages that some progress can be envisioned in the difficult area of automatic abstracting.

In theoretical linguistics, the importance of sublanguage is only now beginning to be appreciated. Even if sublanguage grammars can be related to the grammar of the full standard language, sublanguages behave in many ways like autonomous systems. As such, they take on theoretical interest as microcosms of the whole language. In particular, the theoretical problem of relating linguistic form to communicative function comes into sharper focus when individual sublanguages are examined.

More than one of the authors in this volume has mentioned the relationship between sublanguage research and current investigations into language for special purposes (LSP). Although LSP work has historically had different practical goals, such as language pedagogy and document design, many possibilities exist for a symbiotic relationship. Sublanguage research stands to gain from the data and insights provided by LSP endeavors; in exchange it offers to strengthen the theoretical foundation of LSP through a better understanding of sublanguage grammars.

ORGANIZATION OF THIS VOLUME

The papers collected in this volume were presented at the Workshop on Sublanguage, held at New York University on January 19-20, 1984. The purpose of the workshop was to bring together leading North American researchers in the field of computational linguistics who have substantial experience in one or more of the following areas:

The general theory and description of sublanguage as a linguistic phenomenon,

the linguistic description and computer processing of particular sublanguages, the automation of procedures for discovering and describing the particular syntactic, semantic and lexical properties of individual sublanguages.

Although most of the papers do not deal exclusively with only one of these areas, our grouping in this volume (and at the conference) reflects the primary concern of each author's contribution.

The first chapter in the theoretical section of this volume is Naomi Sager's keynote talk, "Sublanguage: Linguistic Phenomenon, Computational Tool." Sager's major concern is with using linguistic methods to reveal the close correspondence between grammatical organization of a sublanguage (including facts about word distribution) and the information-bearing properties of that same sublanguage. Her definitions of sublanguage and analysis methods are based on more than 15 years' experience in sublanguage research, especially in the fields of medicine and pharmacology. One of the significant contributions of the work reported here is a method for measuring the amount and complexity of information contained in a sublanguage. By way of example, Sager compares two sublanguages from the medical domain with respect to their information density and complexity, using such parameters as the frequency and distribution of operator words in sentences.

The second author concerned primarily with sublanguage theory is John Lehrberger. "Sublanguage Analysis" presents a rather abstract and algebraic view of the field, focusing primarily on the relation of individual sublanguages to the standard language. One of Lehrberger's primary analysis tools is the paraphrase relation, and the analysis of the ways in which sublanguage sentences may be paraphrased in the standard language. Another concern here is with the notion of "formattability" of sublanguages (and its use as a means of comparing sublanguages). A third topic discussed is the distinction between natural and artificial or constructed sublanguages, with particular concern for the sublanguages that are found in the domains of mathematics and computer science. Lehrberger's discussion of these topics poses a large and intriguing set of questions that should be of special interest to theoretical linguists.

Another chapter with a theoretical perspective is "The Status of Telegraphic Sublanguages" by Fitzpatrick, Bachenko and Hindle. The primary question this chapter raises is whether sublanguages can be considered as relatively independent syntactic systems with internal consistency, or whether sublanguage syntax must be described in reference to the standard language. The authors use two phenomena in the telegraphic sublanguage of equipment casualty reports to support the former hypothesis. This contrasts with the more frequently espoused view, which can be discerned in a number of other papers in this volume. Clearly this question is of both theoretical and practical importance and constitutes one of the major issues to which we return later.

The fourth and final paper from the theoretical session is Jerry Hobbs' "Sublanguage and Knowledge." This chapter represents a point of view on sublanguage markedly different from most of the other papers in this volume. It does not take as primary data linguistic usage, but rather the knowledge behind that usage. In particular, Hobbs shows how the linguistic presuppositions that must be used to understand certain sentences can guide the selection of facts to be added to a knowledge base. The knowledge base is part of an information retrieval system that matches the semantic structure of queries to relevant parts of a semantically coded medical reference text. Hobbs argues that the kind of axiomatization approach he proposes is necessary for stating critical relationships between facts (in the knowledge base). Although some axioms of knowledge have direct counterparts in terms of sublanguage selection statements, certain more complex statements seem to require the expressive power of first-order logic, which has no obvious equivalent in sublanguage description. Furthermore, argues Hobbs, sublanguage description is often complicated by cases of metonymy (see also the chapter by Hirschman), which must be regularized by an appeal to common sense or expert knowledge.

The second, and largest, group of papers are united in their primary concern with linguistic data in the context of applied language processing systems. Although important theoretical questions are raised in this section as well, their overriding preoccupation with practical problems has dictated this grouping.

First among the "applied" papers is the report by Walker and Amsler on "The Use of Machine-Readable Dictionaries in Sublanguage Analysis." Here, the authors report on a system that determines the subject domain of newspaper articles by using the semantic codes available in a large machine-readable dictionary. To the extent that the article represents a single domain, it is usually possible to determine the domain (and hence disambiguate most polysemous words) by statistical procedures. Extensions of this approach to technical sublanguages and refinements in the semantic marking system are discussed. Although many problems remain in providing and refining the data necessary to apply this approach on a high-volume basis, it is almost certain that near-term applications exist.

Carol Friedman's "Sublanguage Text Processing — Application to Medical Narrative" gives a very detailed account of the use of distributional techniques for setting up a sublanguage grammar and for converting text (in the domain of clinical records) to a structured data form. Each sentence pattern is mapped to a separate information format, with the result that the formatted natural language data can be queried in relational database systems. This chapter will be particularly useful for readers who are not already familiar with the details of the method of information formatting practiced by NYU's Linguistic String Project.

One chapter included in the applied section is actually a generalization of work carried out in at least two domains. Elaine Marsh reports on "General Semantic Patterns in Different Sublanguages," drawing on the experience of the NYU group in analyzing medical discharge summaries, as well as her more recent participation in a project for processing equipment casualty reports. After giving a detailed account of the semantic patterns found in reports on equipment failures, she compares those patterns with the medical reports on human health maintenance, aiming to describe a higher level "domain of failures." She also notes some similarities to a special-purpose programming language used to describe requirements for automatic test equipment. Marsh concludes by comparing the semantic patterns of sublanguages with the frame and script structures used in knowledge representation work. It may be interesting for the reader to compare Marsh's view of sublanguage structures as knowledge representations with Hobbs' claims, cited previously.

In "A Sublanguage for Reporting and Analysis of Space Events," Christine Montgomery and Bonnie Glover describe a sublanguage that functions as a medium for communicating both factual reports about space vehicle events (launches, re-entries, etc.) and analytical comments about those events. These two levels of space event discourse, the report level and meta level of commentary on the reports, have distinct linguistic properties, giving rise to the question of whether one or two sublanguages are present. The authors also deal extensively with the problem of representing different levels of meta-event in the space event reports, where different degrees of confidence may be assigned to statements, depending on whether they constitute direct or indirect reports.

Tim Finin's chapter on "Constraining the Interpretation of Nominal Compounds in a Limited Context" is a continuation of work carried out on the UNCLE system, in which semantic interpretations were built for nominal compounds in a technical domain. Here, Finin introduces the use of discourse context as a way of filtering the many possible interpretations for compounds. Whereas earlier work focused on three types of local rules that use lexical information to interpret nominals, Finin now proposes to add rules that treat nominals as referring expressions and use discourse constraints on reference to establish the most likely connection between previously mentioned objects and a newly introduced object.

George Dunham presents an unusual sublanguage case study in "The Role of Syntax in the Sublanguage of Medical Diagnostic Statements." In this written sublanguage, typical syntactic constructions are limited in usage, but certain sublanguage-specific devices are prominent. The sublanguage is telegraphic (lacking true verbs, for example) and makes heavy use of nominalizations. This case is particularly interesting, Dunham says, because it shows how the typical role of syntax as a framework for semantic interpretation is taken over by pragmatically based discourse rules. He goes on to sketch some of the semantic rules for this sublanguage in a higher-order logic.

The third topic area of this book involves discovery procedures for sublanguages and sublanguage properties. First, Jonathan Slocum presents his quantitative work on identifying and adapting to a sublanguage's syntactic properties. Slocum compares two distinct varieties of text (German technical manuals and sales brochures) by measuring the number of rule applications made by the analysis grammar of a large automatic translation system. Measures based on automatic rule applications are also used to check the amount of variation among different samples of the same type of text. Slocum proposes to use the characteristic frequency of rule applications in each type of text to assign weights to syntactic rules differently when processing different sublanguages, thus increasing the likelihood that the preferred parse for the analyzer is the correct one. These same data on frequency can serve as a basis for dynamically "guessing" the type of text in which an analyzer begins to parse.

A more general approach to the discovery problem is outlined by Lynette Hirschman in "Discovering Sublanguage Structures." Hirschman considers the "portability problem" (adapting existing systems to new domains) to be critical, now that limited-domain systems have had some initial success. If some of the characteristics of a new sublanguage can be discovered automatically, then the considerable effort of describing a new domain can be reduced. Hirschman reviews some recent work in the automatic acquisition of sublanguage semantic classes using clustering techniques and points out some of the unsolved problems and limitations of a statistical approach. She discusses the problem of circularity, which arises from the attempt to automate discovery procedures (i.e., we need the grammar to fully automate the discovery process, whose goal is to establish the grammar). The solution must involve "bootstrapping" through successive iterations. It is important to note that Hirschman's view of sublanguage grammar is much more semantic than Slocum's, concerning as it does semantic word class co-occurrence.

Some Major Issues in Sublanguage Theory and Applications

A number of theoretical and practical issues cut across the grouping just described. Perhaps the most general of these is how sublanguages, viewed as linguistic systems, relate to the much larger system of standard language. Only Lehrberger discusses this question directly and at length. But several authors, including Sager, Fitzpatrick et al., Marsh, Slocum and Hirschman, provide some relevant insights. Most authors take the view that sublanguages, despite the occurrence of specialized structures, can be viewed as derivable (through general types of deletion, etc.) from the standard language, at least on the syntactic level. If Fitzpatrick et al. are correct in their opposing view, then organizational principles for each sublanguage must be considered as possibly specialized. This would give a more pessimistic outlook on the possibility of "porting" sublanguage systems to new domains.

A second theoretical problem with practical consequences for computational linguistics is the relationship between sublanguage syntax and semantics. In many of the sublanguages discussed, syntactic information seems to be too impoverished to play a primary role in analysis (cf. Dunham, Finin, Hobbs). The problem of compound nominals is a case in point. These authors stress the need for using not only semantic class information, but also information from discourse context, to establish the proper meaning relationship between words found in text. Many of the other authors (cf. Sager, Marsh, Fitzpatrick et al., Friedman), while not discounting the interest of other information, seem to indicate that the data from word distribution (essentially syntactic information) can reveal enough semantic information (through word grouping) to clarify most of the problems of meaning relationship. To some extent, the conflicting views may be a function of the authors' different processing goals.

DISCUSSION QUESTIONS

During the discussion period of the conference, participants were asked to express their views on a number of questions (selected in advance) of practical importance.

1. There was general agreement that, except for highly circumscribed sublanguages such as weather reports, we are currently not able to obtain correct sentence analyses with high reliability. (By this, we mean the correct determination of all operator-operand and host-adjunct patterns for at least 90% of the sentences in a text.) Reaching this goal is important if we are to develop useful applications involving more complex sublanguages. Is there any clear evidence of progress in this direction?

The discussion of this question raised a number of points:

There are a growing number of sublanguages that can be analyzed with some success, if not high reliability—medical discharge summaries, equipment failure reports, maintenance manuals, intelligence reports. Slocum, in particular, cites performance in the 80% range on telephone system manuals.

There are problems of scale in achieving this objective. Substantial work in analyzing the lexical, syntactic and semantic properties of sublanguages has been required to achieve even the current measure of success. Much more work will be needed to develop these systems further for complex domains.

The steady improvement in "question-answering systems" (natural language database interfaces) gives hope of similar progress in sublanguage text analysis; however, text analysis is more difficult, and so success here will be slower in coming.

Even when no complete sentence analysis can be obtained, useful processing (e.g., generation of information formats) can be done using sentence portions that can be analyzed.

Progress in sublanguage analysis cannot be gauged by success in parsing alone. There has been much greater progress in the last few years, for example, in understanding how to represent the information in a sublanguage text in a database.

2. What information about a sublanguage and its domain is needed to attain the goal of reliable correct sentence analysis?

The general answer of the discussants was "everything," including the lexical, syntactic, semantic, and discourse properties of the sublanguage. The papers of the workshop focused largely on syntactic and semantic properties; much of the exchange in the discussion session was on the use of discourse properties. Among the issues raised were: (a) the need for discourse analysis to handle anaphora; (b) the need for an understanding of discourse structure in order to generate text; (c) representation of different levels of discourse structure: paragraph structure, "top level" macrostructure, etc.; (d) different types of discourse constraints: continuity of focus, parallelism between sentences, etc.

It was agreed that although discourse properties will be important for sublanguage analysis, they are as yet poorly understood by comparison with syntactic and semantic properties. In particular, it is unclear how to use feedback from discourse analysis in order to increase the reliability with which we understand individual sentences. The one suggestion in this regard was that texts with different sections in different styles (e.g., manuals with descriptive sections and sets of instructions) have different grammars for different styles.

The discussion also turned to the issue of which properties might be shared by different sublanguages. It was suggested that texts concerning the same domain should share vocabulary and semantic patterns, while those involving the same function (e.g., telegraphic messages, sets of instructions) should share syntactic characteristics.

3. Can sublanguage characteristics be discovered in an automatic or semi-automatic fashion for a new domain?

The chapters by Slocum and Hirschman describe initial efforts at developing such discovery procedures. One problem brought out in the discussion of these papers concerns circularity: one needs good sentence analyses in order to compute sublanguage properties, and one needs to know sublanguage properties in order to obtain good sentence analyses. It was suggested that this circle might be broken by identifying "unproblematic" sentences within a corpus — say, those that can be unambiguously parsed without sublanguage information — and using them to start the discovery process.

The discussion of discovery procedures also brought out the trade-offs between simpler constraints and more powerful ones. Simpler constraints, such as word selection constraints, are relatively easy to discover for new domains and are also straightforward to represent and use in processing systems. But the representations and processing strategies used for these simpler constraints are too weak to deal with such phenomena as sublanguage-dependent presupposition. Presupposition requires more complex representation schemes (such as the first-order logic proposed by Hobbs) and computationally more expensive processing strategies. Much more experience is needed before the roles and relative advantages of various formalisms can be assessed.

ACKNOWLEDGMENT

The Workshop on Sublanguage Description and Processing, at which the papers in this volume were presented, was supported in part by a grant to New York University from the National Science Foundation, Division of Mathematics and Computer Science (grant NSF-MCS-83-01197).

1 Sublanguage: Linguistic Phenomenon, Computational Tool

Naomi Sager
Linguistic String Project
Courant Institute of Mathematical Sciences
New York University

ABSTRACT

A sublanguage is characterized by distinctive specializations of syntax and the occurrence of domain-specific word subclasses in particular syntactic combinations. The Linguistic String Project of New York University has studied several sublanguages in detail over the past 15 years and developed computer methods for obtaining the relevant word classes and relations from samples of syntactically analyzed domain sentences. The methods are illustrated in application to articles in the lipoprotein literature. It has also proved possible to measure such features as the quantity, density, and complexity of information in the sentences of contrasting sublanguages.

The special word-classes and relations of a particular sublanguage provide the basis for a variety of natural language processing applications that would not be practicable in the language as a whole. For example, it is possible (with difficulty) to process full texts in a sublanguage and convert the free-text information into a structured form suitable for fact retrieval and data summarization. The information structures arrived at in such processing are similar in certain respects to data models used in database management systems, and suggest the possibility of adapting such systems for the management of natural language-derived databases.

INTRODUCTION

Without language there would be culture, no means of recording and transmitting the knowledge necessary to survival, nor the means to register, hence to develop, thought. Here, we consider the ability of language to carry information. In the use of language within specific (primarily technical) domains (Kittredge & Lehrberger, 1982), it is a highly developed, highly specialized tool, an essential part of the very technology its role is to record. Yet in considering the use of language within specialized areas of knowledge, where it is stripped of literary niceties and totally dedicated to the communication of information, we also have the opportunity to witness in a relatively pure form some of the mechanisms by which language fulfills its broader function of transmitting all verbal culture.

For example, the grammar of the language as a whole has numerous instances of compacting by deletion ("zeroing") where a shorter, less regular sentence form is created that is paraphrastic to the fuller form. (*It is considered to be harmless ↔ It is considered harmless*). Various sublanguages make extensive use of this process, presenting so-called ill-formed input to language processing programs, that is, syntactic forms that are not found as sentences in the language as whole. In a sublanguage text it is clear that a dropped word in such a form is the one that would occur in the corresponding position in the fuller sentence using the same words (e.g. *patient* as subject of the occurrence *is on folic acid* in the sublanguage of patient documents). Because the word classes and patterns of word-class occurrence are more narrowly defined in a sublanguage, with clear semantic values attaching to each syntactic position within a form, we see more sharply than in the language as a whole how departures from regularity are made possible by the existence of linguistic expectations as to which words combine to make well-formed ocurrences in the language of the discourse.

Thus, while our concern in sublanguages is with the restricted use of language in narrow domains, our studies also cast light on processes that are at work in the language as a whole.

FUNDAMENTAL CONCEPTS

Definition of Sublanguage

What is a sublanguage; how is it defined? Informally, we can define a sublanguage as the language used by a particular community of speakers, say, those concerned with a particular subject matter or those engaged in a specialized occupation (Bross, Shapiro & Anderson, 1972). This corresponds to the way a language is identified as the mutually understandable verbal communication of some community, often geographically bounded. Faced with the difficult problem of defining the boundaries of a given sublanguage, we may take comfort in the fact that even whole natural languages sometimes have fuzzy edges, seen in the shading of dialects across border areas and in the uncertainties as to what constitutes a well-formed sentence within a well-defined language like English in some cases.

A technical approach to language definition defines a language as the set of all sentences than can be generated by its associated grammar. In the case of artificial languages, the grammars can be stated as a set of formal definitions. In the case of natural languages, we may aim for a formal generating grammar similar to those used to define artificial languages; but whatever the formal constructs are, they must generate just those sentences that a native speaker accepts as belonging to the language.

A formal characterization of a whole language requires at least two levels of word classification. Gross syntactic formulas for well-formed sentences are obtained in terms of categories such as noun, verb, adjective (defined in part on morphological grounds); a more refined syntactic characterization uses grammatical subclasses, such as singular, plural, count-noun, etc. The subclasses are grammatical because, regardless of the particular words that satisfy a gross syntactic formula, whether they make a sensible utterance or not, an educated speaker will by and large reject as incorrect an occurrence that violates the stated well-formed combinations of the grammatical subclasses in a given syntactic formula (*The book was interesting, *Book was interesting, *The book were interesting*).

But, as is well known, this two-level grammatical characterization still leaves untreated a major feature of natural language, the fact that for a given sentence form, say a simple NOUN-VERB-NOUN (subject-verb-object) form, not every sentence obtained by substituting a class member for the class symbol in the syntactic formula constitutes an equally acceptable sentence of the language, even if the substituted words satisfy all grammatical subclass constraints (*John loves Mary, Misery loves Company, Company loves misery, Clouds love chocolate, etc.*). This is the phenomenon known linguistically as *selection*.

The distinguishing feature of sublanguage is that over certain subsets of the sentences of the language the phenomenon of selection, for which rules cannot be stated for the language as a whole, is brought under the rubric of grammar. In a sublanguage, selectional word classes have relatively sharp boundaries, reflecting the division of real world objects into classes that are sharply differentiated in the domain. Refined syntactic formulas stated in terms of these classes reflect the types of relations the objects named in these classes can have to each other and thereby provide a semantic characterization of the discourse in the given domain, using grammatical methods of description.

Sublanguage Grammar

The restrictions on word combination on the sublanguage level are grammatical in the sense that a speaker of the sublanguage can say with reasonable assurance whether a given sentence is a *possible* utterance in a discourse in the given area, independently of whether it is true or false. The more structured the knowledge in a given area, the sharper the constraints on what can reasonably be said. Hence, the sublanguage phenomenon is most marked in scientific and technical areas, where the discourse proceeds on the basis of some body of already well-established laws or practices.

Although the sentences of a sublanguage are a subset of those in the parent language, the sublanguage grammar is not a subset of the grammar of the parent language and in fact intersects it, as Harris (1968) points out in the first treatment of sublanguage as a linguistic phenomenon. Some rules (in terms of the special word classes of the sublanguage) are not satisfied by sentences that are part of the parent language (e.g., to use Harris' example, *Hydrochloric acid was washed in polypeptides* is not a sentence of biochemistry though still a sentence of English), while some rules of the parent language do not apply in the sublanguage (e.g. colloquial forms defined for the whole language may not occur in a science sublanguage).

Science sublanguages may be studied using a corpus drawn from the published literature in the field. In this case, the sublanguage sentences are indeed a subset of the sentences of the parent languages. However, the notion of sublanguage has also been applied to informal communications in technical areas, where the "sentences" may be so shortened for rapid communication that they may not qualify as grammatical utterances in the parent language. A modificiation of the orginal definition of *sublanguage* in Harris (1968) may have to be developed to cover these cases.

METHODS OF ANALYSIS

Sublanguage Word Classes

The first step in obtaining a sublanguage grammar is to determine the domain-specific noun classes, and, close upon this task or in conjunction with it, the verb and other linguistic operators that co-occur with them in elementary structures. In some domains, the noun classes are virtually given by established classifications within the science or by the organization of data in a database to which sublanguage sentences (in this case, questions) are to be addressed. It is also possible to obtain the sublanguage word classes by grouping the words of sublanguage texts into classes on the basis of their occurrence in similar environments. For example, it has been shown that the domain-specific noun and verb classes can be obtained simultaneously by a clustering program that operates on a sample of transformationally analyzed sublanguage sentences (Hirschman, Grishman & Sager, 1975). The illustration of sublanguage analysis that is presented here utilized a computer-aided method of obtaining a sublanguage grammar where the main sublanguage noun classes were provided by a scientist working in the field.

The domain of this sublanguage is lipoprotein kinetics. Lipoproteins are the molecules that serve as the transport system for cholesterol and other lipids in the body. The journal literature from which the texts of this sublanguage are drawn treats such topics as cholesterol turnover and the metabolic pathways of the lipoproteins under various conditions of diet, disease, and other factors, as studied both in humans and experimental animals. We undertook this sublanguage study with the aim of arriving at information structures that would help to organize portions of the literature for use by scientists engaged in mathematical modeling in this area (Sager & Kosaka, 1983).

Co-occurrence Patterns

To obtain the domain-specific co-occurrence patterns, we first manually analyzed a sample of the textual material and entered the syntactic sentence trees into the computer in parenthesized list form. The type of analysis used was a modified form of *operator-argument* grammar (Harris, 1982). In the operator-argument sentence tree, every node corresponds to a word or phrase of the sentence (sometimes restored from a zeroed occurrence or morphologically transformed), and the dominance of one node over others immediately below it has the interpretation of predication.

An example of an operator-argument tree for a sentence from this literature (Brown, Kovanen & Goldstein, 1981) is shown in Fig. 1.1. The sentence reads: "For export of triglycerides and cholesterol, the liver incorporates the lipids into VLDL (300–800A)." VLDL stands for *Very Low Density*

BKG 2.9.1 FOR EXPORT OF TRIGLYCERIDES AND CHOLESTEROL,
      THE LIVER INCORPORATES THE LIPIDS INTO VLDL (300-800A).

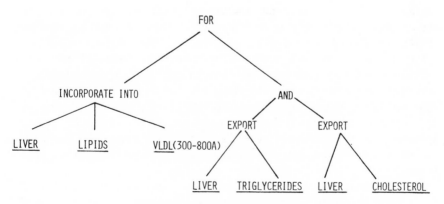

FIG. 1.1   Lipoprotein sentence tree.

*L*ipoproteins. The tree has three operator occurrences whose arguments are sublanguage nouns, corresponding to the elementary sublanguage sentences: (1) *the liver incorporates lipids into VLDL*; (2) *the liver exports triglycerides*; and (3) *the liver exports cholesterol*. The first of these operators with its arguments is connected by *for* to the other two, which are joined by *and*. Thus it is asserted that one activity of the liver is *for* (i.e. in the service of) another: It incorporates lipids into the lipoprotein VLDL in order to export them. In this type of grammatical analysis the syntactic relations obtained for a sentence correspond to the informational relations among the words of the sentence.

Note that in the operator-argument tree of Fig. 1.1 two zeroed occurrences of *liver* have been restored, one (along with the verb *export*) due to zeroing under the conjunction *and*, and one due to the nominalization of *export* and its occurrence (under *for*) as a sentence adjunct to the main clause where *liver* is the explicit subject. These zeroings are grammatically reconstructable. By contrast, *the lipids*, which in this sentence is a referential noun phrase referring to *triglycerides and cholesterol*, has not been replaced by these nouns. A full informational expansion would have four operator occurrences, cross linked (*For export of triglycerides, the liver incorporates triglycerides into VLDL,* and *For export of cholesterol, the liver incorporates cholesterol into VLDL*). This sublanguage-dependent referential resolution cannot be assumed in the analysis that is to produce the sublanguage grammar. Nor, as it turns out, is it needed for producing the sublanguage grammar, since *lipids* (as classifier) and *triglycerides* and *cholesterol* are all in the same sublanguage noun class with regard to their occurrence under particular classes of operators.

It will be noticed that in Fig. 1.1 the sublanguage nouns (*liver, lipids, VLDL, triglycerides, cholesterol*) occupy the bottom-most nodes of the operator-argument tree. It is a striking fact that when sublanguage text sentences are syntactically analyzed in operator-argument form, the sublanguage vocabulary is always found at the bottom nodes of the tree. Fig. 1.2 illustrates this fact by showing the location of the sublanguage vocabulary in the operator-argument trees of three consecutive sentences from Brown et al. (1981). (The second tree of Fig. 1.2 corresponds to the sentencee tree in Fig. 1.1; the articles and parenthesized modifier are not represented.) The squares and circles show the placement of words of the sublanguage vocabulary: white squares for the class of ORGAN/CELL words, black squares for the class of LIPIDS, white circles for LIPOPROTEINS, and black circles for ENZYME words. Nouns of the sublanguage vocabulary always occur in the bottom-most tree nodes and never in the top-most nodes. Sublanguage-specific verbs or predicates are the immediate operators on sublanguage nouns.

Having the operator-argument trees in the computer, we entered separately a list of the main sublanguage noun classes and their members, some of the main ones being:

AP	apoprotein	e.g.	apoprotein B, apoprotein C
LI	lipid	e.g.	cholestrol, triglyceride, cholesterol ester
LP	lipoprotein	e.g.	chylomicron, VLDL (very low density lipoprotein), HDL (high density lipoprotein)
EZ	enzyme	e.g.	LPL (lipoprotein lipase), LCAT
OR	organ/cell	e.g.	liver, peripheral tissue, fibroblast cell
HO	hormones	e.g.	insulin
RC	receptors	e.g.	LDL receptors

It was then straightforward for a program to substitute class names for class-member occurrences in the sentence trees and to make a table of the operator-argument tuples, sorted alphabetically by operator or by the sublanguage class of each argument.

Figure 1.3 shows a portion of a sublanguage operator-argument table generated from our data. In the first column are the operators, mostly verbs, or verbs in nominal form, that relate ORGAN/CELL words to LIPID words; for example, for ARG1, an ORGAN-CELL word, we have the operator-argument tuples corresponding to the elementary sublanguage sentence oc-

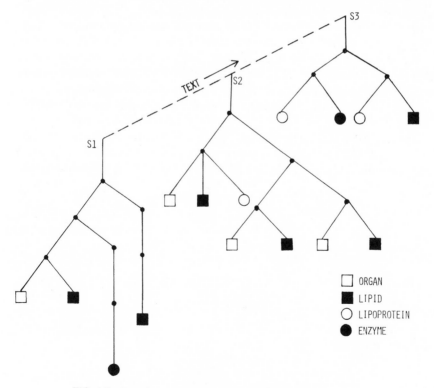

□ ORGAN
■ LIPID
○ LIPOPROTEIN
● ENZYME

FIG. 1.2   Location of sublanguage vocabulary in sentence trees.

OPERATOR	ARG1			ARG2		
DEMAND OF-FOR	/OR	=	LIVER	/LI	=	CHOLESTEROL
EXPORT OF	/OR	=	LIVER	/LI	=	CHOLESTEROL
TAKES UP	/OR	=	LIVER	/LI	=	CHOLESTEROL
SYNTHESIZES	/OR	=	LIVER	/LI	=	CHOLESTEROL
RELY ON	/OR	=	EXTRAHEPATIC CELLS	/LI	=	CHOLESTEROL
USE	/OR	=	CELL	/LI	=	CHOLESTEROL
EXPORT OF	/OR	=	LIVER	/LI	=	TRIGLYCERIDES

FIG. 1.3   Portion of operator-argument table.

currences: *The liver has a demand for cholesterol, The liver exports choles-terol, The liver takes up cholesterol, The liver synthesizes cholesterol, The liver relies on cholesterol, The cell uses cholesterol, The liver exports triglyc-erides,* and so on. The same argument word-classes appearing in the opposite order define a related class, as shown in Fig. 1.4, where the data is drawn from the same file as in Fig. 1.3. Here the operators are *are delivered to, are transported to, originate in, excretion into, is delivered to, the exit of-from.*

We can combine operator classes that have the same number and type of arguments but a different order of arguments by establishing a primary order and marking those members that require a different order as inverses. Thus, a single ORGAN-LIPID operator class is obtained from the data illustrated in Figs. 1.3 and 1.4.

The computer-generated tables of subclass co-occurrence patterns provide the material for the most elementary (linguistically, the *kernel* or K-level) portion of the sublanguage grammar. From the lipoprotein kinetics literature

OPERATOR	ARG1			ARG2		
ARE DELIVERED TO	/LI	=	TRIGLYCERIDES	/OR	=	ADIPOSE TISSUES
ORIGINATE IN	/LI	=	LIPIDS	/OR	=	LIVER
ARE TRANSPORTED TO	/LI	=	CHOLESTERYL ESTERS	/OR	=	CELLS
EXCRETION INTO	/LI	=	STEROL	/OR	=	BILE
IS DELIVERED TO	/LI	=	CHOLESTEROL	/OR	=	LIVER
THE EXIT OF-FROM	/LI	=	CHOLESTEROL	/OR	=	BODY

FIG. 1.4   Operator-argument table (continued).

as represented in our file, we have obtained some 40 kernel-types, where a kernel type (K-type) is defined as a sublanguage operator class and its argument classes in terms of about a dozen sublanguage noun classes. Some of these kernel level relations are illustrated in Fig. 1.5. Figure 1.5 also illustrates that, within each operator class, semantically distinct subsets can be distinguished.

Sublanguage Sentence Types

While the co-occurrence patterns of sublanguage-specific word classes (the K-types of the sublanguage grammar) are the primary means of distinguishing and characterizing the sublanguage, these forms are often a part of larger sentential structures that are regular throughout the sublanguage texts, and they constitute a second level of sublanguage description.

```
V-EZ      ------------------ LIPOPROTEIN LIPASE ACTIVITY

V-LP      ------------------ LDL IS POLYDISPERSE; LDL IS HETEROGENOUS

V-LILI    ------------------ TRIGLYCERIDE EXCHANGES WITH CHOLESTEROL

V-LIOR  ----- 1. FROM ----- THE EXIT OF CHOLESTEROL FROM THE BODY
               2. TO ------- CHOLESTEROL ESTERS ARE TRANSPORTED TO CELLS
               3. IN ------- LIPIDS ORIGINATE IN LIVER
               4. SYNTH ---- THE LIVER SYNTHESIZES CHOLESTEROL
               5. NEED/USE - THE CELLS RELY ON CHOLESTEROL; LIVER DEMAND FOR CH.

V-LILP  ----- 1. FROM ----- CHOLESTEROL ESTER IS REMOVED FROM LDL
               2. TO ------- CHOLESTEROL BINDS TO HDL
               3. IN ------- TRIGLYCERIDES ARE CARRIED IN CHYLOMICRONS

V-LPEZ    ------------------ VLDL PARTICLES INTERACT WITH LIPOPROTEIN LIPASE

V-LPLP    ------------------ THE CONVERSION OF IDL TO LDL
```

LEGEND TO FIGURE 5: V-EZ   OPERATOR ON ENZYME CLASS
                     V-LP   OPERATOR ON LIPOPROTEIN CLASS
                     V-LILI OPERATOR ON 2 OCCURRENCES OF LIPID CLASS
                     V-LIOR OPERATOR ON LIPID AND ORGAN/CELL CLASSES
                     V-LILP OPERATOR ON LIPID AND LIPOPROTEIN CLASSES
                     V-LPEZ OPERATOR ON LIPOPROTEIN AND ENZYME CLASSES
                     V-LPLP OPERATOR ON 2 OCCURRENCES OF LIPOPROTEIN CLASS

FIG. 1.5   Some lipoprotein sublanguage relations.

For example, in the medical sublanguage of patient documents, we can distinguish a large number of co-occurrence patterns in the elementary subject-verb-object and host-modifier relations. These patterns combine to form a small number of inclusive sentence types that represent the main types of events in the course of a patient's illness and treatment (Friedman, this volume). The patient document can be seen to be composed of a sequence of these sentence-type occurrences with explicit linguistic connectives between them and with associated time expressions that provide the chronology of the events (Hirschman & Story, 1981). The sublanguage grammar, stated up to the level of these event-representing sentence types, provides the structural units of the discourse.

In science sublanguages, where the linguistic data are given in journal articles or other published texts, the existence of characteristic sentence types involving more than the kernel-level co-occurrence patterns is even clearer. In the first such sublanguage that we analyzed in some detail, using texts from the literature on the mechanisms of pharmacological action of digitalis and digitalis-related drugs, the kernel-level elementary sentence types had characteristic adjuncts stating certain conditions on the observations, often also quantity operators, and a distinguished noun class (the drug words) that occurred with a causal verb operating on one of the kernel sentences (Sager, 1972). Texts were found to be composed primarily of sequences of such occurrences (sometimes in reduced form) under a complicated structure of conjunctions and co-reference.

The structure of the larger sentence types of the lipoprotein kinetics sublanguage shown schematically in Fig. 1.6, involves the addition to the K-types of "slots" for sublanguage material that occurs variously in adjunct status (i.e. as modifiers) or as the subject of operators on the kernel sentences. Sublanguage word classes on this level include classes for diseases, elements of diet, human/animal subjects and particular physiological variables.

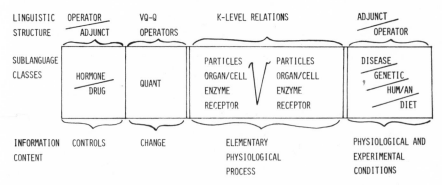

FIG. 1.6   Schematic of sentence types in lipoprotein kinetics experimental literature.

These classes occur linguistically most often as adjuncts and can be interpreted in such texts as given conditions for the observations reported. However, where the reported investigation varied these conditons, members of these classes may occur as operators, as illustrated in the text analyzed in the next section. Several other sublanguage classes, principally the hormone and drug class, also occur linguistically as either adjunct or operator, but more frequently as operator, corresponding to their role as controls on the elementary physiological processes described by the K-level relations.

In addition, there are quantity operators on nouns and verbs that may introduce an intermediate structure between a sublanguage operator (or English operator) and its arguments. Further, sentences in this sublanguage are rich in local modifiers, which are introduced as adverbial phrases or as relative clauses (mainly, reduced) and compound nouns. The main logical structure of each sentence is most clearly seen when local modifiers are associated with the element they modify and are not made a part of the main branching structure of the sentence tree.

SUBLANGUAGE SENTENCE TYPES IN DISCOURSE

To illustrate the role of sublanguage sentence types in an informational representation of sublanguage texts, the first paragraph of an abstract from the lipoprotein literature (Grundy, 1975), which is shown in Fig. 1.7, is shown in analyzed form in Fig. 1.8.

Studies were carried out on the effects of polyunsaturated fats on lipid metabolism in 11 patients with hyptertriglyceridemia. During cholesterol balance studies performed in eight patients, the feeding of polyunsaturated fats, as compared with saturated fats, caused an increased excretion of endogenous neutral steroids, acidic steroids, or both in most patients. Increases in steroid excretions were marked in some patients and generally exceeded the decrement of cholesterol in the plasma compartment. The finding of a greater excretion of fecal steroids on polyunsaturated fats in hypertriglyceridemic patients contrasts to the lack of change in sterol balance previously reported for patients with familial hypercholesterolemia: however, other workers have found that polyunsaturated fats also enhance steroid excretion in normal subjects.

FIG. 1.7   Sample Text.

In Fig. 1.8 the entire paragraph is seen to consist of successive occurrences of a particular case of the lipoprotein sentence type, as follows:

DIET | V | VQ ‖ LI V OR ‖ HUMAN | DISEASE
‖ LI V   ‖

S#	C	Meta	C	C	DIET	V	VQ	LI	V	OR	HUMAN	DISEASE
1.1.1		Studies carried out			puf	affect		lipid	metabolism		in 11 patients	with HTG
1.1.2a					feeding of puf	caused	increased	endogenous neutral steroids	excretion (into)	(feces)	in most patients (of 8 pts)	(")
b				,	"	"	"	e. acidic steroids	"			
c				or	"	"	"	both e. neutral and acidic steroids	"			
d			as compared with		(feeding of) sf	(not caused)	(increased)	(")	(")	(")	(")	(")
e	during	studies performed						cholesterol	balance		in 8 pts	(")
					on puf		increases marked	steroid	excretions (into)	(")	in some pts (of 8)	(")
1.1.3a	and				(")		(")	(")	(")	(")	(")	(")
			generally exceeded		(")		the decrement	cholesterol	in	the plasma compartment		

12

	the finding of		on puf		steroids	excretion	fecal	in pts	HTGic
1.4a	the finding of		on puf		steroids	excretion	fecal	in pts	HTGic
b	contrasts to	greater (than)	(not on puf)		(")	(")	(")	(")	(")
c	previously reported		(on puf)?	lack of change in	sterol	balance		for pts	with FHC
d	; however	other workers have found that	puf	enhance	steroid	excretion	(")	in subjects	normal

Abbreviations:

S#	=	Sentence number
C	=	English conjunction
Meta	=	Scientist-verb (metalanguage)
puf	=	Polyunsaturated fats
sf	=	Saturated fats
VQ	=	Quantity

HTG	=	Hypertriglyceridemia
FHC	=	Familial hypercholesterolemia
LI	=	LIPID class
OR	=	ORGAN/CELL class
V	=	verb form

FIG. 1.8 Sublanguage sentence types in sample text.

The kernel-type (mainly a LIPID-ORGAN relation but in some cases a LIPID word with a predicate) is enclosed between double bars; and the outer columns contain the classes that extend the kernel, occurring either with an operator (V) or as an adjunct. VQ stands for a quantity operator such as *increase, decrease*. The logical structure of the text is carried by the English language connectives shown in the conjunction (C) columns.

INFORMATIONAL PROPERTIES OF SUBLANGUAGES

Different sublanguages clearly differ in their gross syntactic structure and in the structure of their characteristic sentence types, stated in terms of sublanguage word classes and operators. In addition to these qualitative differences, it is possible to compare sublanguages quantitatively in regard to properties they all share to some degree, such as the amount and complexity of the information in sublanguage sentences.

The operator-argument representation provides a basis for such measurements. Because every operator represents a predication on its argument(s), the number of operators in a sentence provides a rough measure of the amount of information in the sentence, not including the operators that would appear if resolved references were substituted for the referential expression. The new, or manifest, information given by the sentence is what is measured by counting the number of operators in the sentence.

Informational complexity of sentences is also related to the number of operators contained in the sentence, but the structure among operators is also important. For example, a sentence composed of a linear sequence of simple (K-level) assertions connected by *ands* is intuitively less complex than a structure that has the same number of operators but several of them logical operators on K-structures (compare *A1 and A2 and A3 and A4 and A5* (Ai = simple assertions) with *If both A1 and A2 then A3*). To account for this feature, we include the maximum depth-of-nesting as a factor in the measure of complexity.

Two very different sublanguages (clinical reporting in patient records and lipoprotein kinetics in the experimental literature) were compared (Gordon & Sager, 1985) using in part the variables defined in Table 1.1, where the results of the comparison are given in terms of ratios of the average values of the variables in each sublanguage corpus. Literature sentences were about three times as long as record sentences (a ratio of 3.21), with somewhat less than three times as many operators (a ratio of 2.37), making for an almost equal density of information (a ratio of 1.24). However, the reductions that made for compactness were not the same in both cases. With regard to the measure

TABLE 1.1
Informational Properties of 2 Sublanguages Compared

LITERATURE CORPUS = 62 SENTENCES
RECORDS CORPUS   = 113 SENTENCES

			LITERATURE : RECORDS RATIO OF AVERAGE VALUES
W	=	NUMBER OF WORDS IN SENTENCE	3.27
O	=	NUMBER OF OPERATORS IN SENTENCE, MEASURES THE AMOUNT OF MANIFEST INFORMATION	2.37
W/O	=	RATIO OF WORDS TO OPERATORS, MEASURES THE INVERSE OF INFORMATIONAL DENSITY	1.24
D	=	MAXIMUM DEPTH OF NESTING, OVERALL	2.10
D_{LOC}	=	LOCAL MODIFIER TREES, MAXIMUM DEPTH OF NESTING	13.0
O * D	=	PRODUCT OF O AND D, MEASURES THE SENTENCE INFORMATIONAL COMPLEXITY	4.17

of sentence complexity, the most striking difference is in the complexity of the local modifiers, with the literature showing an average maximum depth of nesting in adjuncts thirteen times as great as the records. The overall complexity as measured by the product of the number of operators and the maximum depth of nesting was over four times greater in the literature than in the records, that is, one third more than the ratio of sentence lengths. As sentences get longer the increase in complexity of information is not a linear function of length.

SUBLANGUAGE ANALYSIS AS A COMPUTATIONAL TOOL

Sublanguage analysis has great utility in natural language processing and its applications. Sublanguage co-occurrence patterns help to resolve syntactic ambiguity. Sublanguage sentence types lead to the formulation of target structures for semantic representation. A sublanguage grammar may eliminate ambiguity in some structures of the parent language. Sublanguage structures may also suggest larger patterns that include representations of subfield knowledge not explicit in the sublanguage text.

Sublanguage analysis provides a bridge between sentence analysis and discourse analysis. It provides forms in terms of which sublanguage discourses are seen to have a repeating structure. It may be that further work on sublanguage texts will bring into the sublanguage grammar some of the large informational patterns that now seem special to each discourse. For example, in patient documents it may be possible to identify certain event sequences, occurring under certain types of connectives or time-order relations, that correspond to more complex events, such as the patient response to treatment. As a linguistically identified, patterned occurrence such a higher level structure could be added to the sublanguage grammar.

At the same time, it is clear that extensions of sublanguage grammar toward discourse patterns and the study of discourse processes go hand in hand. In order to recognize the regular occurrence of sublanguage sentence types in a discourse, we often have to perform discourse-level operations, such as reference resolution and special transformations whose justification, in part, is the discourse regularity obtained. Conversely, without a repertoire of sublanguage sentence types to help in reference resolution and to provide the skeleton of discourse regularity, it is difficult indeed to extract such patterns from a text.

To bring together the many aspects of language analysis into a single working system is a challenging task. Sublanguage analysis is a welcome, new, powerful tool to aid in this endeavor.

ACKNOWLEDGMENTS

This research was supported in part by National Library of Medicine grant number 1-RO1-LM03933, awarded by the National Institutes of Health, Department of Health and Human Services, and in part by National Science Foundation grant number IST81-15669 from the Division of Information Science and Technology.

REFERENCES

Bross, I. D. J., Shapiro, P. A., & Anderson, B. B. (1972). How information is carried in scientific sub-languages. *Science, 176,* 1303–1307.

Brown, M. S., Kovanen, P. T., & Goldstein, J. L. (1981). Regulation of plasma cholesterol by lipoprotein receptors. *Science, 12,* 628–635.

Gordon, D., & Sager, N. (1985, August). A method of measuring information in language, applied to medical texts. *Information Processing & Management, 21* (4), 269–289.

Grundy, S. M. (1975). Effects of polyunsaturated fats on lipid metabolism in patients with hypertriglyceridemia. *The Journal of Clinical Investigation, 55,* 269–282.

Harris, Z. S. (1968). *Mathematical structures in language.* (Sec. 5.9). New York: Wiley (Interscience).

Harris, Z. S. (1982). *A grammar of English on mathematical principles.* New York: Wiley (Interscience).

Hirschman, L., Grishman, R., & Sager, N. (1975). Grammatically-based automatic word class formation. *Information Processing and Management, 11,* 39–57.

Hirschman, L., & Story, G. (1981). Representing implicit and explicit time relations in narrative: In *Proceedings of the Seventh International Joint Conference on Artificial Intelligence (IJCAI 81), 1* (pp. 289–295).

Kittredge, R., & Lehrberger, J. (Eds.). (1982). *Sublanguage: Studies of language in restricted semantic domains.* Berlin: de Gruyter.

Sager, N. (1972). Syntactic formatting of science information. *AFIPS Conference Proceedings, 41* (pp. 791–800). Montvale, NJ: AFIPS Press. (Reprinted in R. Kittredge & J. Lehrberger (Eds.) (1982), *Sublanguage: Studies of language in restricted semantic domains* (pp. 9–26). Berlin: de Gruyter.)

Sager, N., & Kosaka, M. (1983). A database of literature organized by relations: In R. Dayhoff (Ed.), *Proceedings of the Seventh Annual Symposium on Computer Appliations in Medical Care (SCAMC 7)* (pp. 692–695). Silver Spring, MD: IEEE Computer Society.

2 Sublanguage Analysis

John Lehrberger
Quebec, Canada

ABSTRACT

The current notion of a sublanguage of a natural language has developed through studies of texts in specialized fields, particularly technical and scientific texts. The practicality of computerized information retrieval and automatic translation of certain sublanguage texts depends on the simplified structure of these sublanguages compared with the structure of the language as a whole. They were not constructed as formal languages but grew through the use of a natural language for communication in limited fields. One way of viewing the structure of a sublanguage is, then, in terms of the structure of the natural language of which it is a part. This paper examines sublanguage structure in terms of restrictions on and deviations from the structure of the natural language. These restrictions and deviations may be lexical, syntactic, or semantic and may involve discourse structure as well as sentence structure. In addition to providing a means for describing the sublanguages of a natural language, the point of view adopted here provides insight into the properties of the natural language itself.

SOME COMMON ASSUMPTIONS

In mathematics we are often presented with a system A, which is described as an independent system, only to learn later that is really a subsystem of a larger system, B. Similarly, a sublanguage of a natural language might be described as an independent system or as a subsystem of the natural language. In practice, when we analyze a sublanguage of a natural language L, we normally use the grammar of L, implicitly or explicitly, as a guide in describing the sublanguage. In principle, we could build the sublanguage grammar strictly on the basis of the sublanguage texts, ignoring the grammar of L. Zellig Harris (1968) introduced a precise characterization of *sublanguage* in linguistics by analogy with *subsystem* in mathematics. There a subsystem can be readily defined in terms of restrictions on the sets and operations of the system of which it is a part. In the case of a sublanguage of a natural language, the relation between part and whole is not so clear-cut. To see why this is so, let us begin by examining some of the commonly held beliefs concerning that relation. Perhaps the most obvious assumption is the following:

(i) A sublanguage of a natural language L is part of L.

At first glance (i) appears to be a tautology. In support of this assumption, we note that speakers of L who do not understand some text in a sublanguage of L can, nevertheless, recognize that the text is "in L" (we have all seen technical articles that strike us as incomprehensible, but which we unhesitatingly label as basically English). It is tempting to skip lightly over (i). Of course, it may also be tempting to assume that the grammar of a sublanguage of L must be a subgrammar of the grammar of L – an assumption that is not supported by the facts, as we shall see. Perhaps, then, we should take a second look at (i).

There is an ambiguity in linguistics concerning the use of the expression *the natural language L*. It is not always clear whether this refers to the "whole" language, the standard language, the language associated with the competence of an ideal speaker in an ideal community, or something else. Suppose, in this paper, we take it to mean the whole language, including within its scope any sentences recognized by native speakers as being "in L" even though they may consider them a little odd in some way or another. This would seem to place (i) on firmer ground; we will leave it that way for the moment.

Another common assumption is that sublanguages deal with restricted subject matter:

(ii) A sublanguage is identified with a particular semantic domain.

Sublanguage analyses that have been carried out so far have dealt with texts limited to specific fields, usually technical or scientific fields. Harris (1968) has used the term sublanguage more generally for "proper subsets of the sentences of a language closed under some or all of the operations defined in the language" (p. 152). This gives no indication of any semantic limitations. In fact, Harris has even outlined the construction of an "information sublanguage" whose semantic domain is no more restricted than that of the natural language itself (this will be discussed further later). He refers to those sublanguages with restricted semantic domains as *subject-matter sublanguages* and points out an important feature of such sublanguages, namely, that they do not contain the sentences of their own metalanguage (Harris, 1976, p. 276). The natural language does contain its own metalanguage, the grammar of the language.

Closely related to (i) and (ii) is an assumption about the manner in which sublanguages originate:

(iii) A sublanguage of a natural language L grows in a natural way through the use of L, albeit in special circumstances.

The idea here is that, unlike an artificial language, a sublanguage is not constructed, but comes into being gradually as L is adapted for a particular purpose. In accordance with (ii), the usage that gives birth to the sublanguage is that of specialists in a certain subject communicating with each other about that subject. (iii) reflects the state of affairs in the case studies that have been conducted so far; but there is no reason, a priori, for dismissing constructed languages from consideration — a point we return to later.

Real texts that are said to be in a given sublanguage, X, are not assumed to consist only of sentences from X. Assumption (iv) is another way of putting the matter:

(iv) What we refer to as *sublanguage texts* usually contain some material that does not belong to the sublanguage proper.

This extra material may occur as whole sentences interspersed among those of the sublanguage proper or as matrix expressions under which sentences or expressions of the sublanguage proper are embedded. For example, in a geometry text we may find:

(1) Pythagoras proved the theorem that now bears his name in the sixth century B.C. He was able to show that the area of the square on the hypotenuse of a right triangle equals the sum of the areas of the squares on the other two sides.

The first sentence of (1) is not, properly speaking, a sentence of geometry, but of history. The second sentence consists of a sentence of geometry ("the area of the square on the hypotenuse . . .") embedded under a matrix expression ("He was able to show that"). If one is investigating the linguistic properties of geometry textbooks, these two levels of text soon become apparent on syntactic as well as semantic grounds. This is a general pheomenon in real texts from restricted semantic domains. Typically, a text consists of a mixture of discourse *within* a particular domain and metadiscourse *about* it.

It could be argued that any type of material whose occurrence is widespread in texts from a given field belongs to the sublanguage of that field. After all, metadiscourse constitutes a substantial portion of many texts, and even a grammar designed only for parsing texts from a restricted domain must take this into account. Consequently, a researcher's sublanguage grammar may include more than a grammar of the sublanguage proper.

The use of the term sublanguage proper can be avoided and the notion of sublanguage grammar clarified by keeping in mind the distinction between sublanguage and discourse (see, e.g., Harris, 1982). A sublanguage is a theoretical construct. If L' is a subject-matter sublanguage with semantic domain D, the sentences of L' are just those that state the properties and relations of D. But it is from actual discourse that we form our idea of L', and not all of the material in the discourse expresses the properties and relations of D. Now when we write a grammar for natural language processing, we know that it is actual discourse that must be processed; consequently, our so-called sublanguage grammar turns out to be more comprehensive than a grammar of the theoretical construct L'. However, if the discourse analysis on which our grammar is based taken into account the distinction between discourse and metadiscourse, then that grammar will have a component corresponding to a grammar of L', along with rules for handling the metadiscourse and its relation to the rest of the discourse.

Before stating the next assumption, I would like to comment further on (i). If, in (i), L is taken to be the whole language, then presumably it subsumes many varieties of speech and writing, including an indefinite number of sublanguages. That being the case, what would a grammar of L be like? And how would one go about describing a sublanguage formally as a subsystem of L? From a practical point of view, with such an interpretation of L, a grammar of L is not likely to be available. What is likely to be available, however, is a grammar of the standard language (or dialect).[1] It will be described in the school grammar books and generally recognized even by those who do not use it very well. Granting the existence of a standard language, say Lstd, we may state the following hypothesis:

(v) Whatever can be said in a sublanguage of a natural language L can be paraphrased in Lstd.

We might add as a footnote to (v) the assumption that any deviant grammatical constructions peculiar to the sublanguage in question can be replaced by constructions of Lstd. Carrying out this replacement would be no simple

---

[1]There may be more than one standard language, in which case a choice can be made on the basis of some criterion such as wide acceptance for use in scientific or technical writing, etc., depending on the particular sublanguage field.

task. For example, extreme cases of deletion resulting from shared knowledge among specialists in a given field often require for their explanation discourse rules or pragmatic principles beyond the scope of a normal sentence grammar. The specialists themselves may be able to render the paraphrases without difficulty; the problem for computational linguistics is how to formalize such paraphrase relations.

A POINT OF REFERENCE

A sublanguage L' of a natural language L can be viewed as resulting from restrictions on and deviations from the grammar of Lstd. The relation between L, L' and Lstd is then as shown in Fig. 2.1. The intersection of L' and Lstd contains those sentences of L' that can be described in terms of restrictions on the grammar of Lstd; the remainder of L' contains sentences that deviate from the grammar of Lstd in some way, although they are considered L'-grammatical. Assumption (v) in the preceding section suggests that L' can be mapped into Lstd in such a way that the image of each sentence of L' under the mapping is a paraphrase of that sentence. The problem of specifying the image of a sentence of L' in the intersection is trivial (use the same sentence), but the rules of correspondence may be very complex for the remaining sentences. These rules involve correspondences between deviant constructions in L' and their standard language counterparts. For example, deviant constructions frequently result from deletions that are acceptable in L', but not in Lstd. This can be seen in (2).

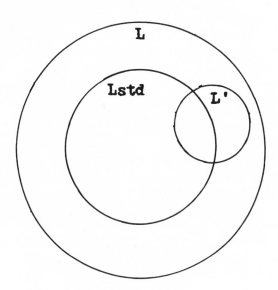

FIG. 2.1

(2)		Refill		tank		if	fluid level		low
L':		V		N [sg, count]		SC	NP		A
Lstd:		V	DET	N [sg,count]		SC	NP	BE	A

The required paraphrase is obtained from the structural correspondences by substituting *the* for DET and *is* for BE ('Refill the tank if the fluid level is low'). Clearly, after the structural correspondences have been obtained the substitution of words for the class symbols may still present problems. Thus one might object that in (2) DET could yield *a* as well as *the* in the first clause. This particular problem, which involves a pragmatic principle, will be discussed further in the next section.

The question of paraphrasing becomes very complicated when we attempt to formalize the paraphrastic mapping in a principled way. The claim that for sentences of L' already in Lstd the problem of finding the appropriate paraphrase is trivial assumes that the only goal is to map L' into Lstd, preserving meaning. But it may also be desirable to imposed other constraints on the mapping. A given sentence can be paraphrased in many ways; the selection to a particular paraphrase depends on the ultimate goal: What do we expect to learn from the resulting set of sentences? What properties of L' (or L) are we looking for? In addition to the preservation of meaning, constraints might be imposed for the purpose of eliminating redundancy, for recovering deleted material, for normalizing the vocabulary (choosing appropriate synonyms), for making presuppositions explicit, for selecting operators having the greatest freedom of occurrence, and so forth. Even if L' is a subset of Lstd (i.e., a sublanguage with no "deviant" sentences), the specification of a paraphrase for each sentence of L' in Lstd might still be far from trivial. This can be seen, e.g., in the paraphrase component of the CO-OP system, a natural language question-answering system (see McKeown, 1983). A question posed in perfectly normal standard English may be paraphrased in this system in such a way as to make the presuppositions of the original question explicit or to clarify alternative interpretations of an ambiguous question.

Harris has dealt with the problem of selecting a representative from each equivalence class of sentences (under paraphrase) with the goal of establishing an *information sublanguage*, {I}, which carries all the objective information that can be carried by the whole language. In this case the mapping is into the sublanguage, not from it. At any rate, the mapping is accomplished by means of transformations extant in the grammar of the language (not by transformations introduced as ad hoc devices just to obtain the desired result). {I} is not a subject-matter sublanguage; it may be described as a report sublanguage, and it is closed under the nonparaphrastic transformations. Harris (1969) claims that "Investigation of what kind of information can be born in language, and how language can be modified to carry other kinds of information, is made possible by analysis of the structure of this report sublanguage, in which every item of structure is relevant to the informational burden that language carries" (p. 2).

The construction of such an information sublanguage for a natural language is a formidable enterprise, but for a subject-matter sublanguage it becomes more practicable; that is, an information sublanguage {I'} could be constructed for a subject-matter sublanguage L' such that: (a) {I'} is a sublanguage of L'; (b) {I'} is capable of carrying all the objective information carried by L'; and (c) {I'} contains no paraphrastic operators (their role being to derive the sentences of L'-{I'} from {I'}). Harris (1969) comments: "Sharper versions of an information-processing structure may be found, if an {I} system is constructed for the sublanguages of particular sciences, where much dictionary paraphrase (due to semantic overlapping in the vocabulary) can be isolated and eliminated, so that the correlation of structure and report becomes sharper, and the particular relations of the science would be brought out sharply" (p. 76).

We cannot explore the details of Harris's {I} system here; the notion is introduced at this point merely to give an example of a serious attempt to provide a principled method, within a theory of language, for selecting a representative for each paraphrastic set of sentences—a kind of normalization that eliminates the redundancy due to paraphrase. The advantage of this approach is the close correlation of structure and objective information in the resulting {I} system, which then serves as a base for generating the language itself, using only paraphrastic transformations. Anything sayable in the language can be represented in this base; hence there are no subclass restrictions on the primitive arguments of the predicative operators in the base. Particular nouns are not excluded as arguments of a verb; such restrictions arise in discourse within restricted domains. Within this theory the gross structures of the languages (such as NVN, etc.) can then be interpreted as *envelopes* of all the structures with subclass restrictions ($N_iV_jN_k$, etc.) in particular sublanguages.

Earlier it was pointed out that there are two different approaches to the study of a sublanguage, depending on whether it is viewed as an independent system or as a subsystem. Perhaps greater economy could be obtained in describing some sublanguages of a natural language L by treating them as independent systems rather than situating them in L and relating them to Lstd. The independent approach may be advantageous for some practical applications restricted to particular domains. For other purposes it may be more revealing to describe the sublanguage in terms of the structures and operations of the larger system. There are, for example, applications involving hierarchies of sublanguages (L' L" . . .) and there can be considerable overlap between sublanguages in different hierarchies. Even sublanguages with quite different semantic domains may have much in common grammatically, and this relatedness can be expressed in a uniform manner against the common background of Lstd. Some such uniform representation would certainly be useful in establishing a general typology of sublanguages within a given language. In processing texts from diverse fields it is common to find many metadiscourse expressions of the same type (e.g., intentional expressions and indirect quotation devices), which are well known and described in the grammar of Lstd. "Practical" grammars are therefore likely to be linked with the grammar of Lstd at this level in any event. Another case where reference to Lstd would be advantageous is the use of paraphrase in practical applications. The development of a general method for paraphrasing texts from different fields might be simplified if each relevant sublanguage were described in terms of the structures and operations of Lstd and the texts then rendered in Lstd. Finally, if the study of sublanguages is considered as just another aspect of the study of linguistic variation within a language, along with dialects styles and registers, then Lstd can serve as a common point of departure in that study.

SOURCES OF RESTRICTIONS AND DEVIATIONS

The restrictions and deviations that characterize a sublanguage may be lexical, syntactic or semantic and may involve discourse constraints as well as constraints on sentences in isolation. Lexical restrictions may consist of the exclusion of large parts of the total vocabulary of the language due to restricted subject matter. In fact, there is a tendency to think of any sublanguage as having a special vocabulary related to a particular semantic domain. However, in the definition of a sublanguage as a proper subset of the sentences of a language, closed under some or all of the operations of the language, there is no mention of restricted semantic domain. We could take as a sublanguage of English, for example, the subset of sentences containing no passives, the subset containing no past tense, and so forth; that is, in transformational terms, the set of sentences derivable without certain transformations, but using the full vocabulary of English. Of course, if a word "enters" the language only as a result of a certain transformation and that transformation is not applicable in the sublanguage, then the word will not be in the sublanguage vocabulary. But this kind of lexical restriction, unlike the wholesale vocabulary reduction that results from restricting the semantic domain, can be specified on strictly syntactic grounds.

In addition to overall reduction in size of vocabulary, restricting the semantic domain affects word usage in a variety of ways (see Lehrberger, 1982a, for examples.) There may be a reduction in the number of parts of speech (noun, verb, adjective, etc.) to which a given "word" is assigned, as well as the number of senses it has within a given part of speech. Thus many instances of homography are eliminated, with a consequuent reduction of ambiguity and a substantial improvement in the prospects for automatic analysis. The number of semantic word-subclasses needed for general linguistic analysis is not known, but an examination of the literature on this subject suggests that it could be quite large. In a subject-matter sublanguage, on the other hand, the number may be relatively small because of the restricted semantic domain. It is questionable whether there are any semantic groupings that are required for the analysis of all sublanguages. One immediately thinks of the old standbys such as *abstract* and *concrete*, but even these are of questionable value in the domain of pure mathematics, since all mathematical objects are abstract. Although semantic subclasses of nouns have been used to great advantage in parsing texts from certain fields, their use in the analysis of arbitrary texts, independent of semantic domain, is more problematic.

Aside from the possible restriction on the number of parts of speech to which a given word belongs in a subject-matter sublanguage, the grammatical usage of a word can be affected in other ways. In a study of computer software manuals, for example, the verb *halt* was found to occur in the explanatory texts with reference to programs' "stopping" ("The program halts when return is typed"), but it did not occur in the imperative (*Halt the program! *Halt!) even though many other verbs did occur in the imperative ("Look at the loops as a whole," "Do not assume that the first error is the only one in the program"). Grammatical usage of words not only is restricted, but also deviates occasionally from normal usage outside the sublanguage. Thus, in the same software manuals the verb *save* occurred with an *into* complement ("Only the creator of the public workspace can save into it," "One may save only into one's own library or into a public library,") along with the more normal usage ("It is not possible to save a workspace in another user's private library"). Of course, if the computer scientist steps out into the real world and says "Let's save our money into the bank," (s)he will be speaking ungrammatically.

Grammaticality in a subject-matter sublanguage is determined by whatever officially prescribed or implicit norms of usage exist among the specialists in the subject-matter field. When these norms conflict with those of the standard language, we have a case of sublanguage-grammatical sentences that are ungrammatical in Lstd. Thus "Rain Sunday" must be counted as a grammatical sentence in the sublanguage of weather bulletins, but not in Lstd, and "Check reservoir full," "Check fluid level indicator is registering correctly" are considered grammatical in aircraft maintenance manuals, but not in Lstd. Viewed from inside the sublanguages, there is no question of deviant structures in these examples: the sublanguages are internally consistent; they have their own grammars and can be treated as independent systems. But if we look at the sublanguage as part of a large, composite entity (the whole natural language), then sublanguage structures that do not conform to the standard grammar can legitimately be described as deviant. Alternatively, they could be considered as *marked structures* — contextually determined variants — with restricted subject matter being one aspect of *extralinguistic context*. Whichever term is used, we emphasize the part–whole relation, using Lstd as a point of reference.

An important factor determining restricted or deviant use of language in a text is the purpose for which the text is intended. This can affect both vocabulary and grammar. Within different texts from a given field, or within different parts of a single text, there may be characteristic lexical patterns, depending on the purpose of the text (or section of the text). For example, daily weather bulletins in Canada were found to have a vocabulary on the order of 1,000 words, aside from place names, whereas weather synopses were estimated to have a vocabulary of from 2,000 to 4,000 words (see Kittredge, 1983). Both types of texts deal with the same subject matter, weather conditions, but the purpose of the former is to report the latest forecast as concisely as possible, whereas the purpose of the latter is to give a general summary with less emphasis on brevity. Compare, for example, (3) and (4):

(3) Mostly cloudy today. Snow beginning early this afternoon and ending early this evening. Snowfall accumulation 1 to 3 inches. Highs today near 30. Lows in the teens.

(4) Variable skies and isolated showers were reported overnight and this pattern is forecast to continue through this morning across Southern Ontario. The weak disturbance responsible for this weather will move east of the region by tonight allowing skies to clear once again. High pressure will dominate the weather picture on Thursday bringing sunny skies, light winds and temperatures several degrees above seasonal normals.

The use in (4) of expressions like *were reported, is forecast, responsible for, dominate,* and *weather picture* is avoided in (3), where only the bare facts of the forecast are reported without any dressing. Clearly, grammar as well as vocabulary varies with text purpose. The telegraphic style of (3) is absent from (4), where only complete sentences (from the point of view of the standard grammar) are used.

The effect of text purpose on grammar also shows up in the difference beween instructions for carrying out a procedure and the description of an object or its function. This type of difference is found in aircraft maintenance manuals, for example, where telegraphic style prevails in sections whose purpose is to instruct maintenance personnel in procedures for installing, removing, checking, and repairing parts of the aircraft, but not in those sections whose purpose is to describe the aircraft parts and their functions. Compare, for example, (5), which describes the function of a certain relief valve, and (6), which gives instructions for its removal:

(5) A hydraulic filter relief valve is installed in the filter head in order to bypass the filter element in the event of fluid flow restriction causing a pressure differential of 100 psi between the filter inlet and outlet.

(6) (a) Depressurize hydraulic system.
(b) Disconnect pressure and return lines from filter head.
(c) Remove two attaching bolts from the filter head and remove assembly.
(d) Break lockwire and remove relief valve from filter head.
(e) Cap all open lines and ports.

An obvious grammatical difference here is the use of imperatives in the instructions (6), but not in the description (5). Another factor that stands out very clearly is the effect of text purpose on sentence length. Each instruction in (6) is short, which sometimes results in ambiguity, as in (b) where we do not know whether *return line* is a noun phrase or verb + object. Sentence length is not, in itself, a grammatical element, but it is an indicator of grammatical complexity.

Flow charts are used in many fields to describe a procedure or an operation diagrammatically. The text in these diagrams consists almost entirely of yes-no questions, imperative sentences and the words *yes, no*. Telegraphic style is usually employed.

Knowing the purpose of a text sometimes helps in disambiguating the text and rendering the correct paraphrase. For example, in the discussion of the sentence (2) *Refill tank if fluid level low* in the preceding section, it was pointed out that *Refill tank* could be paraphrased as either *Refill the tank* or *Refill a tank*. Our assumption was that (2) involved deletion of *the*, but this needs some justification since there are many similar sentences resulting from deletion of *a*:

(7) (a) See (a) doctor if (the) pain persists.
(b) Take (a) sedative if (it is) needed.
(c) Send (a) money order, not (a) check.
(d) Please include (a) recent photo with (your) application.

One possibility is that *the* is implied in (2) by a previous mention of *tank*, since the definite article can be used with a noun for anaphoric reference. However, the following example shows that this alone is not sufficient justification:

(e) (The) license must contain (the) licensee's *photo*. Please include (a) recent photo with (your) aplication.

What actually determines that *the* is the missing article in (2) is a principle of specificity. The purpose of the text that includes (2) is to provide a mechanic with instructions for carrying out a task in maintaining a vehicle. At each step the mechanic's attention is directed to a specific part of the vehicle on which he is working. Consequently, if an instruction is of the form VN, where V is a verb such as *drain, fill, refill, remove, replace, check, lubricate, loosen, tighten,* and so on and N is a noun denoting some part of the vehicle, then the specificity requirement permits us to assume that VN has been derived by deletion of the definite article. This can be extended to V NP, where NP is a determinerless noun phrase denoting some part of the vehicle.

Generally speaking, text purpose affects text structure in fairly predictable ways. It is important to bear in mind when dealing with subject-matter sublanguages that given a set of texts from the same subject-matter field, structural homogeneity is not to be expected if text purpose is not the same throughout. In addition to the subject matter, one must take into account whether the purpose of the text is to describe an object or its function, to instruct the reader in carrying out a task (maintenance manuals, cook books), to present logical argumentation (proving theorems or solving problems), to persuade the reader without resorting to logic (some advertising), to request information (questionaires), to make predictions (weather forecasts) or to provide explicit unambiguous documents for legal use. The relation between text purpose and text structure is complex: although the choice of lingusitic elements may be affected, it is not simply a matter of a given purpose determining a specific structure. There are, however, certain tendencies such as the use of telegraphic style, the use of imperatives, the absence of or restriction to questions, the absence of certain tenses, absence of or frequent use of passives, and the use of certain types of pronominalization or coreference.

DISCOURSE ANALYSIS

The principle of specificity discussed earlier allows us to draw certain conclusions about the structure of individual sentences but it is a principle underlying an entire discourse. As mentioned, a sublanguage is a set of sentences, and we analyze discourse to arrive at a description of those sentences. Our knowledge of the properties of whole discourses in a sublanguage field is an integral part of our knowledge of the sublanguage itself. One such property, important in sublanguage analysis, is textual cohesion. Texts from various fields have characteristic sentence-linking devices for providing this cohesiveness. Texts in logic and mathematics make heavy use of sentence connectives such as *therefore, consequently, it follows that, hence, as a consequence, by, thus, so* and the often misleading *clearly.* A text consisting of a sequence of instructions for carrying out some task may use only a few connectives like *then, next,* and *after,* indicating time sequence rather than logical consequence. Continuity may be achieved by repetition of words or phrases, often with reduction of endocentric phrases to their heads, and pronominalization. In the telegraphic weather bulletins there is little explicit linkage between successive sentences.

An interesting case of textual cohesion, or lack of it, occurs in the sequence of comments included in a computer program (see Lehrberger, 1982b). The comments, written in a natural language, do not affect the execution of the program, which, of course, is written in some constructed programming language. Let us consider the sequence of comments itself as a natural language text. For example, (8) accompanies a program for building a tree (Wirth, 1976, pp. 197–198) and (9) accompanies a program for solving systems of simultaneous linear equations (Wiener & Sincovec, 1982, pp. 254–257).

(8) stack
     first integer is number of nodes
     dummy
     pop
     push

(9) This procedure is hidden from user
     LU__FACTOR
     We initialize subscript array
     This procedure is invisible to the user
     MATRIX__INVERSE
     The matrix A will be changed by LU__FACTOR

These "texts" are coherent only if read along with their respective programs. In general, if a text T, consisting of the comments on a computer program, is taken together with the lines of the program to which the comments refer, the result is a coherent text; but the program lines are not, in fact, part of T, and are not normally in the same language as T.[2] It might be throught that the sit-

---

[2]Note, however, that in (8) technical terms such as *pop* and *push* from the programming language are part of the programmer's English vocabulary in their technical sense. As such they are used freely in program comments to explain what is happening inside the program, where the terms actually affect the execution of the program. Thus, English words that were incorporated into programming languages with a very special sense have re-entered English with this new sense via the community of computer scientists.

uation is the same as that in a math or physics book, where mathematical proofs and derivations are interspersed with explanatory text, but there is a difference. In the latter case, the cotinuity of the explanatory text is always of the utmost concern to the author and, consequently, the explanatory text is coherent in a way that T is not. The reader must understand the formulas and equations in order to extract the full meaning of the text, but even without that degree of understanding there is sufficient textual cohesion to produce a feeling of naturalness, for example, when read by someone concerned with style rather than content. A more suitable comparison with T is furnished by the sequence of comments made by an editor in the margin of a manuscript; and just as the editor's comments could be expanded to form a commentary in a literary review (including some excerpts from the manuscript), so T could be expanded to form an explanation of the program in a textbook on computer software. In either case the expanded commentary would, presumably, contain the elements of textual cohesion that are necessary to produce acceptable discourse.

The comments included in computer programs may or may not form a sublanguage—the matter needs further study. In any event, this case brings out an interesting point about sublanguages and sublanguage discourse: there may be sublanguages identified entirely on the basis of texts that lack the cohesiveness we expect in natural language discourse. However, once we have identified such a sublanguage, it is not difficult to imagine constructing cohesive discourse from sentences that conform individually to the sublanguage grammar and vocabulary. If the vocabulary lacks the sentence connectives normally employed for this purpose, it may be necessary to lean more heavily on the use of other devices such as repetition of coreferential expessions in adjacent sentences.

Discourse analysis takes into account the presence of word-recurrence patterns in the successive sentences of a discourse. A sublanguage grammar describes the relations between word classes (and subclasses) within sentences and shows that certain elements are available in those sentences for producing textual cohesion; discourse analysis reveals the actual use of these elements in producing coherent discourse. Special features of discourse structure may result from shared knowledge and assumptions on the part of specialists. On the other hand, discourse structure may reflect the relations between the objects or events of a particular subject matter or science, an aspect that is elaborated on in the remainder of this section.

A fundamental property of discourse structure, brought to light by Harris in the course of his work on transformations and discourse analysis in the 1950s, is particularly significant for the automatic analysis of sublanguage texts. It is succinctly described in Harris (1963):

> Discourse analysis is a method of seeking in any connected discrete linear material, whether language or language-like, which contains more than one elementary sentence, some global structure characterizing the whole discourse (the lin-

ear material), or large sections of it. The structure is a pattern of occurrence (i.e., a recurrence) of segments of the discourse relative to each other; . . . Discourse analysis, then, finds the recurrence relative to each other of classes of morpheme sequences, given a segmentation into morpheme sequences by a suitable grammar, and having the intention that *the classes set up are such that their regularity of occurrence will correspond to some relevant semantic interpretation for the discourse. [italics added.]*

Harris developed a "double array," represented in tabular form, showing the correlation between the recurrent classes and a semantic interpretation for the discourse. Entries in a given column of the table have the same informational role in the domain of discourse, as well as some grammatical similarity, but are not mutually substitutable; each row of the table is a sentence of the transformed discourse. He first applied a transformational analysis to "normalize" the original text, reducing the dissimilarities among the various sentence structures. This consists not only of replacement by kernel sentences, but also the combining of kernel sentences in some cases. A small portion of a sample text follows and the resulting table is shown in Table 2.1

The Structure of Insulin as Compared to that of Sanger's A-Chain*

The optical rotatory power of proteins is very sensitive to the experimental conditions under which it is measured, particularly the wavelength of the light which is used. Consequently single measurements of optical rotation do not give an adequate description of rotatory properties, though they have often proved very useful in the characterization of proteins and the detection of changes in structure in solution. The diversity of the factors which affect optical rotation is in many ways an advantage, for the variation of each parameter yields a separate source of experimental information (Harris, 1963, p. 20).

---

*By K. Linderstrom-Lang & John A. Schellman reprinted from *Biochemica et Biophysica Acta*, XV (1954), 156–157.

Table 2.1 is only a segment of the complete table, and it has been simplified by omitting two columns; just enough is included here to illustrate the general method. In the final stage of analysis, this information is organized into more compact tables, eliminating redundancy and showing the general structure of the article without all the linguistic elements. We cannot here enter into the details of Harris's analysis, we can only note that the end result is the merging of the linguistic and informational structure of the article. This general method has been extended and refined by Naomi Sager and her colleagues at NYU in their work on sublanguages. The tabular representation of the transformed discourse is referred to as an *information format*. Adopting this terminology, let us say that if a discourse (or section of a discourse) can be represented in such a manner, then it is *formattable*; and if this is generally the case for discourses in a given sublanguage, let us call it a *formattable sublanguage*. Formattability, in this sense, may be viewed as a kind of global

TABLE 2.1
Partial discourse analysis table

P	C	H	V	R	W	K	Metadiscourse
1		Insulin	has	structure			compared with 2
2		Sanger's A-Chain	has	structure			compared with 1
3		Proteins	have	optical rotatory power	very sensitive to	the experimental conditions	
4	wh	Proteins	have	optical rotatory power	measured under	the experimental conditions	
5	particularly	Proteins	have	optical rotatory power	very sensitive to	the wavelength of the light which is used	
6	Consequently			rotatory properties			are not given adequate description by single measurements of optical rotation
7	though						the latter has often proved very useful in the characterization of proteins
8	and						. . . in the detection of 9
9				structure	changing in	solution	
10		Proteins	have	optical rotation	affected by	a diversity of factors	
11	In many ways					a diversity of factors	is an advantage
12	for						the variation of each parameter yields a separate source of experimental information

restriction, a restriction at the level of a discourse structure. The sentences that are mapped into a particular format need not all have the same structure; the mapping may be thought of as a kind of normalization of the original sentences, which eliminates many structural differences while preserving meaning (or objective information). Of course, we should not dismiss the possibility that there are discourses in which the sentences are sufficiently simple and regular to be placed directly in a format without normalization.

Formattability is, in fact, a matter of degree: there may be a single format for all texts in a highly restricted sublanguage, or there may be several formats in the case of a subject-matter sublanguage covering a broad field; there may be just one format for a particular discourse or separate formats for identifiable sections of the discourse. Information concerning the formattability of sublanguages and the kinds of formats involved could be used as a tool in the classification of sublanguages. And the relevance of formattability for computational linguistics is evident: it gives a clear indication of the tractability of sublanguage texts for the purpose of natural language processing in such fields as information retrieval, machine translation, and text generation.

SUBLANGUAGE, ARTIFICIAL LANGUAGE, NATURAL LANGUAGE.

Natural languages and computer programming languages once seemed as far apart as the people who spoke the former and the machines who spoke the latter. With the development of higher level programming languages the gap has narrowed, and there is now talk about closing the gap altogether. So we witness the progression of artificial languages in the direction of natural language, as suggested in (10):

(10) binary machine language
       assembly language
       .
       .
       .
       BASIC
       .
       .
       .
       PASCAL
       .
       .
       .
       ADA
       .
       .
       .
       query languages
       .
       .
       .
       English

If we were to apply the same criteria for complexity to these formal languages and to various "natural" sublanguages of English, members of the sublanguage list probably would not all lie beyond the point on the scale corresponding to the most complex of the formal languages. It would be interesting to see the extent of the overlap. The development of natural language question answering systems is of particular interest here; thus Warren and Pereira (1982) state their goal as "providing practical computer systems that will answer questions expressed in precisely defined subsets of natural language" and "to so constrain natural language that it becomes a formal, but user-friendly, query language" (p. 110). Here we have an example of the increasing interplay between constructed formal languages and natural language.

Natural language is many-faceted and a hotbed of innovations. Some of the developments within natural languages tend to blur the boundary between them and the increasingly complex artificial languages. Within certain fields norms for reporting information have come into being which drastically affect the style of writing, although the resulting texts are still considered as part of the natural language. The existence of such norms (whatever their origin), combined with restricted subject mater, offers fertile ground for the growth of well defined sublanguages. It is for these natural language subsets that the goal of writing descriptively adequate grammars is most likely to be realized — a goal that has proven so elusive for natural languages in general.

If a descriptively adequate generative grammar can be written for a sublanguage, then, ignoring its natural language origin, it can be looked upon as a *constructed* language. The term consructed has generally been used interchangeably with *artificial*, standing in opposition to *natural*. The distinction between constructed and natural is clear when we compare the formal language of arithmetic or first order predicate logic with English, or when we compare programs in PASCAL with the English text explaining those programs in a PASCAL user's manual. But in the case of certain sublanguages the distinction is not so clear. Thus Moskovich (1982) notes that the sublanguage of rational nomenclature of organic compounds, a language created artificialy by chemists, "has features both of a natural and of an artificial language" (p. 195).

It is tempting to constrain our use of the term sublanguage so that a sublanguage of a natural language is, in some sense, natural — as (i) and (iii) earlier seem to suggest. But how does one decide whether specialized texts read like natural language? And when we consider constructed languages that use the resources of a natural language, we may wonder just how far they can deviate from ordinary usage and still be considered part of the natural language. The distinction between natural and artificial in the domain of sublanguages is fuzzy at best; this should come as no surprise to those linguists who perceive natural language as having fuzzy boundaries anyway.

At the beginning of this chapter we started with an "obvious" assumption: (i) A sublanguage of a natural language L is part of L. We appear to be left with a nagging doubt about just what it means to say that a sublanguage is *part of* a natural language. We may adopt a liberal attitude toward natural language when confronted with a sublanguage candidate of dubious natural credentials and say to its sponsor: "True, this little language that you have identified (or constructed) and which uses a subset of English vocabulary, some grammatical structures of English and a few other things, is certainly far removed from ordinary English; but it is based on English and can be considered as English, though somewhat on the fringe." Or we may attempt to formalize our notion of what constitutes natural language text and then say with some confidence: "This little language that you have identified (or constructed) . . . is not, strictly speaking, a sublanguage of English, but is rather an independent system." Our answer to the question "What is a sublanguage?" hinges on which of these attitudes we adopt. Of course, if we define a sublanguage of L as a subset of the sentences of L closed under some or all of the operations of L (assuming the existence of a formal grammar of L in which these operations are specified), the matter is settled. However, as more and more sublanguages are proposed (which I expect to be the case), my guess is that the question of sublanguage boundaries will remain very much alive.

The application of sublanguage theory has begun to gather momentum; further examination of this theory and its role in a theory of natural language is sure to follow. The increasing number of sublanguage grammars will provide data for an in-depth study of how sublanguages are related to each other and to the standard language and will enable us to identify groups of sublanguages with common characteristics. These developments should yield additional insight into the use of language in special circumstances and may even give us a better handle on what kind of system, or set of interrelated systems, natural language is.

Up to now the main impetus for sublanguage research has been the computational tractability of certain scientific and technical texts. It may be time now to look at some other areas as well. For example, the assumption that sublanguages are subsystems (in the mathematical sense) of the natural languages raises some interesting questions.

What is the status of proposed linguistic universals in sublanguages?

Do any of the "deviant" sublanguages violate hypothesized universals because of the deviant structures?

What about the learnability of sublanguages? There is an active field, ESP, devoted to teaching English for special purposes, and an ESP journal. One of the main concerns is the teaching of job-specific English to foreign students. There must surely be a wealth of data in this field that would be of interest to sublanguage researchers; likewise, ESP can surely benefit from research on sublanguages.

Can any of the language systems being taught to apes be interpreted as sublanguages of natural languages? (Perhaps as subject-matter sublanguages with domains such as food and play?)

Finally, if we accept that the grammar of a sublanguage of L need not be a subgrammar of the grammar of L, but that the grammars only intersect, what is the situation like as that intersection approaches 0? It may be that this boundary question is of more than theoretical interest.

REFERENCES

Harris, Z. S. (1963). *Discourse analysis reprints.* The Hague: Mouton.

Harris, Z. S. (1968). *Mathematical structures of language.* New York: Wiley (Interscience).

Harris, Z. S. (1969). *The two systems of grammar: Report and paraphrase.* TDAP 79, University of Pennsylvania Linguistics Department, Philadelphia.

Harris, Z. S. (1976). On a theory of language. *Journal of Philosophy, 73,* (10), 253–276.

Harris, Z. S. (1982). Discourse and sublanguage. In R. Kittredge & J. Lehrberger (Eds.), *Sublanguage: Studies of language in restricted semantic domains* (pp. 231–236). Berlin: de Gruyter.

Kittredge, R. (1983, March). *Sublanguage-specific computer aids in translation.* Technical report to Translation Bureau of Canada.

Lehrberger, J. (1982a). Automatic translation and the concept of sublanguage. In R. Kittredge & J. Lehrberger (Eds.), *Sublanguage: Studies of language in restricted semantic domains* (pp. 81–106). Berlin: de Gruyter.

Lehrberger, J. (1982b). *Linguistic aspects of software manuals.* Social Sciences and Humanities Research Council of Canada, Project Number 410-81-0249.

McKeown, K. R. (1983). Paraphrasing questions using given and new information. *American Journal of Computational Linguistics, 9*(1), 1–10.

Moskovich, W. (1982). What is a sublanguage? In R. Kittredge & J. Lehrberger (Eds.), *Sublanguage* (pp. 191–205). Berlin: de Gruyter.

Warren, D. & Periera, F. (1982). An efficient easily adaptable system for interpreting natural language queries. *American Journal of Computational Linguistics, 8* (3–4), 110–122.

Wiener, R. & Sincovec R. (1982). *Programming in ADA.* New York: Wiley.

Wirth, N. (1976). *Algorithms + data structures = programs.* Englewood Cliffs, NJ: Prentice-Hall.

3 The Status of Telegraphic Sublanguages

Eileen Fitzpatrick
Joan Bachenko
Don Hindle
AT&T Bell Laboratories
Murray Hill, New Jersey

ABSTRACT

Sublanguages used for telegraphic communication are viewed as fragmentary versions of the standard language. Thus, a sublanguage grammar is difficult to describe because it must comprise the rules and lexicon of the standard language along with sublanguage options whose occurrence is unpredictable.

Our analysis of the Navy message sublanguage suggests that this view is incorrect. The grammar we propose describes the gapped object, passive, and middle verb data that is characteristic of telegraphic messages. The core of this description is a sublanguage-specific constraint that allows verbs to be transitive or intransitive but not both. If the rules that describe our data presuppose this constraint, the result is a more accurate and simpler grammar than one that assumes these data to be fragments of the standard language. The mechanisms we propose for the sublanguage grammar are (a) independent of Standard English, and (b) interdependent. This situation argues that we view a telegraphic sublanguage as a complete system rather than a fragmented version of the standard language.

INTRODUCTION

Sentences like those listed below distinguish telegraphic sublanguages such as those found in military messages, medical reports, and headlines from the standard language:

(1) a. Attempt to deliver on 05 April.
   b. No shipyard test performed.
   c. She took for five days.
   d. Pain noted in hands and feet.
   e. Shut-ins can grow indoors with lights. (*The Miami Herald,* 7/21/78)
   f. Stiff opposition expected to casketless funeral plan. (*The Toronto Star,* 4/7/76)[1]

There are currently two views of the relation between the standard language and these telegraphic sublanguages. One view is that the sublanguages are ill-formed with respect to the standard language, that is, the sentence fragments that characterize telegraphic communication are in the same general category as ungrammatical phrases like *We is.* The work of Sondheimer and Weischedel (1980), Kwasny and Sondheimer (1981), and Hayes and Mouradian (1981) is representative of this view.

The other view holds that telegraphic sentences are reduced forms of standard language sentences and that these forms are perfectly acceptable within the pertinent domain. The work of Lehrberger (1982), Marsh and Sager (1982), and Marsh (1983) is representative of this view. In fact, both Marsh and Lehrberger point out that the sentence fragments that characterize telegraphic narrative occur also in the standard language in certain contexts. Marsh gives the example of the fragment *the sentence ambiguous* occurring in Standard English as a complement in *She found the sentence ambiguous.*

This reduced sentence view takes us a long way towards being able to handle telegraphic data because it regards sentence fragments as patterns to be expected, and because the research that assumes this view is aimed at identifying the fragment patterns for a particular domain. However, both of the existing views on telegraphic narrative have the same empirical approach to sentence fragments. Both assume that a fragment is the result of deletions and that the interpretation of a fragment proceeds by filling in the deletions and so converting it into a full standard form. In other words, both views assume that a telegraphic sentence is dependent on a full standard language sentence.[2] For example, Sondheimer and Weischedel (1980) propose two kinds

---

[1]Examples (1a)–(1b) are taken from navy casualty reports, reporting shipboard equipment failures; (1c) is a clinical report example discussed in Hirschman and Sager (1982); (1d) is a clinical report example discussed in Marsh (1983); (1e)–(1f) are taken from Columbia Journalism Review (1980).

[2]This is not the stated position of Hayes and Mouradian (1981), who view fragments as "themselves complete utterances given the context in which they occur." However, their Flexible Parsing, by relaxing the requirements of the standard language to get a successsful parse, proceeds under the assumption that the fragments contain omissions.

of rules: rules used in normal processing, and meta-rules, which apply "to the rules of the first sort in order to relate the structure of ill-formed input to that of well-formed structures" (p. 48). And Marsh (1983) states: "The fact that the fragment types can be related to full English forms makes it possible to view them as instances of reduced SUBJECT-VERB-OBJECT patterns from which particular components have been deleted" (p. 99).

The grammar of a telegraphic sublanguage, according to this assumption, has no internal consistency independent of the standard language. Thus, the rules that mark the sublanguage as different from the standard language cannot be directly connected to each other; rather they have only an indirect connection through the standard language. This approach makes the grammars of these languages difficult to describe, inasmuch as the grammar has to comprise the rules and lexicon of the standard language along with sublanguage options whose occurrence is unpredictable. In addition, this approach forces a grammar that relies on deletion to make an incorrect prediction in the area we have examined: that of gapped and moved objects.

Our work on the telegraphic narrative of Navy messages suggests that we look at the opposing assumption, namely, that a sentence fragment is a full form rather than the result of deletions. In other words, we should view telegraphic sublanguages as languages that exhibit an internal consistency independent of the standard language. This assumption entails that the rules that mark the sublanguage as different from the standard language are directly connected to each other.

In the second section, we discuss one rule difference between the Navy sublanguage and Standard English involving verb transitivity. In the third section, we discuss four instances in which rules of the sublanguage are directly dependent on this difference rather than on Standard English rules. We also discuss how this assumption of rule interdependency compares with the assumption that telegraphic sentences are the residue of deletions. In the fourth section, we summarize and describe our implementation of the sublanguage grammar.

TRANSITIVITY IN ENGLISH AND IN NAVY TELEGRAPHIC NARRATIVE

In Standard English, a large number of verbs are both transitive and intransitive, as is *grow* in (2):

(2) a. Shut-ins can grow plants.
    b. Shut-ins can grow.

In our Navy message data, however, there are no verbs that are transitive in one example and intransitive in another: transitive verbs always require a noun phrase object. This was true for a corpus of 219 sentences that we used for implementation. This corpus contained 92 different verbs. Approximately 70 more sentences were checked to confirm this requirement. We call this requirement of sublanguage verbs, the *verb transitivity constraint*. This requirement is a constraint on lexical description that prohibits intransitive options for transitive verbs.

We cannot prove by a verb count (regardless of the size of the count) that the transitivity constraint exists within the Navy sublanguage. But there are two points about this sublanguage that make such a constraint plausible.

The first point follows from Harris's (1968) claim that the semantic domain of a sublanguage forms a subset of the semantic domain of the standard language. That the semantic domain of a sublanguage is smaller than the semantic domain of the standard language means that many of the lexical options occurring in the standard language will not occur in the sublanguage. For example, in Standard English, the verb *procure* can be either transitive, as in *He procured work,* or intransitive, as in *They procure at the airports.* In the Navy message narrative, however, the verb *procure* has the transitive form, as in *Attempt to procure parts locally,* but the intransitive form, which deals with procurement for illicit purposes, is out of place in a description of shipboard equipment failures.

The second point in favor of the constraint is that assuming such a constraint as a working hypothesis allows the grammar to make the right predictions with respect to the data involving transitive and intransitive verbs. In the next section we discuss these data as well as how the sublanguage grammar, by incorporating the verb transitivity constraint, provides an empirically correct and simple description of these data.

RULE INTERDEPENDENCY IN THE NAVY SUBLANGUAGE

We consider here four phenomena that arise in the Navy sublanguage: the gapping of noun phrase objects, passivization, the formation of the middle construction, and apparent syntactic ambiguity. Each of these phenomena depends on the verb transitivity constraint for a correct analysis.

Gapped Objects

Our Navy sublanguage corpus contains the following examples of object gapping, with a "__" inserted to represent the gap:

(3) a. 72 manhours expended to correct __.
    b. Attempt to procure __ locally to deliver __ on 05 April.

c. Ship's tech will repair __.
d. System currently unable to process __.

The fact that the verbs *correct, procure, deliver, repair,* and *process* realize only the transitive option in the Navy sublanguage allows the object noun phrases in the above examples to be gapped because the sublanguage grammar will never interpret these verbs as intransitive.

We are assuming that the sublanguage semantic component plugs in the appropriate noun phrase where the syntactic component has identified a gap. This differs from the assumption that these object gaps are simply syntactic deletions of the full noun phrase objects of Standard English; the possibility of a gapped object in the sublanguage depends on the assumption that the verb never realizes its intransitive option in the sublanguage. This assumption is not true for Standard English and hence could not be true for the syntactic deletion approach.

There is an empirical consequence to the assumption of a gapped object rather than a deleted one in the examples of (3). The consequence may be illustrated with the verb *procure*. In Standard English, this verb has a transitive sense, meaning "to obtain or secure" and an intransitive sense, meaning "to obtain for the purpose of prostitution". If the sublanguage grammar incorporates the assumption that objects can be deleted from fuller, standard language constructions, then the grammar will analyze the phrase *to procure locally* as both a Standard English transitive construction with a deleted object and a Standard English intransitive construction with no change in analysis between the standard language and the sublanguage. In contrast, if the sublanguage grammar incorporates the assumption that verbs are either transitive or intransitive, but not both, then the grammar will analyze *procure* only as a transitive with a syntactically empty object.

As we indicated, the expectation that messages about shipboard equipment failure will include information about prostitution is absurd, as anyone doing sublanguage research senses. The approach to this problem on the part of researchers who assume that the sublanguage represents deletions of standard language forms has been to block the unwanted reading of *to procure locally* at the semantic level. This approach, however, misses the generalization that the verbs are constrained as to transitivity. By missing the generalization, this approach is unable to describe the wider range of missing object data that includes passives and middles.

Passivization

In Standard English, many verbs must be specified as both transitive and intransitive, as discussed previously. Only some of these verbs have a distinctive passive form, e.g., *taken, begun, flown, grown, spoken.* Most verbs have the same form for the past and the passive: either an -*ed* suffix or the same irregular form, as in *The ship left, The ship was left.*

In the Standard English passive, the logical noun phrase object occupies the subject position. Thus when a verb with an ambiguous past/passive form is encountered without a following noun phrase, it may either be that the verb is transitive and its lexical object is the subject of the sentence or that the verb is a past tense intransitive. This is an important difference for the semantic represenation of the information contained in the sentence. In Standard English, the difference between the passive form of the verb and the past tense is signaled by the presence of the copula, as the b. examples in (4)-(6) demonstrate:

(4) a. The ship attacked.
    b. The ship was attacked.

(5) a. The ship left.
    b. The ship was left.

(6) a. No test performed well enough to identify the bad transistors.
    b. No test was performed well enough to identify the bad transistors.

The distinctive fact about the passive construction in the Navy sublanguage is that there is normally no copula.[3] (This fact is true for telegraphic sublanguages in general, as (1b), (1d) and (1f) demonstrate.) The examples in (7) demonstrate this fact:

---

[3] Our corpus contains 54 instances of passivization, 37 of which have no copula. Examples of the remaining 17 are given below:

(i)   Temporary repairs have been made by ship's force.
(ii)   Upper half of antenna damaged beyond repair when antenna was lowered.
(iii) Request facility in Barcelona be assigned to rewind motor.
(iv)   Arrange tech assistance for repairs to be accomplished.
(v)   Motor controller was wired improperly by shipyard personnel.
(vi)   Problem appears to be caused by one or more of two hydraulic valves.

While our explanation for the absence of the copula makes no claim about cases where the copula is present, it would be interesting, for sublanguage purposes, to determine if the presence of *be* in these sentences is arbitrary. In (i), apparently, the perfect *have* forces the copula. Our data contains 7 examples where another word in the auxiliary forces the appearance of the copula.

Our data contains 6 examples like (ii), where the occurrence of the passive in an embedded sentence with a lexical subject forces the appearance of the copula.

The examples (iii)–(iv) are distinct in that the passivized verb indicates a future action. Without the copula, these sentences would imply that the action took place in the past.

As far as we can determine at present, the presence of the copula in (v) and (vi) is arbitrary.

(7) a. No Norfolk Naval Shipyard test performed subsequent to work.
  b. 72 manhours expended.
  c. Stock requisition shipped.
  d. Pinhole leak found in drain line during lite off.
  e. Work request submitted.
  f. USS Piedmont assigned for repairs.
  g. P(lanned) M(aintenance) S(ystem) not covered.
  h. Crankshaft scoured.
  i. Further investigation required.
  j. Hydraulic cylinder lost by Norfolk Naval Shipyard during overhaul.
  k. Overhaul not completed due to missing cylinder.
  l. Improper repair work performed.
  m. No parts required.

If we assume that these telegraphic sentences are the result of deletions, then we leave the sublanguage grammar with no way to distinguish between the passives and past tense intransitives. If the sentences in (7) were ambiguous, then this situation would be the desirable one. However, the sentences in (7) are not ambiguous: they are understood only as passives. For the most part, it is possible to determine this from the pattern of selectional restrictions. For example, *Stock requisition shipped* cannot be intransitive because stock requisitions cannot ship in the intransitive sense that a sailor can ship on the USS Piedmont. A sublanguage grammar that incorporates copula deletion must use this selectional information to eliminate the intransitive readings, as it must to eliminate the intransitive/gapped object ambiguity we discussed above.

However, this grammar will miss a generalization about the sublanguage, namely, that the existence of gapped objects and noncopula passives is dependent on the transitive/intransitive distinction among verbs. Moreover, it will make an incorrect prediction about the data.[4] The sentences in (6) provide one example of this incorrect analysis. As the sentences in (6) show, the verb *perform* can be both transitive and intransitive in Standard English. Furthermore, the examples in (6) show that the noun *test* can function selectionally either as the subject or the object of *perform.* Therefore, a sublanguage grammar that incorporates copula deletion will assign two analyses to *No test performed,* one with an intransitive verb and one with a passivized transitive verb. In other words, the deletion analysis predicts that

---

[4]Additionally, in terms of parsing, the use of selectional restrictions to eliminate the potential ambiguity problems that arise in (7) is a costly solution. In writing the parsing grammar, it requires a great amount of human intervention to determine the appropriate selectional restrictions. In parsing, it requires a constant cost in machine time to do a correct selectional match between a verb and its subject and objects.

No test performed is ambiguous in the sublanguage. This sentence, however, is not ambiguous in the message narrative: it is understood only as a passivization. On the other hand, a sublanguage grammar that incorporates the transitivity constraint will correctly assign a single analysis to the sentences in (7), including the sentence *No test performed* because all the verbs in (7) are transitive in the Navy message narrative. The verb transitivity constraint thus allows us to account for noncopula passives.

More significantly, the constraint explains why the copula is absent in certain cases. In Standard English, the copula is necessary to distinguish the past tense intransitive from the passive transitive. In the sublanguage, however, the copula is not necessary; the transitive/intransitive ambiguity never arises because the verb transitivity constraint prevents passivized transitive verbs from being wrongly interpreted as intransitives.

This observation provides an additional argument for a sublanguage grammar that incorporates the transitivity constraint. It explains why the copula, rather than some other preverbal element, is absent: the copula can be absent in this grammar because it is not needed to distinguish the transitive senses of a verb from the intransitive ones. In contrast, a sublanguage grammar in which passive fragments are treated as cases of copula deletion offers no explanation for why the copula, but no other preverbal element, is deleted. For example, this latter grammar has no explanation for the fact that (8b) is not a possible sublanguage sentence, even though (8a) is:

(8) a. Temporary repairs have been made by ship's force.
    b. *Temporary repairs been made by ship's force.

Apparent Problems with the Passive.   There appears to be a difficulty with our treatment of gapped objects and passives. From what we have said so far, it appears that the grammar analyzes the verbs in (7) both as passives *and* as verbs with gapped objects, because the verbs in (7) are all transitive verbs, to which both object gapping and passivization can apply. This is a potentially serious problem. A sentence such as *Ship attacked* could be assigned two analyses with opposite readings: the gapped object reading, *Ship attacked something,* and the passive reading, *Ship was attacked.*

However, this problem does not arise in the message narrative because gapped noun phrase objects do not occur with verb forms that are ambiguously past and passive. Thus, although our corpus contains 54 passive constructions, including 37 telegraphic passives, it contains only the following examples of gapped objects.[5]

---

[5]Gapped object examples like the sentence in (i) appear often in the message narrative, though not in our corpus:

(i) 72 manhours expended to correct ____

These examples are consistent with the data in (9) in that *correct* is not a past/passive form.

(9) a. Attempt to procure __ locally
   b. Attempt . . . to deliver __ on 05 April
   c. Ship's tech will repair __
   d. System currently unable to process __

The distinctive feature of the verbs that precede the gapped object is that none of them exhibits an *-ed* suffix. This means that if a transitive verb occurs without an object to its right and the verb has an *-ed* suffix or an irregular form that is ambiguously past and passive, then the verb is always understood as a passive.

That this type of ambiguity could arise and that the message narrative works out a way to avoid it provides additional support for our analysis. Stronger support will be provided if, in an analysis of a larger corpus, we find examples such as the data (1c), *She took for five days,* which comes from a medical report processed by the Linguistic String Parser. Example (1c) is a case of a past tense verb followed by a gapped object. This is exactly what our hypothesis predicts should occur with verbs like *take* because its past tense, *took,* is not ambiguous with its passive form, *taken.*

There is also a small set of apparent counterexamples to our passive analysis per se. The sentences in (10) exemplify this set:

(10) a. Ship's service air capacity reduced 50%.
    b. No deficiencies projected end of fiscal year.

In these examples, we have a passivized, transitive verb. According to our analysis, these verbs should have no noun phrase to their right because the noun phrase objects for which they are lexically specified occur as the subjects of these verbs.[6] However, an additional constituent that may be a noun phrase appears in each case.

In both examples of (10), it is clear that the problem arises because we expect a preposition between the verb and the noun phrase. Avoidance of prepositions is a common feature of the Navy sublanguage. We expect that an analysis of the circumstances under which prepositions may be absent in the sublanguage will give us an analysis of data such as (10) that is consistent with our analysis of passives in general.

The Middle Construction

There are certain verbs that, in a given sublanguage sentence, appear to be intransitive, but in which the subject of the verb actually functions as the ob-

---

[6]If the verb is lexically specified to take two noun phrase objects, as is *issue* in (i), then this problem does not arise because the second noun phrase is expected:

(i) Subject Named Man issued government transport request from Baltimore to Bermuda.

ject of the verb. These verbs are often referred to as middle verbs. Our data contain the following examples of this type of verb:

(11) a. Troubleshooting will resume.
    b. A five inch split in hull opened.
    c. . . . causing latch to extend in mid-cycle.

Middle verbs are specified as transitive in the lexicon and treated in the same way as passives, i.e., the subject of the verb is taken as the object.[7] When a middle verb occurs in the past tense, as in (11b), it is impossible to tell whether it is a passive form or a middle form in our data. Treating the middle form as analagous to the passive in terms of transitivity allows us to capture this fact.

Syntactic Ambiguity

In Standard English, the fact that verbs are both transitive and intransitive may result in ambiguity. The well-known sentence, *Flying planes can be dangerous,* is an example of such ambiguity. The transitive *fly* occurs in *Flying planes is dangerous;* the intransitive *fly* in *Flying planes are dangerous.* We would expect a sublanguage used for technical communications to avoid ambiguity. Incorporating the verb transitivity constraint into the Navy sublanguage grammar ensures that it will avoid the *Flying planes* type of ambiguity.

The sentence (12), from our corpus, is an example of the potential transitive/intransitive ambiguity:

(12) Failed klystron. Unable to radiate continuous wave 1.

In Standard English, the phrase *Failed klystron* has two readings: one in which *failed* is an intransitive left modifier of *klystron,* such that the klystron is doing the failing; the other in which *failed* is a transitive verb and *klystron* is its object, such that *klystron* is understood as some sort of test and the noun phrase that is functioning as the subject of *failed* is understood as failing that test. A klystron being an electron tube, the latter reading is not possible.

A sublanguage grammar that allows object deletion on Standard English sentences must allow both syntactic analyses because *fail* is both transitive and intransitive in Standard English. A deletion grammar must thus block the transitive reading of (12) by putting selectional restrictions on *fail* to en-

---

[7]This is the approach to middles taken by Burzio (1981) within the Government-Binding framework (Chomsky, 1981) of generative linguistic theory.

sure that *fail* will reject as objects nouns having the selectional properties of the noun *klystron*. Again, this is time consuming and fails to capture the generalization captured by the transitivity constraint.

In contrast, the Navy sublanguage data indicate that the verb *fail* is only intransitive in the sublanguage, as the following sentences illustrate:

(13) a. Screen regulator diodes failed.
      b. Drum ejectors failed to function.

Therefore, a sublanguage grammar that incorporates the transitivity constraint will block the transitive reading of *fail* in *failed klystron* on a purely syntactic level. We thus avoid the problems attendant on a selectional check while maintaining the generalization captured by the transitivity constraint. We also provide additional motivation for the transitivity constraint: it is a method of cutting down ambiguity in a technical area.

CONCLUSION

Our goal has been to define the status of the grammar of a telegraphic sublanguage with respect to the grammar of the standard language. In attempting to do so, we have compared the assumption that the grammar of a telegraphic sublanguage consists of the grammar of the standard language plus certain deletion rules with a logically opposite assumption, namely, that the grammar of a telegraphic sublanguage consists of a subset of the rules of the standard language plus certain interdependent rules that are peculiar to the sublanguage. Both the rule interdependence and the sublanguage-specific nature of the rules indicate a partially independent status for the grammar of the sublanguage with respect to the standard language.

On the basis of the data in our Navy message corpus, we proposed a transitivity constraint on the lexical options of the sublanguage verbs such that a verb is specified as transitive or intransitive, but not both. We argued that the rules that handle several types of missing object data are dependent on this constraint. We showed that, if a grammar of the Navy message sublanguage incorporates this constraint, it can handle the missing object data more accurately and in a more revealing fashion than a grammar that assumes the rules of the standard language plus certain deletion rules. Specifically, a sublanguage grammar that incorporates the verb transitivity constraint provides an account of sublanguage noncopula passives in certain cases where a sublanguage grammar that does not have this constraint fails. One of these cases involves the verb *perform,* discussed previously. Furthermore, a grammar that incorporates the transitivity constraint provides a simpler account of gapped objects, middle verbs, and potential verb/modifier ambiguity than a grammar that assumes deletion rules operating on the standard language; the former grammar obviates the need for selectional checks for these constructions.

Finally, a grammar that incorporates the transitivity constraint explains why the copula, but no other preverbal element, can be absent from sublanguage passives. The explanation is that, in contrast to the situation in Standard English, the copula is not needed to distinguish the transitive occurrence of a verb from its transitive occurrence. The transitivity constraint requires that a transitive option on a verb preclude an intransitive option, and vice versa, depending on the verb's usage in the sublanguage. A sublanguage grammar that assumes deletion rules operating on the standard language has no explanation for why some elements are candidates for deletion whereas others are not.

To summarize, we have shown that a grammar that describes the missing object data as dependent on a verb transitivity constraint is superior to a grammar that describes these data as the result of deletions of standard language forms. This rule interdependence, and the fact that the constraint is sublanguage-specific, indicate a partially independent status for the sublanguage grammar with respect to the standard language. In other words, the sublanguage has a life of its own with respect to the data we have described.

We should mention, finally, how the sublanguage options we have discussed are handled in the NRL Deterministic Parser, known as Fidditch (Hindle, 1983). Fidditch has the capacity to tailor its grammar rules and lexicon to a specific sublanguage. Sublanguage is a switch that causes the sublanguage lexicon to be checked and checks rules for the presence or absence of the sublanguage feature. With a sublanguage turned on, the lexical lookup function checks first for a special sublanguage lexical entry before using the standard language lexical entry for a word. The verb transitivity constraint is thus built into each verb in the lexicon. Also, rule tests specified for a sublanguage that is switched on are evaluated, and if true, then the specified action is taken. For the Navy sublanguage, the rule tests include a check for a transitive verb that lacks an object. If the value of the test is true, then an empty noun phrase object is inserted into the parse.

The aspects of the Navy message sublanguage that we have discussed here have been fully implemented in the Fidditch parser.

ACKNOWLEDGMENT

The research on which this chapter is based was done while the authors were working at the Computer Science and Systems Branch, Information Technology Division, Naval Research Laboratory, Washington, DC.

REFERENCES

Burzio, L. (1981). *Intransitive verbs and Italian auxiliaries.* Unpublished Ph.D. dissertation. Cambridge, MA: MIT Press.

Chomsky, N. (1981). *Lectures on government and binding.* Dordrecht, the Netherlands: Foris Publications.

Columbia Journalism Review (ed.). (1980). *Squad helps dog bite victim.* Garden City, NY: Doubleday.

Hayes, P. J. & Mouradian, G. V. (1981). Flexible parsing. *American Journal of Comparative Linguistics* 7(4), 232–242.

Hindle, D. (1983). User manual for Fidditch, a deterministic parser. Naval Research Laboratory Technical Memorandum #7590-142.

Hirschman, L. & Sager, N. (1982). Automatic information formatting of a medical sublanguage. In L. Kittredge & J. Lehrberger (Eds.), *Sublanguage: Studies of language in restricted semantic domains.* Berlin: de Gruyter.

Kwasny, S. C. & Sondheimer, N. K. (1981). Relaxation techniques for parsing ill-formed input. American Journal of Comparative Linguistics.

Lehrberger, J. (1982). Automatic translation and the concept of sublanguage. In R. Kittredge and J. Lehrberger (eds.) *Sublanguage: Studies of language in restricted semantic domains.* Berlin: de Gruyter.

Marsh, E. (1983). Utilizing domain-specific information for processing compact text.*Proceedings of the Conference on Applied Natural Language Processing.* Association for Computational Linguistics, Santa Monica, CA.

Marsh, E., & Sager, N. (1982). Analysis and processing of compact text. *COLING-82 Abstracts: Proceedings of the Ninth International Conference on Computational Linguistics* (pp. 201–208). Prague.

Sondheimer, N. K. & Weischedel, R. M. (1980). A rule-based approach to ill-formed input. *COLING-80 Abstracts: Proceedings of the Eighth International Conference on Computational Linguistics*, Tokyo.

4 Sublanguage and Knowledge

Jerry R. Hobbs
SRI International
Menlo Park, California

ABSTRACT

In conjunction with a project for information retrieval from a medical textual data base, we have encoded a fairly large knowledge base of facts (about 1000 axioms) ranging from low-level commonsense knowledge to mildly arcane medical knowledge. A methodology is described for constructing such a knowledge base in a principled way. Facts are selected for the knowledge base by determining what facts are linguistically presupposed by a text in the domain of interest. The facts are then organized into clusters according to their logical dependencies and encoded as predicate calculus axioms. We are currently devising pragmatic processes that use such a knowledge base to interpret medical discourse. Among these is a process that seeks to bring a predicate and its arguments into congruence. At the simplest level, this merely checks selectional constraints; in more complex cases, it seeks to resolve examples of metonymy. It is argued that sublanguage constraints that are usually encoded as selectional constraints on predicate-argument pairs are in fact a surface manifestation of these deeper pragmatic processes operating on such a domain-specific knowledge base.

INTRODUCTION

Over the last year and a half we have been building a fairly large knowledge base for a natural language processing system. This effort may be viewed as an alternative to, or perhaps as alternate perspective on, the sublanguage approach to text processing. Instead of specifying constraints particular to a sublanguage, one axiomatizes in a formal language some of the knowledge in the underlying domain. In this paper I first set the context by describing the system we ultimately hope to construct. A knowledge base is an important component of the system. The methodology used in building the knowledge base is then discussed: first, the method of selecting the facts to be encoded followed by several observations on the internal organization of the knowledge base. Examples are given of two ways in which the knowledge base will be used in discourse processing. Finally, this approach is compared to, and, primarily, contrasted with the sublanguage approach.

The work described in this paper has been carried out as part of a project to build a system for natural language access to a computerized medical textbook on hepatitis, the HKB (Bernstein, Siegel, & Goldstein, 1980). The intent is that the user will ask a question in English, and rather than attempting to answer it, the system will return the passages in the text relevant to the question. As illustrated in Fig. 4.1, the English query is translated into a logical form by the DIALOGIC system, a syntactic and semantic translation component (Grosz et al, 1982). The textbook is represented by a *text structure*, consisting of, among other things, summaries of the contents of individual passages expressed in a logical language. Inference procedures, making use of a knowledge base, seek to match the logical form of the query with some part of the text structure. In addition, they attempt to solve various pragmatics problems posed by the query, including the resolution of coreference, metonymy, and the implicit predicates in compound nominals.

Several examples demonstrate just how rich the knowledge base must be for this application. In one of the target dialogs we have collected, the user asks the question,

Is saliva infective?

It happens that the relevant passage is about the *transmission* of hepatitis B virus by saliva. The knowledge base must therefore have an axiom relating *infective* and *transmission*.

Similarly, the question

Can a patient with mild hepatitis go on a strenuous rock climb?

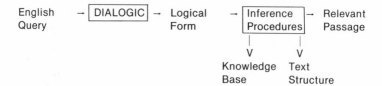

FIG 4.1.   Structure of the Text Access System.

is answered by a passage whose heading is "Management: Requirements for Bed Rest." The rather indirect relation between *strenuous* and *bed rest* must be encoded in the knowledge base.

In addition to matching the query with the text structure, the system is intended to solve various discourse problems, such as the problem of co-reference resolution. Consider the two successive queries:

Could this episode be a reactived form of his prior disease?
How can I confirm this possibility?

The definite noun phrase *this possibility* refers to the operand of *could* in the first sentence. To resolve it, we must have encoded the relation between *possibility* and *could*.

A large knowledge base is necesary. But how large? Unfortunately, there is no limit. Discourse can require arbitrarily detailed world knowledge for its interpretation. If you know that John's maternal grandmother's maiden name is Davis, you will be able to understand the compound nominal in the sentence

John has a Davis smile.

It is of course impossible to encode this much knowledge. What we would like is a knowledge base that is richer than the simple sort hierarchy that most natural language processing systems have, but does not include facts as detailed as John's maternal grandmother's maiden name. More particularly, we would like to develop a principled methodology for building intermediate-sized knowledge bases for natural language applications. This paper describes such a methodology, developed in the course of constructing a knowledge base of about one thousand "facts" for the text access system.

One way to build the knowledge base might have been to analyze the queries in the target dialogs we had collected to determine what facts they seem to require, and to put just these facts into our knowledge base. However, we were interested in discovering general principles of the selection and structuring of such intermediate-sized knowledge bases, principles that would give us reason to believe our knowledge base would be useful for unanticipated queries.

Thus we have developed a three-stage methodology:

1. Select the facts that should be in the knowledge base by determining what facts are linguistically presupposed by the medical textbook. This gives us a very good indication of what knowledge of the domain the user is expected to bring to the textbook and would presumably bring to the text access system.

2. Organize the facts into clusters and organize the facts within each cluster according to the logical dependencies among the concepts they involve.

3. Encode the facts as predicate calculus axioms, regularizing the concepts, or predicates, as necessary.

In this paper only the first two stages are discussed since they are most relevant to the study of sublanguages.

Before we continue, it may help orient the reader if three examples of facts and their corresponding axioms are given. The knowledge base includes commonsense knowledge, which everyone knows, and medical knowledge, usually known only by experts. An example of the former is the lexical decomposition inference for the predicate *produce*:

If x produces y, then x causes y to exist.

$(\forall x,y)(\exists e)$ produce $(x,y) \to$ cause (x,e) & exist' (e,y)[1]

The following is a medical fact that everyone knows:

Food can be the medium for the transmission of an (etiologic) agent.

$(\forall x,y)(\exists e,z,w)$ food(x) & agent $(y) \to$ possible(e) & transmit'(e,x,y,z,w)

The knowledge base also includes midly arcane knowledge about medicine, such as:

The lobules of the liver move bilirubin from the blood stream into the bile.

(1) $(A x,y)(E z,w)$ lobule(x) & blood-stream$(y) \to$ bilirubin(z) & bile(w) & move (x,z,y,w)

SELECTING THE FACTS

A useful system needs a large vocabulary. Moreover, when trying to axiomatize a domain, without a rich set of predicates and facts to be responsible for, one does not get a feel of coherence. One's efforts seem ad hoc. Therefore, the first step in building the knowledge base is to make up a large list of words, or predicates, or concepts (the three words are used interchangeably here), and a large list of relevant facts about these predicates. The

---

[1] The mildly nonstandard aspects of the logical notation used in this paper are described in Hobbs (1983, 1985). In this formula, e is an event or self argument, standing for y's existence. In general, if p(x) means that p is true of x, then p'(e,x) means that e is the condition of p being true of x.

words or predicates we chose were the (about 250) predicates from the text structure and the (about 80) additional content words that occurred in our target dialogs. Inasmuch as the knowledge base is intended to link the dialogs and the text structure, this seemed to be the bare minimum.

Because there are dozens of facts one could state about any one of these predicates, we were faced with the problem of determining those facts that would be most pertinent for natural language understanding in this application. Our principal tool at this stage was a full-sentence concordance of the HKB, displaying the contexts in which the words were used. Our method was to examine these contexts and to ask what facts about each concept were required to justify each of these uses. Morphologically related (and not so related) words were considered as evidence for a single underlying predicate. Thus, the words *vary, varied, varying, variable, various, variation* and *variety* were all seen in this application as decomposable into expressions involving the predicate *vary*, and *oral* was viewed as related to the predicate *mouth*.

The three principal linguistic phenomena we looked at were predicate-argument relations, compound nominals, and conjoined phrases. As an example of the first, consider two uses of the word *data*. The phrase *extensive data on histocompatibility antigens* seems to presuppose that the reader knows the fact about data that it is a *set* (justifying *extensive*) of particular facts *about some subject* (justifying the *on* argument). The phrase *the data do not consistently show* . . . points to the fact that data is assembled to support some conclusion. To arrive at the facts, we ask questions like "What is data that it can be extensive or that it can show something?" For compound nominals, we ask: What general facts about the two nouns underlie the implicit relation? Thus, for "casual contact circumstances" we posit that contact is a concomitant of activities, and the phrase "contact mode of transmission" leads us to the fact that contact possibly leads to transmission of an agent. Conjoined noun phrases indicate the existence of a superordinate in a sort hierarchy covering all the conjoined concepts. Thus, the phrase *epidemiology, clinical aspects, pathology, diagnosis, and management* tells us to encode the facts that all of these are aspects of a disease, and *renal dialysis units and other high-risk institutional settings* tells us that a renal dialysis unit is a high-risk setting.

To illustrate the method, let us examine various uses of the word *disease* to see what facts they suggest:

destructive liver disease: A disease has a harmful effect on one or more body parts.

hepatitis A virus plays a role in chronic liver disease: A disease may be caused by an agent.

the clinical manifestations of a disease: A disease is detectable by signs and symptoms.

the course of a disease: A disease goes through several stages in time.

infectious disease: A disease can be transmitted.

a notifiable disease: A disease has patterns in the population that can be traced by the medical community.

We emphasize that this is not a mechanical procedure but rather a method of discovery that relies on our informed intuitions. Because it is largely background knowledge we are after, we can not expect to get it directly by interviewing experts. Our method is a way of extracting it from the presuppositions behind linguistic uses.

The first thing our method gives us is a great deal of selectivity in the facts we encode. Consider the word *animal*. There are hundreds of facts that we know about animals. However, in this domain there are only two facts we need. Animals are used in experiments, as seen in the compound nominal *laboratory animal*, and animals can have a disease, and thus transmit it, as seen in the phrase *animals implicated in hepatitis*. Similarly, the only relevant fact about *water* is that it may be a medium for the transmission of disease (*waterborne hepatitis*). Similarly, all that is relevant about alcohol is that it is consumed by and may be harmful to people, as indicated by the phrase,

prescription regarding alcohol intake.

By this method, we often find the differences in the meaning of a word in general English and in the sublanguage of this application. For example, the word *history* in this application does not refer to a record of past events, but only to a record of past episodes of disease in a patient. The word *vertical* in this application does not mean perpendicular to the horizon, but rather refers to the transmission of disease from a mother to a foetus. In addition, concepts must be categorized in different ways. For example, we do not want to say that persons are animals, for almost none of the inferences are the same for the two. A person cannot be a laboratory animal, and an animal cannot be a patient (in this application). One of the few relevant properties they share is that both can be the source of an infection.

The method leads us toward generalizations we might otherwise miss, when we see a number of uses that seem to fall within the same class. For example, the uses of the word *laboratory* seem to be of two kinds:

1. laboratory animals, laboratory spores, laboratory contamination, laboratory measurements, laboratory methods.
2. a study by a research laboratory, laboratory testing, laboratory abnormalities, laboratory characteristics of hepatitis A, laboratory picture.

The first of these rests on the fact that experiments involving certain events and entities take place in laboratories. The second rests on the fact that things are learned there.

A classical issue in lexical semantics that arises at this stage is the problem of polysemy, and the concordance method suggests solutions. Should we consider a word, or predicate, as ambiguous, or should we try to find a very general characterization of its meaning that abstracts away from its use in various contexts? The rule of thumb we have followed is that if the uses fall into two or three distinct, large classes, the word is treated as having separate senses; whereas if the uses seem to be spread all over the map, we try to find a general characterization that covers them all. The word *derive* is an example of the first case. A derivation is either of information from an investigative activity, as in *epidemiologic patterns derived from historical studies*, or of chemicals from body parts, as in *enzymes derived from intestinal mucosa*. By contrast, the word *produce* (and *product*) can be used in a variety of ways: a disease can produce a condition, a virus can produce a disease or a viral particle, something can produce a virus ("the amount of virus produced in the carrier state"), intestinal flora can produce compounds, and something can produce chemicals from blood ("blood products"). All of this suggests that we want to encode only the fact that if x produces y, then x causes y to come into existence. The word *distribute* is an intermediate case. We could view it as having three senses: an abnormal condition is distributed through tissue, a disease is distributed through a population, and various degrees of severity are distributed through a set of cases. Or we could characterize it in the abstract terms of a condition or property's being distributed among the elements of a system. I favor a single, more general predicate, where possible.

The polysemy problem is complicated by another issue — metonymy. For example, we can talk about both "managing a pathological condition" and "managing a patient". There are three ways we could view this situation. (a) *Manage* is a polysemous word. There is a sense *manage1*, wich means to manage a pathological condition, and a sense *manage2*, which means to manage a patient. (b) We could say that there is only one word *manage* but that it has disjunctive selectional constraints. If x manages y, then either y must be a pathological conditon or y must be a patient. A difficulty with this approach is that different inferences will be drawn from "x manages y," depending on which disjunct is true of y. (c) We could say that we have an example of metonymy, or referring to an entity by referring to something functionally related to it, and that the apparent referent must be coerced into the intended referent. Here it could go either way. We could say that one can manage only a pathological condition, and when we encounter "manage a patient," we must coerce it into "manage *a pathological condition* in a patient." Or we could say that one can manage only a patient, and when we encounter "manage a pathological condition," we must coerce it into "manage *a patient wih* a pathological condition." I have chosen to view *manage* in the last of these ways, and in general I favor the metonymy approach over the ambiguity approach.

Similar choices face us with the pair "transmit an agent" and "transmit a disease," and the pair "exposed to an agent" and "exposed to a disease." In both cases the etiologic agent has been chosen as the canonical argument of the predicate.

ORGANIZING THE KNOWLEDGE BASE

The second stage in building a knowledge base is to sort the facts into domains and to organize the facts within each domain. The aim of this step is to discover gaps and logical dependencies in the knowledge base. A general principle is that we should not use a predicate in an axiom unless that predicate is characterized, though not necessarily defined, elsewhere in the knowledge base, in a set of axioms.

Sorting the facts into natural domains, or clusters (cf. Hayes, 1985), is for the most part fairly straightforward. For example, the fact "If x produces y, then x causes y to exist" is a fact about causality. The fact "The replication of a virus requires components of a cell of an organism" is a fact about viruses. The fact "A household is an environment with a high rate of intimate contact, thus a high risk of transmission" is in the cluster of facts about people and their activities. The fact "If bilirubin is not secreted by the liver, it may indicate injury to the liver tissues" is in the medical practice domain.

Problems sometimes arise, however. Concepts can span two domains, like *strain*. Viruses come in types, such as the hepatitis A virus and the hepatitis B virus, generally defined by the disease they cause. But within each type there may be several strains, definable by properties involving laboratory tests. Only viruses come in strains in this application, but the concept of strain rests on an understanding of the nature of classification systems. Thus, it is unclear whether we should consider *strain* to be a concept in the viruses domain or in the medical science domain. Inasmuch as the division into domains is primarily a heuristic aimed toward achieving elegant axiomatizations, a reasonable rule of thumb is to choose the domain in which it would exert the most influence on the formal statements of other facts.

It is useful to distinguish between commonsense domains, which would be useful for most natural language applications, and medical knowledge. Among the commonsense domains are space, time, belief, modality, normality, and goal-directed behavior. But at the very foundation of the knowledge base is a domain that might be called *naive topology*. The medical knowledge includes clusters of facts about viruses, immunology, physiology, disease, and medical practice and science. The cluster of facts about people and their activities lies somewhere in between these two.

We are taking a rather novel approach to the axiomatization of commonsense knowledge. Much of our knowledge and our language seems to be based on an underlying topology, which is then instantiated in many other areas, like space, time, belief, biological systems, social organizations, and so on. We have begun by axiomatizing this fundamental topology. At its base is set theory, axiomatized along traditional lines around the predicates *member* and *subset*. Some common ways of talking about predication are then axiomatized, in a way that is abstracted away from content. These include the locutions *having a property* and *being in a state*. This is required for such concepts as *related to, associated with, aspect, sharing a property,* and *differ*. Next a theory of granularity is encoded, in which the key concept is "x is indistinguishable from y with respect to granularity g." The progressive tense and the contrasting uses of *at* and *in*, among other things, require such a theory. Next a *scale* is defined as a partial ordering with an associated granularity. A theory of scales is developed to the point that such words as *minimal, limit,* and *range* can be characterized.

Next there is an axiomatization centered around the notion of a system, which is defined as a set of entities and a set of relations among them. In the system cluster, we provide an interrelated set of predicates enabling one to characterize the structure of a system, producer-consumer relations among the components, the function of a component of a system as a relation between the component's behavior and the behavior of the system as a whole, and distributions of properties among the elements of a system. The applicability of the notion of system is very wide; among the entities that can be viewed as systems are viruses, organs, activities, populations, and scientific disciplines.

Among the other naive topological concepts that are given (perhaps overly simple) axiomatizations are the idea of the location of an entity with respect to scale or system; change of state, as required for such words as *acquire, appear,* and *continue*; and, following up on a suggestion by Hayes (1985), a cluster of facts centered around the notions of enclosure and causality, building toward such words as *produce, resist,* and *penetrate*.

Other general commonsense knowledge is built on top of this naive topology. The domain of time is seen as a particular kind of scale defined by change of state, and the axiomatization builds toward such predicates as *regular* and *persist*. The domain of belief has three principle subclusters in this application: learning, including such predicates as *find, test,* and *manifest;* reasoning, explicating predicates such as *leads-to* and *consistent*; and classifying, with such predicates as *distinguish, differentiate,* and *identify*. The domain of modalities explicates such concepts as *necessity, possibility* and *likelihood*. The domain of normality deals with such concepts as *abnormal, disturbance,* and *recovery. Finally, in the domain of goal-directed behavior, we characterize such predicates as help, care,* and *risk.*

The lowest level of the knowledge base having explicit medical content includes the domains of viruses, immunology, physiology, and people and their activities. Within physiology there are sublevels for biochemistry, cells, tissues and body fluids, and organs and bodily systems. The facts about bio-chemistry are primarily of a classificatory nature. Those about cells and tis-sues concern their interactions with each other, with etiologic agents, with the immunological system, and with bodily fluids. The facts about organs and bodily systems concern primarily their structure and functions, such as ax-iom (1).

People and their activities is of course a huge domain, but for this applica-tion, the only facts we need to know about people are that they have bodies, they are aware of certain abnormal conditions in their bodies, their activities bring about contact with other people and hence possibly the transmission of disease, and their activities consume bodily resources that could be used for recovery instead. We also need certain notions of instrumentality, for words like *instrument* and *equipment*. An activity, such as eating, is defined as a system of actions. An environment, such as an institution, household, or school, is defined as a system of people and associated activities.

The disease domain is defined here primarily in terms of a temporal schema. A virus or other agent enters a body; the immunological system re-sponds; there is an incubation period during which there are no apparent ef-fects; with onset the infection becomes apparent and can be described at the level of tissues and other body parts or at the level of the person as a whole and his or her awareness; and one of several outcomes results.

Above the level of disease is the domain of medical practice, or medical in-tervention in the natural course of the disease. It can be axiomatized as a plan, in the artificial intelligence sense, for maintaining or achieving a state of health in the patient. The different branches of the plan correspond to where in the temporal schema for disease the physician intervenes and to the mode of intervention. Thus, prevention and treatment are intervention be-fore and after onset, respectively. To prevent a disease, one can block its transmission by avoiding certain sorts of contacts, or one can by immuniza-tion prevent the infection from becoming established. Diagnosis is the acqui-sition of the knowledge that is a prerequisite for treatment.

The domain of medical science takes as its subject matter all of the forego-ing. It can be viewed as the discovery and organization of shared knowledge about this subject matter. Discovery is of two types: data collection, such as experiments and surveys; and inducing general principles. Organization in-volves classification and standardization of such things as nomenclature.

It is not clear whether there are general principles for axiomatizing these domains, but certain strategies prove useful. In each of these domains, we be-gin by specifying its *ontology*—the different sorts of entities and classes of entities in the domain—and the *inclusion relations* among the classes. Next we ask what relations and interactions occur among the entities, such as the *react-with* relation between antigens and antibodies in the immunology domain, and for these predicates, we encode the *delineation constraints* on their arguments. The entities in one domain are frequently systems whose components are entities in another domain, as organs are systems of tissues. Where this is the case, *articulation* or *bridging axioms* are written to express the relations between the properties and behavior of the components and the properties and behavior of the system as a whole. We then often want to specify temporal schemas involving interactions of entities from several domains, goal-directed intervention in the natural course of these schemas, and efforts at learning and systematizing all of this subject matter.

The concordance method of the second stage is useful in ferreting out the relevant facts, but it leaves some gaps that become apparent when we look at the knowledge base as a whole. The gaps are especially frequent in commonsense knowledge. The general principle we follow in encoding this lowest level of the knowledge base is to aim for a vocabulary of predicates that is minimally adequate for expressing the higher level, medical facts and to encode the obvious connections among them. One heuristic that proves useful is this: if the axioms in higher level domains are very complicated to express, some underlying domain has not been sufficiently explicated and axiomatized. This consideration has led to a fuller elaboration of the systems domain, for example. Another example concerns the predicates *parenteral, needle,* and *bite,* appearing in the domain of disease transmission. Initial attempts to axiomatize them indicated the need for axioms in the native topology domain about membranes and the penetration of membranes allowing substances to move from one side of the membrane to the other.

Another example of a gap concerns the word *bilirubin.* The concordance method yields only the fact that bilirubin is a chemical. Yet the elimination of bilirubin from the bloodstream is one of the principal functions of the liver, and jaundice, which results from the liver's failure to eliminate it, is an important symptom of hepatitis. This leads us to construct to a fuller explication of the structure and function of the liver.

Within each domain, concepts and facts seem to fall into small groups that need to be defined together. For example, the predicates *clean* and *contaminate* need to be defined in tandem. There is a larger example in the disease transmission domain. The predicate "transmit" is fundamental, and once it has been characterized as the motion of an infectious agent from a person or animal to a person via some medium, the predicates *source, route, mechanism, mode, vehicle,* and *expose* can be defined in terms of its schema. In addition, relevant facts about bodily fluids, food, water, contamination, needles, bites, propagation, and epidemiology rest on an understanding of *transmit.* In each domain there tends to be a core of central predicates whose nature must be explicated with some care and thoroughness. A large number of other predicates can then be characterized fairly easily in terms of these.

USING THE KNOWLEDGE BASE

The ways in which a natural language processing system would use such a knowledge base are described more fully elsewhere (Walker & Hobbs, 1981). Here we consider just two examples — matching with the text structure, since that is the primary aim of the text access system, and resolving metonymy, since that illustrates an advantage of the approach presented here over the sublanguage approach.

Suppose the user asks the question, Can a patient with mild hepatitis engage in strenuous exercise? The relevant passage in the textbook is labeled, "Management of the Patient: Requirements for Bed Rest." The inference procedures must show that this heading is relevant to this question by drawing the appropriate inferences from the knowledge base. Thus the knowledge base must contain the facts that rest is an activity that consumes little energy, that exercise is an activiity, and that if something is strenuous it consumes much energy, and axioms that relate the concepts *can* and *require* via the concept of possibility.

The logical form of the query is the following (certain problems of resolving implicit arguments are assumed to have been solved):

(2) can(P,E) & engage-in'(E,P,A) & patient (P) & with (P,H) & hepatitis(H) & mild(H) & exercise (A,P) & strenuous (A)

The text structure representation of the content of the passage in the HKB is as follows:

(3) require (p,r) & patient(p) & with(p,h) & hepatitis(h) & rest(r)

The following set of axioms allows us to deduce almost a complete match of expressions (2) and (3) by forward chaining and looking for unifiable predications.

If p requires r, then r is necessary for p.
$(\forall \ p,r) \ / \ require(p,r) \rightarrow necessary(r,p)$

If r is necessary for p, then it is not the case that n is possible for p, where n is the nonoccurrence of r.
$(\forall \ r,p)(\exists \ n) \ necessary(r,p) \rightarrow possible(n,p) \ \& \ not'(n,r)$

If p can do r, then r is possible for p.
$(\forall \ r,p) \ can(p,r) \rightarrow possible(r,p)$

If p engages in an activity, then it is p's activity.
$(\forall \ a,p,x) \ engage-in(p,a) \ \& \ activity(a,x) \rightarrow p = x$

If e is exercise by p, then e is an activity by p.
($\forall$ a,p) exercise(a,p) $\rightarrow$ activity(a,p)

If a is strenuous, then a uses much energy e.
($\forall$ a)($\exists$ e) strenuous(a) $\rightarrow$ use(a,e) & energy(e) & much(e)

Much is not little.
($\forall$ e) much(e) $\rightarrow \neg$ little (e)

Rest r by p is an activity by p that uses little energy e.
($\forall$ r,p)($\exists$ e) rest(r,p) $\rightarrow$ use(r,e) & energy(e) & little(e)

The second example of the use of the knowledge base by inference processes involves determining the congruence between a predicate and its arguments. Let us suppose that in the knowledge base there are certain axioms that are written as follows:

($\forall$ x,y) p(x,y) : q(x) & r(y)

This means the same as

($\forall$ x,y) p(x,y) $\rightarrow$ q(x) & r(y)

except that the inference is drawn obligatorily and the text is modified in whatever way necessary to make this inference true. This amounts to treating q and r as conditions the arguments x and y of p must satisfy. Thus our knowledge may contain the rule:

(4) ($\forall$ x,y) exposed-to(x,y) : person(x) & agent(y)

We may state the metonymy resolution operation in something like the following form:

Given "p(A)" in the text,
if "(A x) p(x) : q(x)" is in the knowledge base,
then infer "q(f(A))" from the properties of A in the text
    and transform "p(A)" into "p(f(A))" in the text.

If the coercion function f is the identity, we simply have the checking of selectional constraints. For example, suppose the text refers to

exposure to hepatitis A virus

Then the selectional constraints on the second argument of *exposed-to* expressed in (4), can be verified by forward chaining through the two axioms

(5) $(\forall y) \text{HAV}(y) \rightarrow \text{virus}(y)$
   $(\forall y) \text{virus}(y) \rightarrow \text{agent}(y)$

If we allow more general functions f, then we allow metonymy, and the operation becomes one of coercion. Supposed the text had referred to

(6) exposure to type A hepatitis

Then we could perform the coercion by using the following axiom:

$(\forall z)(\exists y) \text{type-A-hepatitis}(z) \rightarrow \text{HAV}(y) \& \text{cause}(y,z)$

together with axioms (5). Then the expression in the logical form for the sentence would be expanded from

. . . $\& \text{exposed-to}(X,H) \& . . .$

to

. . . $\text{exposed-to}(X,V) \& \text{HAV}(V) \& \text{cause}(V,H) \& . . .$

We have thus expanded the metonymic (6) to

exposure to *the hepatitis A virus that causes* type A hepatitis.

COMPARISON OF APPROACHES

The sublanguage approach to text processing, briefly and too simply, is this. One determines the various subclasses of nouns in the language used in a particular application, and determines for verbs and other operators the subclasses that their arguments must be. One's parser can then use this semantic information about the domain for syntactic disambiguation and other interpretation processes.

The approach described in this paper, which might be called the axiomatization approach, is a generalization of the sublanguage approach. If in a sublanguage we specify that the operator *exposed-to* requires as its subject a noun of subclass PERSON and as its object a noun of subclass (etiologic) AGENT, then we are stating axiom (4) in slightly different terms. Similarly, when we state that the noun HAV is in noun subclass AGENT, we are stating the axioms (5) in different terms.

But sublanguage constraints capture only one-kind of fact about a domain. The axiomatization approach can capture a richer set of facts and constraints, such as the bulk of the facts in the knowledge base. For example, we can state conditions on arguments that are much more complex than simple sort constraints. Consider the predicate *range*. If x ranges from y to z, then x must be a set whose members are located on a scale on which y and z are points, where y is less than z on the scale. This may be stated as follows:

$$(\forall \ x,y,z) \ range(x,y,z) : (\exists \ s) \ set(x) \ \& \ scale(s)$$
$$\& \ on(y,s) \ \& \ on(z,s) \ \& \ y < z$$
$$\& \ (\forall \ w)(member(w,x) \rightarrow (\exists \ u)(on(u,s) \ \& \ at(w,u)))$$

A rule like this will give us a chance of interpreting such examples as

severity can range from mild to fulminant

where we must expand *severity* into "the severity of a set of possible cases of infection." It is not clear how one could express such constraints in the sublanguage approach.

Finally, there is the problem of metonymy. Natural language discourse is riddled with examples of metonymy, and I don't see any obvious ways that metonymy can be handled in the sublanguage approach. In the approach proposed in this paper, it can be handled by a simple extension of the mechanism for checking selectional constraints, as described in the previous sections.

But the sublanguage approach was developed with a view toward computational efficiency. It is a way of transforming an important part of a difficult semantic problem into a problem in which well-understood syntactic methods apply. What can be said about the axiomatization approach in this regard?

I of course view this work as long-term research. The approach will not be computationally tractable in the near future. But is there any reason to believe it will not be a computational disaster in the long run? Three answers occur to me. The first is that parallel architecture will come to our rescue. But this answer is irresponsible unless we ourselves are helping to design the machines we expect to rescue us, and I am not.

A more responsible answer is that it is a viable research strategy first to discover what classes of inferences are used most frequently in sophisticated natural language processing, and only then to work on the optimization of these classes. This contrasts with a more common strategy of devising some class of inferences that look useful in a few examples and beginning immediately to optimize this class. If we are to adopt the suggested strategy, the essential first step is to build a large knowledge base for use in a natural language system, so that we can acquire the necessary experience.

The third answer is that very little is known, beyond anecdotes, about the relation between the complexity properties of inference processes and the structure of the knowledge base they run on. It is generally assumed that the more axioms one has in the knowledge base, the less efficient the inference processes will be. But a simple example shows that this is not necessarily true. Suppose we add one thousand axioms to our knowledge base of the form

Pi → Q, for i = 1, . . ., 1000.

where all the Pi's are different. If our inference processes are entirely backward chaining, we have introduced a computational disaster. On the other hand, if they are entirely forward chaining, we have not made the inference processes less efficient in the least. In order even to begin the investigation of this relationship, we need much more experience with a large knowledge base like the one whose construction is described in this paper.

ACKNOWLEDGMENTS

I am indebted to Bob Amsler and Don Walker for discussions concerning this work. This research was supported by NIH Grant LM03611 from the National Library of Medicine, by Grant IST-8209346 from the National Science Foundation, and by a gift from the System Development Foundation.

REFERENCES

Bernstein, L., Siegel, E., & Goldstein, C. (1980). The hepatitis knowledge base. *Annals of International Medicine, 93,* 165–222.

Grosz, B., Haas, N., Hendrix, G., Hobbs, J., Martin, P., Moore, R., Robinson, J. & Rosenschein, S. (1982). DIALOGIC: A core natural language processing system. *COLING-82 Abstracts: Proceedings of the Ninth International Conference on Computational Linguistics.* (pp. 95–100). Prague.

Hayes, P. (1985). The second naive physics manifesto. In J. Hobbs & R. Moore (Eds.), *Formal theories of the commonsense world*, Norwood, NJ: Ablex.

Hobbs, J. (1983). An improper treatment of quantification in ordinary English. *COLING-83 Abstracts: Proceedings of the 21st Annual Meeting of the Association for Computational Linguistics*, (pp. 57–63). Cambridge, MA.

Hobbs, J. (1985). Ontological promiscuity. *Proceedings of the 23rd Annual Meeting of the Association for Computational Linguistics.* Chicago, IL.

Walker, D. & Hobbs, J. (1981). *Natural language access to medical text.* SRI International Tech. Note 240.

5 The Use of Machine-Readable Dictionaries in Sublanguage Analysis

Donald E. Walker
Robert A. Amsler[1]
Artificial Intelligence and Information Science Research
Bell Communications Research
Morristown, New Jersey

ABSTRACT

Dictionaries contain valuable information that can be used in sublanguage analysis. Some words are, of course, associated uniquely with a particular subject domain; their occurrence in a text identifies it as belonging to that sublanguage. Other words have several senses, each of which may be specialized for a different domain. In this case, it is necessary to disambiguate the appropriate sense for the given context. To determine the subject domains for a set of texts, we have developed a procedure that satisfies both of these cases. It takes advantage of the semantic codes contained on the computer tape (but not in the printed version) of the *Longman Dictionary of Contemporary English*. For a given text, each word is checked against the dictionary to determine the semantic codes associated with it. By accumulating the frequencies for these senses and then ordering the list of categories in terms of frequency, the subject matter of the text can be identified. Our initial work has been done using the *New York Times News Service* wire. We are currently investigating strategies for extending this procedure to produce a more elaborate profile for the text. This work is being carried out within the framework of a more general interest in natural-language and knowledge-resource systems.

[1]This paper was written while the authors were in the Natural-Language and Knowledge-Resource Systems Group at SRI International, Menlo Park, CA 94025.

INTRODUCTION

The objective of the research we are reporting is to explore the feasibility of sublanguage analysis through the lexicon. It is obvious that dictionaries contain information that is useful for this purpose. Some words are, of course, associated uniquely with a particular subject domain; their occurrence in a text serves to identify it as belonging to that sublanguage. Other words have several senses, each of which may be specialized for a different domain. In this case, it is necessary to disambiguate the sense appropriate for the given context.

Our approach to this problem is experimental; it derives from the availability of texts and dictionaries in machine-readable form. The task we are using to focus our efforts is content assessment; we are determining the topic of a text passage by establishing the relative frequency of occurrence of senses associated with the words it contains.

In particular, we are interested in analyzing natural-language texts through the use of machine-readable dictionaries. More specifically, we have been processing stories from the *New York Times News Service (NYTNS)* through the use of subject codes contained in the *Longman Dictionary of Contemporary English (LDOCE)* (Procter, 1978).[2]

Background

To provide a context for this study, it is helpful to consider the research program on Natural Language and Knowledge Resource Systems in which it is embedded. In this program, we are concerned generally with the basic and applied research issues entailed in the development of computer techniques for processing large volumes of textual information in electronic form. More particularly, our objectives are to:

- Create more effective procedures for analyzing *natural-language* data in order to identify and understand the information in large text files.
- Establish computer-based *knowledge resources,* in particular by extracting relevant information from texts and embodying it in special data banks.
- Design and implement prototype text-expert *systems* that exploit the reciprocal relationships between texts and knowledge resources.

The Program is distinctive in that the data files we are analyzing can contain tens of millions of words of text, and the knowledge resources, tens of

---

[2]The *NYTNS* is a copyrighted service provided by the *New York Times* on subscription and made available to SRI International for research purposes. The computer tapes of the *LDOCE* were made available to SRI International for scholarly research.

thousands of knowledge entries. The research methodology derives from work in computational linguistics and artificial intelligence. However, unlike other work on natural-language understanding that is directed toward a representation of the structure of each sentence, our intent is to capture the meaning associated with larger text units. Unlike other work on expert systems that attempts to capture previously unformalized rules of procedure, our concern is with the development of strategies for organizing knowledge that is already expressed in textual form.

Two basic themes can be seen in this research, reflecting the dual interest in natural language and knowledge resources and in their reciprocal relationship. First, knowledge bases can be used to help locate and understand the information that occurs in texts. The research reported here provides an example: a machine-readable dictionary is used to distinguish among the various senses associated with the words in a news wire service, and that information allows the news stories to be categorized into different content classes. Second, texts can provide the basis for developing new knowledge bases or augmenting old ones. Examples are the identification of new terminology or new usages of words in texts in order to update a dictionary, and the extraction of biographical, geographic, and organizational information from text sources to form new specialized "dictionaries," both relevant to our immediate concerns.

Tasks associated with the two themes complement each other. As we develop capabilities for using highly structured reference knowledge, the ability to deal with unrestricted "free text" or more specialized sublanguage data is correspondingly increased. As procedures for recognizing natural-language structures in free text are established, additional entries for knowledge bases can be detected and compiled. The results of project efforts can provide much more sophisticated access to information and much more effective utilization of knowledge.

Approach

The characteristics of our approach can be highlighted by identifying its distinctive features.

First, we proceed from *general to particular*. Beginning with the analysis of unrestricted texts that represent a broad range of sublanguage data, we believe we can provide insights into the features of those sublanguages that can be sharpened by subsequent more specialized study.

Second, we move from *large to small*. By processing large volumes of text, we expect to identify patterns that are not easily discernible in smaller samples. Once they are identified, however, working with smaller and more carefully selected texts can help refine those patterns.

Third, we progress from *surface to deep*. Lexical elements constitute the starting point; they establish the conceptual content of a text. Once a lexical-

semantic base has been created, it is possible to incorporate the other structural aspects — syntactic, compositional semantic, and pragmatic — essential
for understanding.

Fourth, we proceed from *given to new*. Dictionaries and other knowledge
resources are rich repositories of useful information. Determining how to extract and make use of existing material can provide guidelines for determining how the resources should be revised and what new ones need to be
developed.

Fifth, we move from *experimental to theoretical*. The analysis of data,
properly collected, can provide guidelines for sharpening and refining concepts and hypotheses. More important, the development of this science, as
any other, depends on an interplay between theory and experiment. Computational linguistics and artificial intelligence have tended to ignore this need.

THE TEXT AND DICTIONARY SOURCE MATERIALS

The New York Times News Service

The *NYTNS* was selected as the text database for a number of reasons.
First, it provides broad coverage of newsworthy developments in a large
number of different subject areas. Although the language used can certainly
be characterized as standard English, many of the news releases are written
by specialists in styles that could be expected to reflect features of texts in the
corresponding sublanguages. For our initial work, it is, of course, not essential to use samples from different sublanguage literatures. In fact, if we can
demonstrate that the technique works for what Kittredge and Lehrberger
(1982) have referred to as "paraphrases in the standard language," it can be
expected to be even more discriminating for actual use in sublanguage
analysis.

A second reason for selecting the *NYTNS* is that we are making use of a
special feature in the *LDOCE,* the subject coding of word senses for the general vocabulary of English, which is not available in any of the dictionaries
for specialized sublanguages. Further elaboration of this point is provided in
the next section.

We have been collecting material from the *New York Times News Service*
wires for over a year. Over 40 million words of text have been accumulated
during this period. The first requirement in establishing a database was to develop a format that would allow us to store, accumulate, and recover relevant
information for each lexical item in the corpus. To begin, we made the assumption that the only valid delimiters of a lexical item were the nonprinting
ASCII codes, including blank, tab, carriage return, line feed, form feed, vertical tab, and so forth. Any sequence of alphabetic characters, numbers, or

punctuation so delimited was taken initially to be a "word." Spans consisting only of punctuation were identified first. The remainder were classified as numbers or as alphanumerics distinguished by the presence and position of any capitalized letters. Then preceding and trailing punctuation were separated from the numbers and alphanumerics. This procedure creates special problems for certain kinds of abbreviations and for forms, like money, where the punctuation could be taken as inherent. However, it provides a uniform procedure for storing the data, and it does allow recovering all of the information contained in the original source.

Each entry line in the database contains the following sequence of information:

<word> <type> <prepost> <year-month> <day-of-the-month + frequencies> <totals>

where

<word> is the lower-case version of the word;

<type> is one of P, N, I, U, L or the literal word as it appears without case alteration, and

P = pure punctuation,

N = number (optionally + punctuation),

I = initial capital word (+ optional numbers and punctuation),

U = all upper case word (+ optional numbers and punctuation),

L = all lower case word (+ optional numbers and punctuation);

<prepost> is the preceding and trailing punctuation, separated by __, which represents the word itself;

<year-month> is represented as 82-09, 82-10, etc., with full-width digits for sorting; each month is on a separate line;

<day-of-the-month + frequencies> is a letter standing for the day of the month (1 = A, 2 = B, . . . 31 = e) followed by an integer indicating the frequency of occurrence on that day, except that a frequency of one is indicated just by the letter itself;

<totals> is given as two integers separated by a blank, the first indicating the total frequency for the month, the second the number of days on which it occurred.

This sequence facilitates both readability and updating. Two lines from daily frequency files could look as follows:

<word> L __ 82-09A23 23 1
<word> L __ 82-09B12 12 1

and would be updated into

    <word> L __ 82-09A23B12 35 2

by simply finding that the "<word> L __ 82-09" segments matched and then appending the second daily count to the first and adding the two integers together. Since these lines are guaranteed to be in the correct order as a result of a SORT > MERGE (i.e., A comes before B and everything else in the lines to their left is identical due to strategic placement), the update is always an appending of the successive line's information to the previous one's until a difference is found in the "<word> L __", etc. segments.

Some samples from the file, representing various forms of the word *abandon* that appeared in November of 1982, follow. Note in the first entry that the word occurs in lower case form (L), without punctuation, once each on the 1st and 2nd of the month, twice on the 3rd and 4th, etc., for a total of 45 entries on 23 days.

    abandon L __ 82-11ABC2D2GJ2KL4M3NOPQR5S2U3V2W2X3YZ2c2
    d2 45 23
    abandon L __. 82-11L 1 1
    abandoned I __ 82-11C2JP 4 3
    abandoned L "__" 82-11b 1 1
    abandoned L __ 82-11A4B2CDE3FGH2I7JK3L4M2NO3P2Q2R4ST2U2
    V5WX3Y4Z3abc7d4 78 30
    abandoned L __, 82-11DINPW 5 5
    abandoned L __. 82-11HILORTXYZ 9 9
    abandoned L __.' 82-11T 1 1
    abandoned-mine L __ 82-11E 1 1
    abandoning L __ 82-11AG2HI3JSTVYc2d 15 11
    abandoning U __ 82-11S 1 1
    abandonment L __ 82-11ILNOPZc 7 7
    abandonment L __, 82-11M 1 1
    abandonment L __. 82-11N 1 1
    abandons L __ 82-11G2Qc3d 7 4

One advantage of a precise formulation of the symbols of the file is that it preserves every aspect of the forms that occurred in the text so that they can be subsequently identified through special patterns. To test out the procedure, and for subsequent studies described later, we selected 3 months of *NYTNS* stories, representing 8,351,444 words of text. The resulting database has proved to be efficient and easy to use for a variety of purposes.

The Longman Dictionary of Contemporary English

The *LDOCE* (Procter, 1978) is a medium-sized dictionary designed primarily to be used by people for whom English is not their native language. It contains over 55,000 entries that provide a broad coverage of modern colloquial, idiomatic, and technical English. The development of the dictionary was influenced significantly by both linguistic and computational linguistic considerations. It contains an extremely sophisticated system of grammatical codes. The definitions and exmaples are written in a defining vocabulary of approximately 2000 words, which were themselves carefully chosen for relative frequency of occurrence in English and to ensure that the sense used was the main one for that word.

The *LDOCE* contains other useful features, but of particular interest for research on the lexicon is the inclusion of two sets of semantic codes.[3] The first set provides information on semantic markers and selectional restrictions. The second set identifies subject fields that are distinctive for particular senses of words in the dictionary. It is these *subject codes* that we have been using in our research on content assessment.

The *LDOCE* subject codes were derived from a categorization developed by Merriam-Webster but have been augmented in several ways. There are 120 two-letter field codes that mark, for example, areas like medicine (MD) and political science (PL). There are 212 subfield categories that constitute divisions of the basic field codes; for example, physiology is represented as MDZP and diplomacy as PLZD, the Z being used in the third position exclusively as an indicator of subcategorization. The field codes can also be combined so that the designation for meteorology (ML) together with the one for building (CO), that is MLCO, is used to mark the entry *lightning conductor.* Similarly MLGO (meteorology plus geography) marks *temperate* and *torrid,* GOML (the same fields in the reverse order) marks *permafrost* and *drift ice.* In addition, there are 38 locality codes that identify major geographical areas and countries or distinguish areas within them. Thus, U represents Europe and F represents France; combined with meteorology, the code MLUF is applied to *mistral,* a distinctive wind that is characteristic of southern France. The word *typhoon* is marked MLX, meteorology and Asia.

There are over 2600 realized combinations of two, three, and four-letter codes. Out of the 55,000 entries in the dictionary, 18,000 are marked as having specialized subject senses, with an average of 1.3 subject codes per word. Some examples, selected to anticipate the discussion of our content-assessment procedures in the next section, follow:

---

[3] These codes appear on the computer tape containing the dictionary contents but are not present in the printed book. See Michiels (1982) for an extended discussion of this information.

- *heavy:* FO–food, ML–meteorology, TH–theatre
- *rainfall:* ML–meteorology
- *high:* SN–sounds, FO–food, DGXX–drugs and drug experiences, RLXX–religion, ML–meteorology, AU–motor vehicles
- *wind:* ML–meteorology, MDZP–physiology, MU–music, NA–nautical, HFZH–hunting

FORCE4, A PROCEDURE FOR FULL-TEXT CONTENT ASSESSMENT

FORCE4 is a demonstration program showing how the subject codes contained in a machine-readable dictionary can be used as the basis for a full-text, content-assessment system. The program employs a full-screen display format with three windows that contain, respectively: (a) the text being processed, (b) the program's intermediate inferences regarding the syntactic and semantic properties of each content-bearing word in the text, and (c) a running tally of the frequencies of the top subject assignments made to the document on the basis of the cumulative set of content-bearing words that have been analyzed.

The text appears in *Window 1,* which occupies the major part of the screen, beginning at the top left corner. For each content-bearing word in the text, the subject codes are looked up in the *LDOCE.* If the word fails to have a subject code, it is analyzed to determine whether it is the inflected form of some word with a set of subject codes. If subject codes are found, they are

Heavy rainfall and high winds clobbered the California *coast* early today, while a stormsystem in the Southeast dampened the Atlantic Seaboard from Florida to Virginia.	4	ML
	2	FO
	2	MA
	1	TH
Travelers' advisories warned of snow in California's northern mountains and northwestern Nevada. Rain and snow fell in the Dakotas, northern Minnesota and Upper Michigan.	1	SW
	1	DGXX
	1	RLXX
	1	AU
Skies were cloudy from Tennessee through the Ohio Valley into New England, but generally clear from Texas into the mid-Mississippi Valley.	1	MDZP
	1	MU
	1	HFZH

coast = GOZG NA
GOZG = geography; NA = nautical

FIG 5.1.   Example of FORCE4 processing, through the word *coast.*

Heavy rainfall and high winds clobbered the California coast early today, while a storm system in the Southeast dampened the Atlantic Seaboard from Florida to Virginia.	10	ML
	4	GOZG
	4	DGXX
	3	NA
Travelers' advisories warned of snow in California's northern mountains and northwestern Nevada. Rain and snow fell in the Dakotas, northern Minnesota and Upper Michigan.	2	MI
	2	FO
	2	GO
	1	TH
Skies were cloudy from Tennessee through the Ohio Valley into New England, but generally clear from Texas into the mid-Mississippi *Valley*.	1	SW
	1	RLXX
	1	AU
valley = GOZG GOZG = geography		

FIG 5.2.   Example of FORCE4 processing, through the end of the text.

displayed together with their English descriptions in *Window 3* at the top right of the screen.

Fig. 5.1 shows FORCE4 in the course of processing a weather report. The text has been analyzed through the word *coast* (italicized for emphasis here, but in inverse video in actual operation). The most frequent subject code is meteorology (ML) with 4; food (FO) and nautical (NA) both have 2; the rest all have the value 1. Completing the processing of the text yields the results shown in Fig. 5.2. Meteorology (ML) is still the most frequent code with 10; geographical terms (GOZG) and drugs and drug experiences (DGXX) have 4; nautical (NA) has 3; and food (FO) and military (MI) have 2.

A set of more than 100 *NYTNS* stories (a 24-hour sample) was processed against the *LDOCE* codes to determine their subject content. The results were remarkably good, considering that the system has not had any fine tuning or specialization with regard to the text at hand. It works well over a variety of subjects—law, military, sports, radio and television—and a number of different formats—text, tables, two-line abstracts, and even recipes. The subject identification was almost identical for sequences of stories that constituted part of a single text.[4]

The *FORCE4* approach definitely merits further development. However, it is worthwhile to consider the weather example in a little more detail in order to point out some of the current limitations and, in general, to illustrate problems encountered in using machine-readable dictionaries. Strategies for dealing with these problems are discussed in the next section.

First, it is appropriate to consider the words in the text that were marked with subject codes: *heavy, rainfall, high, winds, coast, storm, Southeast,*

---

[4]The news wire services usually break up longer stories, marking the successive segments as continuations.

Seaboard, Virginia, snow, mountains, northwestern, rain, snow, fell, Upper, skies, cloudy, Valley, New, clear, Valley. Two of the words that were marked for meteorology, *heavy* and *high* were actually being used as adjectives modifying *rainfall* and *winds,* respectively, and not in the coded sense. *Seaboard* should have been treated as part of a compound, *Atlantic Seaboard,* and not as a separate word, as should *Upper* with respect to *Michigan* and *New* with respect to *England.* The two *Valleys,* although part of compound expressions, are being used properly as geographical terms.

The following words did not have subject codes (function words and other general vocabulary items are excluded): *clobbered, California, early, today, system, dampened, Atlantic, Florida, Travelers', advisories, warned, California's, northern, Nevada, Dakotas, northern, Michigan, Tennessee, Ohio, England, generally, Texas, mid-Mississippi.* The obvious thing to note is the predominance of state names and other regional designations. The *LDOCE,* like most dictionaries, does not include most proper nouns. *Virginia* is actually coded for its tobacco sense. Most of the rest of the terms probably do not have specialized subject senses, although it is a little puzzling for *Southeast* and *northwestern* to be included, while *northern* is not.

DISCUSSION

There are, of course, a number of conditions that have to be satisfied in order for *FORCE*4 to work well, even at its present, early state of development:

1. The content-bearing words of the text must have entries in the *LDOCE.*
2. The subject-codes for the content-bearing words must include the sense in which the word is being used in the text.
3. The content-bearing words must not also be common function words, for example, like *in* in the sentence, "The tide is in."
4. A sufficient quantity of text must be examined for the topmost subject-code assignments to stabilize (typically more than a sentence, but often less than two paragraphs).
5. The text must be about a single topic, rather than a collection of different topics such as is found in a new summary of major headline stories.

The procedures for content assessment that we have described constitute only the first step in the development of these capabilities. One extremely desirable extension entails *pruning* the spurious sense entries in the text. If we accept the principle that a word with multiple senses, and thus several subject codes, is likely to be used in the text in only one of these senses, then the following procedure can be applied. Take the code with the highest frequency — that would be meteorology (ML) in Fig. 5.2 — and, for all the words so marked, eliminate all of the other codes. The ordering there showed meteorology (ML) as the most frequent code, with 10; geographical terms (GOZG) and drugs and drug experiences (DGXX) had 4; nautical (NA), 3; and food (FO) and military, (MI) 2. After pruning, ML would still be 10, of course; GOZG would remain at 4; DGXX would be reduced to 1; NA would be reduced to 2; FO would be eliminated; and MI would become 1. Note that, if a slightly more radical pruning strategy were invoked – that is, removing a subject code in the list if any instances of it were eliminated – DGZZ, NA, and MI would all be 0, leaving only ML and GOZG, which is, of course, the desired *profile* for the story. It is obvious that much more experimentation is needed to explore these issues more thoroughly.

Returning to qualification 1, regarding the need for the content-bearing words in the text to have entries in the *LDOCE,* we performed an analysis to establish the correspondence between the words present in the 8 million word sample of the *NYTNS* text and the entries in the *Webster's Seventh New Collegiate Dictionary (W7)* (G. & C. Merriam, 1963).[5] Of the 119,630 different word forms present in the *NYTNS* sample and in the *(W7),* 27,837 (23%) occurred in both; 42,695 (36%) occurred only in the *W7*; and 48,828 (41%) occurred only in the *NYTNS.* That almost two thirds (61%) of the words in the dictionary did not appear in the text is not surprising; dictionaries contain many words that are not in common use. That almost two thirds (64%) of the words in the text were not in the dictionary is more problematic. A preliminary analysis of a sample of the *NYTNS* forms that were not in the *W7* reveals the following breakdown (expressing the values in fractional form is intended to show their approximate character): one fourth were inflected forms; one fourth were proper nouns; one sixth were hyphenated forms; one twelfth were misspellings; and one fourth were not yet resolved, but some are likely to be new words occurring since the dictionary was published.

The inflected forms can be accommodated by performing a morphological analysis on the text entries. Hyphenated forms can also be handled, although some of the instances found in the *NYTNS* are more difficult to deal with, raising the question of noun-noun compounds and phrases, a critical issue that will be discussed at more length later. Misspellings are less easy to detect and correct, but recent developments in spelling correction algorithms suggest that some progress is beng made in this area (Durham, Lamb, & Saxe, 1983). The missing proper nouns constitute a more serious problem. As noted in the analysis of the weather text, most dictionaries do not contain the names of people, places, institutions, trade-names, and similar items. Yet these entries are key features of newspaper text and essential for almost any class of documents. Geographical and biographical dictionaries can provide

---

[5]The *W7* was chosen for this study because it has a larger vocabulary; similar results would be expected for the *LDOCE.*

an initial base from which to develop such entries, but it would, of course, be necessary to assign subject codes to them and perhaps to establish new subject codes for them.[6]

Specialized technical dictionaries are one source for the additional vocabulary required. It is also possible to acquire entries from the texts themselves, although obviously at this stage of our understanding it would necessarily be a machine-aided operation. We have done some preliminary work toward this objective. Using the simple criterion of selecting all the words in the *NYTNS* sample that occur at least five times with intial capitals and never occur only in lower case, we were able to create a large file of entries that, although far from exhaustive, certainly contains many candidates for inclusions as proper nouns. Taking advantage of patterns in the text, we made some progress toward identifying cities in the United States as capitalized words preceding state names and followed by a comma. Similarly, the introduction of names in a story is often followed by some explanatory information set off by commas, for example, "John Doe, President of the First State Bank, said . . . ."

With regard to augmentation of the current *LDOCE* subject codes, it is worth remarking that even those that currently exist may need refinement. Certainly, if the *FORCE*4 procedure is to be extended to more technical text or even to more homogeneous text where greater discrimination is desired than that provided by the current coding, parameters will need to be developed that motivate the creation and assignment of additional categories. One potential source for them is the kind of dictionary analysis that Amsler (1980, 1981) performed on *The New Merriam-Webster Pocket Dictionary (MPD)* (G. & C. Merriam, 1964). He created taxonomies of the senses for all the nouns and verbs based on the hand-disambiguated kernel words in their definitions.[7] These taxonomies establish relations among terms that can be exploited in making further dimensional analyses. For example, recognizing that *vehicle* includes *automobile, bicycle, carriage, locomotive, sled, tractor, truck,* and *wagon,* and noting that the definitions refer to parameters reflecting motive force, objects transported, surface medium, and the like, one can begin to organize terms along these lines. The work by Evens et al. (1980) on semantic-relations provides another direction for expansion. On a more technical level, it should be possible to disambiguate medical vocabulary in relation to categories that identify, for instance, organ systems, disease proces-

---

[6]It should be noted parenthetically that both people and places can have sense distinctions that may be important to separate for given contexts. A particular person may be noted as both actor and political figure; a place may be considered in relation to its location as well as for its distinctive resources.

[7]It is more accurate to characterize these structures as "tangled hierarchies" or, more technically, "semi-lattices," because they contain multiply convergent paths between nodes.

ses, taken, for example, from *Medical Subject Headings* (National Library of Medicine, 1980), the *Systematized Nomenclature of Pathology* (1965) and *Systematized Nomenclature of Medicine* (1979), and *Current Medical Information and Terminology* (Gordon, 1971).

In these remarks so far, we have been ignoring one of the major problems in using dictionary entries for content assessment. That is the relative scarcity of multiword entries in a dictionary. The problems of performing semantic analyses of noun-noun compounds are, of course, well known (McDonald, 1982; Rhyne, 1976). Equally difficult is the problem of identifying aggregates of terms that should be treated as units in a *phrasal lexicon* (Becker, 1975; Smith, Bienstock, & Housman, 1982). As noted in the weather text, *Atlantic Seaboard, Upper Michigan,* and *New England* should all have been treated as single entries. Again, working on the *NYTNS* text, we have made a beginning in attacking this problem by identifying groups of frequently recurring words, specifically those bounded by function words and sentence boundaries. The most frequent entries in the resulting lists are candidates for inclusion as multiword "dictionary" entries. The quotation marks indicate our recognition of the departures from current usage that our proposals entail.

REFLECTIONS

The heading of this section was chosen deliberately to acknowledge that our research is far from the stage where we can expect to report definitive conclusions. The development of *FORCE*4, a procedure for assessing the content of stories from the *New York Times News Service* through the use of subject codes in the *Longman Dictionary of Contemporary English,* does illustrate the use of machine-readable dictionaries in the analysis of natural-language texts. To the extent that these stories can be said to constitute examples of sublanguage data—even if only as "paraphrases in the standard language"—as we remarked earlier, we have illustrated the use of lexical information for sublanguage analysis. Certainly, the specialization of word senses is a central element in the emergence of sublanguages, and *FORCE*4 does provide word-sense disambiguation.

This work has begun with a general text and a general dictionary, because they provided an easy entry point that allowed us to carry out experimental studies. At some point it will be essential to process large blocks of text specifically identified as appropriate for particular sets of sublanguages. An analysis of the vocabulary will then allow us to identify the word senses that are distinctive in each sublanguage, providing a basis for establishing appropriate and discriminating subject codes.

It is clear from our research that there are interesting and productive things to be done by exploiting the reciprocal relations between text and dictionary or, more generally, as described earlier, between *natural-language* and *knowledge-resources*. Although *FORCE*4 is only one of the systems we have considered, it does seem to us to provide a promising direction for further research. To state the issue more broadly, we believe that *lexical semantics* (Evens, Litowitz, Markowitz, Smith, & Werner, 1980) and *computational lexicology* (Amsler, 1982) are areas that have not been explored enough in sublanguage analysis and in computational linguistics. We strongly urge that more careful attention be paid to them.

ACKNOWLEDGMENTS

This research was carried out at SRI International, where it was supported in part by grants IST-8208578, IST-8209346, and IST-8300940 from the National Science Foundation, grant LM 03611 from the National Library of Medicine, a contract funding SRI International Project 5383, and Internal Research and Development funds from SRI International.

We wish to express our gratitude to the Longman Group, publishers of the *Longman Dictionary of Contemporary English,* and to G. & C. Merriam Company, publishers of the *Webster's Seventh New Collegiate Dictionary,* for granting us permission to use the computer tapes representing the contents of those dictionaries in our work. More generally, we cannot commend too highly their generosity in support of the research community as a whole. Our hope is that the results of our collective efforts will eventually compensate them for their help. We also thank the New York Times Syndication Sales Corporation for making the *New York Times News Service* available for research purposes.

The processing of the *NYTNS* and the *LDOCE* files and the development of the FORCE4 program were carried out by Amsler with the assistance of Armar A. Archbold, to whom we express our appreciation.

REFERENCES

Amsler, R. A. (1980). The structure of the Merriam-Webster pocket dictionary. Unpublished doctoral dissertation. University of Texas at Austin. (Also TR-164, Computer Science Department, University of Texas at Austin.)

Amsler, R. A. (1981). A taxonomy for English nouns and verbs. *Proceedings of the 19th Annual Meeting of the Association for Compuutational Linguistics* (pp. 133–138). Menlo Park, CA: Association for Computational Linguistics.

Amsler, R. A. (1982). "Computational lexicology: a research program." *AFIPS Conference Proceedings: 1982 National Computer Conference* (pp. 657–683). Arlington, VA: American Federation of Information Processing Societies Press.

Becker, J. (1975). The phrasal lexicon. In R. Schank & B. L. Nash-Webber (Eds.), *Theoretical issues in natural language processing* (pp. 60–63). Menlo Park, CA: Association for Computational Linguistics.

Durham, I., Lamb, D. A., & Saxe, J. B. (1983). Spelling correction in user interfaces. *Communications of the ACM, 26* (10), 764–773.

Evens, M. W., Litowitz, B. E., Markowitz, J. A., Smith, R. N., & Werner, O. (1980). *Lexical semantic relations: A comparative survey.* Carbondale, IL. & Edmonton, Can.: Linguistic Research.

G. & C. Merriam Company. (1963) *Webster's seventh new collegiate dictionary.* Springfield, MA: Author.

G. & C. Merriam Company. (1964) *The new Merriam-Webster pocket dictionary.* New York: Pocket Books.

Gordon, B. L. (Ed.) (1971). *Current medical information and terminology.* Chicago: American Medical Association.

Kittredge, R., & Lehrberger, J. (Eds.). (1982). *Sublanguage: Studies of language in restricted semantic domains.* Berlin & New York: de Gruyter.

McDonald, D. B. *Understanding noun compounds.* (CMU Technical Report CMU-CS-82-102.) (1982). Unpublished doctoral dissertation, Carnegie-Mellon University, Pittsburgh, PA.

Michiels, A. Exploiting a large dictionary data base. (1982). Unpublished doctoral dissertation, Universite de Liege, Liege, Belgium.

National Library of Medicine. (1981). *Medical Subject Headings.* (Rep. No. NLM-MED-80-02), Bethesda, MD.

Procter, P., (Ed.). (1978). *Longman dictionary of contemporary English.* Harlow & London, England: Longman Group.

Rhyne, J. R. (1976). *Lexical rules and structures in a computer model of nominal compounding.* Unpublished doctoral dissertation, University Texas at Austin.

Smith, R. N.; Bienstock, D.; & Housman, E. (1982). A collocational model of information transfer. In A. E. Petrarca, C. I. Taylor, & R. S. Kohn, (Eds.) *Information interaction: Proceedings of the 45th ASIS annual meeting, Volume 19.* White Plains, NY: Knowledge Industry Publications.

Systematized Nomenclature of Medicine. (1979). Chicago: College of American Pathologists.

Systematized Nomenclature of Pathology. (1965). Chicago: College of American Pathologists.

6 Automatic Structuring of Sublanguage Information

Carol Friedman
Courant Institute of Mathematical Sciences
New York University

ABSTRACT

Computer processing of free-text input can be used to obtain a database of patient information that contains in a structured form the relations among the medical events and observations recorded in the narrative. The information in the narrative can be structured by a computerized procedure because the information is expressed in a small number of sublanguage sentence types. For example, there is a treatment sentence type, a test and result sentence type, and a patient state sentence type. Each type is a syntactic relation among medical and English word classes. Once defined from an analysis of sample patient documents, these types can be used as target information structures into which the narrative portions of medical records can be mapped. This paper describes an implementation of text processing that utilizes English syntactic analysis and sublanguage word class combinations to determine to which of the known sublanguage sentence types an input occurrence conforms and to transform the occurrence into a standard form for the information carried by sentences of that type.

One of the goals of our work at the Linguistic String Project is the creation of an automated procedure whereby medical data from the narrative portions of patient documents are mapped into a structured form, making the information in the data available for use as a database. Such a procedure is possible for several reasons:

1. The narrative portions of patient documents form a sublanguage having a grammar that consists of: (a) a syntactic specification that is a modification of the English Grammar; (b) a vocabulary that can be classified into

both general English syntactic categories and semantic categories of the medical domain; (c) a statement of sublanguage sentence types as particular sequences of the semantic word classes in English syntactic relations.

2. The information in the documents falls naturally into a small number of informational sentence types; and the sentence types, as defined by the sublanguage grammar, correspond to the different types of information given in the documents.

3. Complex text sentences are composed of elementary sentences of the stated types, joined by connectives, or relations, between the sentence types.

For example, there is a test + result sentence type for sentences such as *Culture was positive for streptococcus.* And there is a patient-state sentence type for sentences such as *Patient had meningitis.* On the other hand, the sentence, *Impression of meningitis was confirmed by finding cloudy cerebrospinal fluid,* consists of two informational sentence types related to each other. It contains: (a) a test + result sentence type: *finding cloudy cerebrospinal fluid*; (b) a patient-state sentence type under an evidential operator: *impression of meningitis was confirmed.* The relation between (a) and (b) is *by (by means of).*

Another example of a single sublanguage sentence type is the medication type, as in *Patient was given tylenol 2 tabs qid.* However, *mild increased pain for 3 weeks after stopping azathiopine* consists of: (a) a medication sentence type: *azathiopine was stopped;* (b) a patient-state sentence type: *mild increased pain for two weeks.* The relation between (a) and (b) is the conjunction *after.*

Once the elementary units are defined from an analysis of a representative sample of the sublanguage text, they can be used as target structures (which we call information formats) into which the patient-record narrative can be mapped. These formats represent the semantic regularities of the sentences in the documents and therefore allow the system to have certain expectations depending on the sentence types. The systems can determine that a significant field is missing from a format and then use its knowledge of the sentence type to find and fill in the missing information. For example, in the patient-state format for *increased pain*, the format subject which should be either the whole patient, a body part, a body measure, or a body function, is missing. With the knowledge of what type of word is missing the system can search for it in a previous occurrence.

INFORMATION FORMATS FOR CLINICAL NARRATIVE

A format can be thought of as a prototype sentence or a template for a given type of information. The format has certain fixed fields or columns, and some of the fields have subfields.

Figure 6.1 shows a simplified version of the format that corresponds to the treatment-with-medication sentence type (FORMAT3 in the system). The prototype has the following information: Certain hospital personnel treated the patient with a certain medication, in a certain amount, with a certain frequency, and in a certain manner. The fields with an "*" can have modifiers, which will be explained shortly. Figure 6.1 shows a structured form of the sentence *Patient was treated with ampicillin 200 mg/kg/d Q6 hr.* Several other sentences of this type are:

Patient was given IV ampicillin.
Increase aspirin to 20 tabs daily.
Continue penicillamine 500 mg daily.

FORMAT1, shown in simplified form in Fig. 6.2, is the template for general management information. It consists of four fields: an INST (for institutional personnel) field, a PT (patient) field, a VERB-MD (management verb) field, and a VERB (nonsublanguage verb) field. FORMAT1 can be thought of as having the following information: Certain hospital personnel followed a certain management procedure with regard to the patient. Under each column in Fig. 6.2 are examples of words that can be mapped into that column. The sample words under a column all have the same (or similar) medical subclasses. For example, *admit, appointment, check-up,* and *schedule* are all medical management verbs (which we classify as H-VMD). Several sentences that would map into FORMAT1 are:

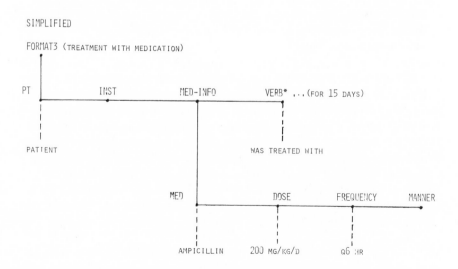

FIG. 6.1   Information format for "Patient was treated with ampicillin 200 mg/kg/d q6 hr."

SIMPLIFIED

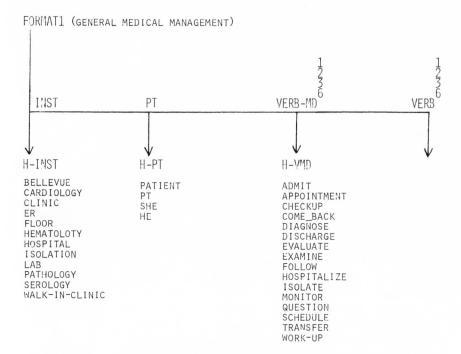

FIG. 6.2   Medical word classes in FORMAT1

Patient was admitted to Bellevue.
Patient was transferred to walk-in clinic.
Pt was discharged.

Two fields in FORMAT1 have numbers next to them, indicating that these fields may have certain modifiers associated with them. These modifiers contain additional information such as evidential status, time, negation, or degree of certainty. The modifiers are also represented in standard templates. Figure 6.3 shows the templates for the time modifiers EVENT-TIME and TIME-ASP. EVENT-TIME contains time information such as *for 2 days prior to admission*. TIME-ASP contains fields for various aspects of time — begin, end, change, repetition, and time period. A modifier is placed immediately to the right of the column it modifies. The remaining modifiers are shown in Fig. 6.4. MODS contains fields NEG for negation, MODAL for nonfactuality, and EVID for evidential information. There is also a BP-MOD for auxiliary bodypart information, a QUANTITY for quanitity information, and a TENSE for tense information. Notice that in Figs. 6.3 and 6.4 some of the modifiers may also have modifiers. Retaining the appropriate

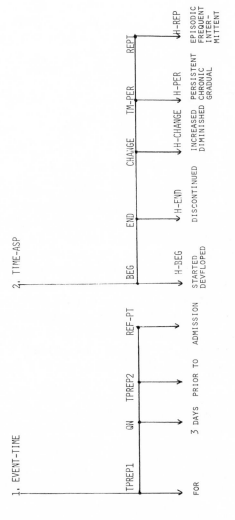

FIG. 6.3 Format modifiers for time information.

89

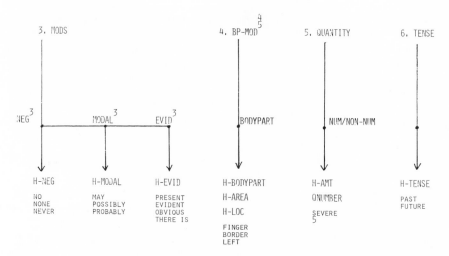

FIG. 6.4   Format modifiers other than time.

hierarchy for the modifiers is important in order to preserve the information content of the narrative. For example, *no fever* is different from *no increase in fever.* In the format of *no fever, no* is the negation modifier of the format field SIGN-SYMPTOM (containing *fever*). In the format of *no increase in fever, no* is the negation modifier of the format field CHANGE (in TIME-ASP containing *increase*); *increase* is in TIME-ASP, modifying the format field SIGN-SYMPTOM (containing *fever*).

Another format (FORMAT2) is shown in simplified form in Fig. 6.5. FORMAT2 contains treatment-without-medication information. There is an INST (institution) field, a PT (patient) field, a VERB-TR (treatment) field, and a nonmedical VERB field. This format contains the following information: Certain institutional personnel performed a certain treatment on the patient. Some examples of FORMAT2 sentences are:

An appendectomy was performed on 5/3/81.
Pt was given chemotherapy.
LMD advised against physiotherapy.

FORMAT4 (see Fig. 6.6) is the test + result sentence type. It is a large format because it covers the spectrum of test and result combinations. Sentences of this type are:

CSF culture showed no growth.
Blood-gases normal.
Chest xray normal.
Culture was positive for streptococcus.
WBC 1000.

FORMAT5 (see Fig. 6.7) contains patient-state information. It is actually a family of formats for such sentences as the following:

Patient has sickle cell disease.
Right shoulder with calcium tendonitis.
Breathing with difficulty.
P.E. essentially normal.
BP was 120/72.

There are four additional formats that are not shown in detail because they do not contain specifically medical information. However, they are described here briefly. FORMAT00 contains English sentential operators, such as: *Doctor felt that . . . ; Her mother noted . . . .* This format usually is connected to another format in the sublanguage. For example, *Her mother noted patient had increasing pain* consists of two formats: an English sentential operator type: *her mother noted;* and a patient-state type: *patient had increasing pain.* FORMAT00 is important because it may affect the factuality of the format it is related to. A second format, FORMAT0, contains patient descriptor information. It has a field PT-DESCR, which has the following subfields: AGE, RACE, SEX, and FAMILY. All the other formats also contain a PT-DESCR field in case that information should occur within a sentence of the given format type (PT-DESCR was omitted from the format figures for simplicity). Another format is FORMAT6, which contains behavioral information such as *Patient worked as a typist.* There is also a template (CONNECTIVE) for housing conjuncts of various types and verbal connectives (verbs connecting two sentence types). Its structure is very simple: CONNECTIVE has one subfield naming the type of connective

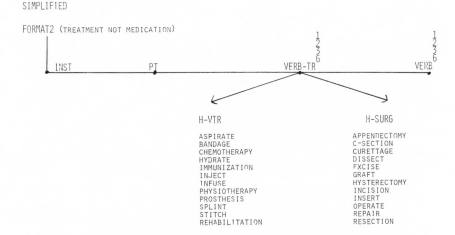

FIG. 6.5   Medical word classes in FORMAT2.

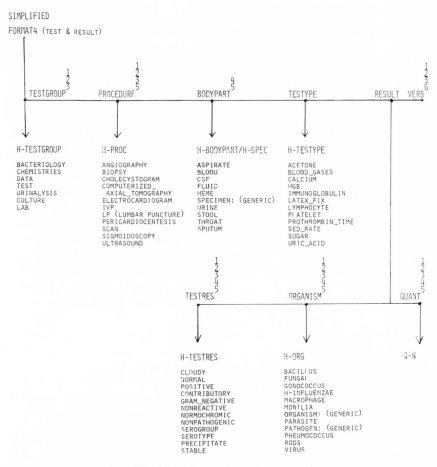

FIG. 6.6   Medical word classes in FORMAT4.

(CONJOINED, SUBORDINATE-CONJ, etc.). This field contains the value of the connective (*and, while,* etc.). CONNECTIVE may also have EVENT-TIME, TIME-ASP, and MODS modifiers.

PROCESSING THE NARRATIVE

The processing has been divided into consecutive modules so that each module performs a distinct logical function and refines the output of the preceding module. Modularizing the process clarifies the steps of the analytic process and permits different and relatively independent implementations for each function. Figure 6.8 shows an overview of all the stages of processing. The modules are described in sequence in the following paragraphs, with greater detail supplied on the sublanguage-dependent stages.

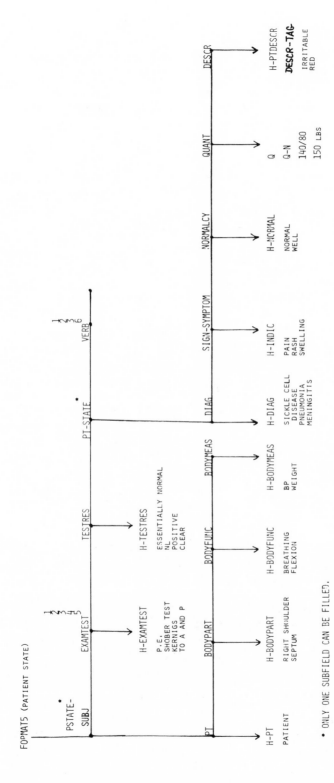

FIG. 6.7 Medical word classes in FORMAT5.

93

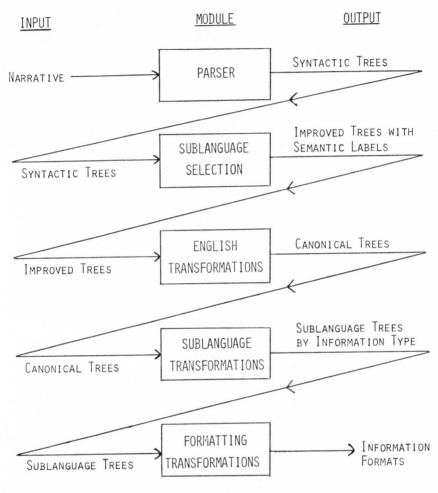

FIG. 6.8   Overview of medical text processing.

The Parser

The first module is the parsing component, which identifies the syntactic structure of the sentences of the narrative. It consists of a top-down parser (Grishman, Sager, Raze [Friedman], & Bookchin, 1973) that uses a broad coverage grammar (Sager, 1981) that has been adjusted for medical texts. An adjustment to the grammar was necessary because of the frequent use of fragmentary and run on sentences in medical documents. The grammar itself consists of syntactic definitions and grammatical constraints such as subject verb agreement. It also contains generalized procedures to handle a very wide range of conjunctional structures (Raze [Friedman], 1976) that are especially frequent in this material.

The parser also uses a lexicon in which words are assigned both English syntactic categories and medical subclasses based on their usage. Figure 6.9 contains some sample dictionary entries. Words are assigned medical sub-classes on the basis of where they occur in assertions relative to other words of the assertion and on the basis of the medical information they contain. For example *pain, rash,* and *fever* all occur in the environment *patient developed__*. They are all informationally disease indicators. Therefore, we assign them the subclass H-INDIC. On the other hand, *joint, arm,* and *leg* all occur in *pain in __*. They are all body part words. Therefore, we assign them the subclass H-BODYPART.

The Semantic Selection Module

The semantic selection module utilizes patterns of medical subclass co-occurrence in particular syntactic relations to give a semantic characterization to the syntactic structures. The patterns are also used to help resolve sublanguage ambiguity and to improve the parse tree. Selection was first implemented in the LSP system as part of the parsing grammar (Grishman, Hirschman, & Friedman, 1982). The selection constraints were list driven for

```
DEVELOPED    TV: (H-GROW, H-BEGIN),
             VEN: (H-GROW, H-BEGIN),


PAIN      N: (H-INDIC, SINGULAR),


IN        P,


LEFT      ADJ: (H-LOC),
          TV,
          VEN,


LEG       N: (H-BODYPART, SINGULAR),
```

FIG. 6.9   Some simplified dictionary entries.

ease of maintenance and portability from one sublanguage to another. The present implementation does selection in two points in the processing: in the selection module and (for conjunctions) in the parsing stage. The list-driven mechanism to determine the sublanguage patterns has been retained from the first implementaton; the use made of the information and the lists themselves have been altered.

In this module, subclass co-occurrence patterns for particular syntactic relations are matched, and the success or failure of the match is recorded along with a semantic characterization of the structures when possible. Figure 6.10 shows some partial entries for the list P-NSTGO-HOST, which consists of subclass co-occurrence patterns for a noun N and its prepositional right adjunct PN. Well-formed N P N subclass sequences are placed in the list P-NSTGO-HOST in the following order (examples, in parentheses, are taken from the first entry to the list P-NSTGO-HOST shown in Figure 6.10):

the preposition P (*in*)
the subclass of the head noun in the PN phrase (H-BODYPART)
the semantic label of the PN phrase (BODYLOC-PN)
the list of the allowable subclasses for the host of the PN phrase (H-INDIC, H-DIAG, . . .)

Consider the phrase *swelling in arm,* where *in arm* is a prepositional right adjunct of *swelling*. The subclass pattern is H-INDIC IN H-BODYPART, and it is on list P-NSTGO-HOST. The success of the match is recorded as follows: *swelling* is assigned a property (i.e. node attribute) called SELECT-ATT, which has the value H-INDIC; *arm* is assigned as a SELECT-ATT with the value H-BODYPART. In addition, the PN structure is assigned an attribute called TYPE-ATT with value BODYLOC-PN.

The recording of a match is important for several reasons. For one, a successful match is preferable to an unsuccessful one. In the phrase *swelling in arm for 2 days, for 2 days* is a prepositional right adjunct of *arm* in the syntactic analysis. The pattern is H-BODYPART FOR NTIME1. The pattern FOR NTIME1 is a recognizable PN pattern; it is a time phrase and in our system is assigned the label TIME-PN. A TIME-PN can not have an H-

LIST P-NSTGO-HOST =

'IN': (H-BODYPART: (BODYLOC-PN: (H-INDIC, H-DIAG,....))
    H-INST: (N-O-TYPE: (H-VTR, H-VMD,....))),

'FOR': (NTIME1: (TIME-PN: (H-INDIC, H-DIAG, H-VTR, H-VMD,....)))',

FIG. 6.10   Partial entries from a selection list.

BODYPART host. However, *swelling* is another possible host for *in 2 days.* This pattern is H-INDIC FOR NTIME1 and is acceptable for this relation. Therefore, this analysis is the preferable one. The parse tree is rearranged to reflect the improved analysis.

The most important reason for recording a successful pattern match of a structure is to provide a semantic characterization of that structure that will be used to obtain its final formatted representation. In our example, *for 2 days* is a time phrase relating to the event *swelling.* In the final format, *for two days* will be mapped into an EVENT-TIME modifier, modifying the format field SIGN-SYMPTOM containing *swelling.*

The recording of the result of a match is important also because it helps to resolve sublanguage ambiguities. A sublanguage homograph is a word that has more than one sublanguage class. For example, *growth* has the subclass H-INDIC, as in *growth is a tumor,* and the subclass H-GROW as in *growth was normal.* Thus, the phrase *normal growth* (where *normal* is a left adjunct of *growth*) has two possible patterns: H-NORMAL H-INDIC and H-NOR-MAL H-GROW. The first pattern match fails, but the second one is successful. Therefore, *growth* in this occurrence is assigned a SELECT-ATT with value H-GROW only. All processing that follows will treat *growth* informationally as an H-GROW word only.

Another example of a sublanguage homograph is *felt.* *Felt* has three subclasses:

H-EXAMTEST as in *No masses felt*
H-VPT as in *Patient felt pain*
VSENT3 (an English sentential operator) as in *It was felt that surgery was
    required.*

In *It was felt that surgery was required,* the object is a sentential object. For the purpose of pattern matching, we give it the value SENTOBJ. There are three verb + object patterns for this sentence corresponding to the three different subclasses of *felt.* The patterns H-EXAMTEST SENTOBJ and H-VPT SENTOBJ fail, but the pattern VSENT3 SENTOBJ succeeds. Therefore, *felt* is assigned a SELECT-ATT with value VSENT3 only, and it will be treated as a sentential operator in all the processing that follows.

A word that has only one medical subclass is not a sublanguage homograph but may still present a problem of sublanguage ambiguity: its usage may or may not be a medical one. That is, a word with a medical subclass may be used in the narrative as an ordinary English word and not as a medical word. This phenomenon occurs most frequently with verbs. For example, *wear* has the subclass H-BEH for behavioral information. In *Patient wore comfortable shoes, wear* is a behavioral verb, but in *the day wore on, wear* is not. When a SUBJECT VERB OBJECT subclass pattern fails, the verb is assigned a SELECT-ATT with value FAIL-SEL, signifying that a sublanguage pattern failed with that verb. This is a signal that the medical subclass of the verb should be ignored and the verb is to be treated as an English syntactic verb only.

A similar procedure is followed when a LEFT-ADJUNCT NOUN subclass pattern fails. A failure in this situation means that the medical subclass of the left adjunct is to be ignored. For example, *white* has the subclass H-RACE. The pattern H-RACE H-PT as in *white female* is acceptable. However, the pattern H-RACE H-RX as in *white pills* is not. In that situation, *white* is not being used to denote the race of the patient or the pills. *White* is assigned a SELECT-ATT with value FAIL-SEL in the latter phrase. Therefore, informationally it will remain as a left adjunct of *pills* in the final format, and the H-RACE subclass will be ignored.

Selection has yet another important function. There are certain words that may be higher order operators or connectives in the sublanguage, joining one basic medical event to another. In the lexicon, these words are given a subclass that we call H-CONN for connective. The following are some examples of connectives:

due to as in headache *due to fever*
from as in *rash from penicillin*
for as in *tylenol for headache*
relieve as in *tylenol relieved pain*
cause as in *fever caused headache*

However, these words may also be used as ordinary prepositions or verbs. For example, in *He visited a clinic for rheumatic patients, for* is not connecting one event to another. Another example is *tylenol for 2 days,* where *for 2 days* is a time phrase associated with *tylenol* and is not a separate event. The selection component determines whether or not words with the H-CONN subclass are connectives. If a word is determined to be a connective, it is assigned a SELECT-ATT with value H-CONN. This characterizes a structure containing a word with a SELECT-ATT equal to H-CONN as being a structure consisting of two separate events related by that connective.

Another case where selection is extremely useful can be demonstrated by the compound noun relation. This is a highly degenerate structure where semantic co-occurrence patterns are used to help determine the basic underlying structure. Consider the pattern H-RX H-INDIC, as in *penicillin rash*. The underlying structure is a Noun + Prepositional Phrase (N P N) with the pattern H-INDIC FROM H-RX, or *rash from penicillin*. This phrase consists of two related patient events and will be treated as such. Now consider the compound noun pattern H-RX H-INDIC, as in *headache remedy*. The underlying structure for this pattern is the N P N phrase H-RX FOR H-INDIC, or *remedy for headache*. In this situation, the H-INDIC (*headache*) is not directly asserted about the patient but is implied, because the patient was given a remedy that was for a headache. Thus, for this pattern, whereas the two related events are H-RX (*remedy*) and H-INDIC (*headache*), the H-INDIC event (*headache*) is marked as implied.

Another pattern, H-BODYPART H-PROC (*chest xray*), can be transformed into H-PROC OF H-BODYPART. However, here the formats are the same for both forms. In both phrases, there is only one medical event *xray* modified by the body part *chest*, with the relation that the *chest* was *xrayed*.

One very important type of selection operates in the parsing stage rather than afterwards (in the selection module). This is sublanguage selection for conjunctional structures. Our grammar handles a rich range of conjunctional structures; therefore, to reduce ambiguity and obtain the best parse possible, it is crucial to restrain possible conjoinings in the parsing stage. In general, nouns or adjectives are allowed to conjoin only if they are in the same subclass or in a class of conjoinable subclasses. These constraints are discussed in greater detail in Hirschman (1982).

THE REGULARIZATION MODULES

The next two modules consist of regularization transformations. They map the structures into canonical forms without changing their informational content. One component consists of general English transformations and the other sublanguage-specific ones. An example of an English transformation is the one that expands conjunctional structures. Thus *patient had fever and chills* is transformed into two assertions: *patient had fever* and *patient had chills*. These two assertions are joined by the connective *and*. An example of a sublanguage-specific transformation is the one that breaks up an assertion into two fragments when there is a connective in the assertion (that is, the connective was assigned a SELECT-ATT with value H-CONN). Thus *headache was due to fever* is transformed into two fragments *fever* and *headache* connected by the relation *be due to*.

As a result of these two stages of processing, the original narrative sentences are structured into elementary assertions or fragmentary assertions joined by connectives, and, most importantly, these assertions conform to the basic sentence types of the sublanguage. Thus, the various linguistic forms that were used in the narrative to express the medical information have been reduced to standard forms: basic medical events and their relations. At this point, the particular sentence type that is occurring can be determined by the presence of its characteristic subclasses in the elementary assertion and fragment.

The Formatting Module

It is the function of this component to map the structured trees into the appropriate information formats. When the narrative reaches this module, it has been structured into elementary or fragmentary assertions joined by connectives. Each assertion corresponds to a basic sentence type of the sublanguage, and each connective structure contains the type of connective (subordinate conjunction, coordinate conjunction), its value (i.e. *while, and*), and possibly modifier information. For each assertion and connective, the formatting component builds the appropriate format and maps the words of the assertion (or the connective) into the appropriate fields of the format. The mapping itself is a fairly straightforward procedure. In general, the syntax directs the order of the mapping, and the semantic subclasses (not the original subclasses but the subclasses assigned by the selection module) determine which fields the words are to be placed in. The processing in the preceding modules has broken each sentence into its component medical events and labeled them accordingly, so that the correct format can be built for it. Once the format is built, the semantic labels on the words (SELECT-ATT values), and phrases (TYPE-ATT values) are sufficient to drive the mapping, except for a few cases that are treated differently.

The LSP had a first implementation of medical formatting that produced a single composite format (Hirschman & Sager, 1982). In the present implementation, the mapping transformations produce individual formats for the different medical sentence types and are list driven, making this component easy to modify and also adaptable for other sublanguages. One list establishes correspondences between the semantic subclasses and the nonmodifier fields of the format. For example, a word that has the SELECT-ATT H-INDIC is mapped into the SIGN-SYMPTOM field of FORMAT5. Another list establishes correspondences between the semantic subclasses and the modifier fields of the format. In this case, however, the proper modifier must be built and inserted next to the appropriate format field. In addition to the list driven transformations, the formatting component also has some sublanguage-specific transformations. These involve mostly quantities and units such as *10 years old, 100 mg, 150 lbs,* and *3 days ago,* which map into one of the fields AGE, DOSE, QUANT, EVENT-TIME, or RESULT.

The important result of formatting the narrative is that the medically significant informational fields for all the various ways of reporting the information are the same. Figure 6.11 illustrates this by showing that the significant fields are filled identically for various forms of reporting *pain in leg.*

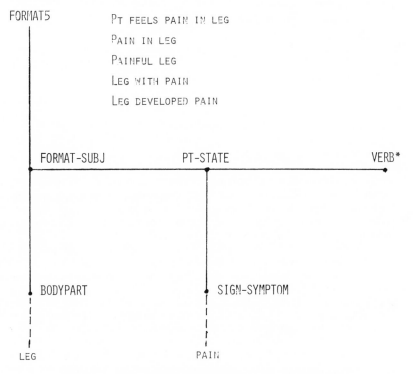

FIG. 6.11 Format for various linguistic forms of "pain in leg".

CONCLUSION

This paper has described an implementation of medical text processing based on English parsing and a medical sublanguage grammar. After parsing, sublanguage co-occurrence patterns are checked for well-formed subclass combinations in the syntactic relations given by the parse, and the parse tree is adjusted to reflect the preferred patterns. Structures are labeled according to their semantic content, and, where a word is in more than one medical subclass, the class conforming to its usage in the given context is selected. Sentences or phrases that contain more than one medical event (*fever due to headache*) are separated into two elementary structures joined by a connective. Finally, the semantically labelled elementary structures are mapped into *information formats*, which are generalized sublanguage sentence forms for housing the different types of patient information in the documents. The patient information that was originally given in narrative form is now organized and codified according to medical categories, so that it can be queried in terms of the medical categories and relations in the material.

ACKNOWLEDGMENTS

This research was supported in part by National Library of Medicine grant number l-RO1-LM03933, awarded by the National Institutes of Health, Department of Health and Human Services.

REFERENCES

Grishman, R., Sager, N., Raze (Friedman), C., & Bookchin, B. (1973). The lingusitic string parser. *AFIPS Conference Proceedings, 42,* (pp. 427–434). Montvale, NJ: AFIPS Press.

Grishman, R., Hirschman, L., & Friedman, C. (1982). Natural Language Interfaces Using Limited Semantic Information. *COLING 82: Proceedings of the Ninth International Conference on Computational Linguistics* (pp. 89–94). Amsterdam: North Holland.

Hirschman, L. (1982). Constraints on noun phrase conjunction: A domain-independent mechanism. *COLING 82 Abstracts* (pp. 129–133). Prague.

Raze (Friedman), C. (1976). A computational treatment of coordinate conjunctions. *American Journal of Computational Linguistics,* microfiche 52.

Sager, N. (1981). *Natural language information processing: A computer grammar of English and its applications.* Reading, MA: Addison-Wesley.

Hirschman, L., & Sager, N. (1982). Automatic Information Formatting of a Medical Sublanguage. In R. Kittredge & J. Lehrberger (Eds.), *Sublanguage: Studies of language in restricted semantic domains* (pp.27–80). Berlin: de Gruyter.

7 General Semantic Patterns in Different Sublanguages

Elaine Marsh
Navy Center for Applied Research in Artificial Intelligence
Naval Research Laboratory
Washington, D.C.

ABSTRACT

A comparison of the semantic word class co-occurrence patterns in two different domains, a class of Navy messages about shipboard equipment failure and a set of medical discharge summaries, discloses that, despite superficial differences, the sublanguages share semantic relationships among classes of objects. A set of general semantic patterns is proposed. The semantic patterns, which are contextually determined and which represent stereotyped situations, can be considered instances of frames. By sequencing the semantic patterns, scriptal knowledge about discourse structures in a sublanguage can be represented. The domains of discourse of the different sublanguages can be viewed as sister nodes in a generalization/specialization hierarchy of discourse domains. The parent node represents the general *domain of system failures*. The shared/ different semantic patterns of the sublanguage are shown to correspond to the relative positions of the discourse domains in the hierarchy. As supporting evidence, the domain of discourse of an artificial language, IEEE ATLAS programming language (for describing electronic signal failures), has also been placed in the hierarchy; its semantic patterns are a specialization of the patterns of its parent domain (equipment failures).

INTRODUCTION

A sublanguage is characterized by limited subject matter, lexical, syntactic, semantic and discourse properties, and text structure properties that are distinct from those of the standard language. Sublanguages under study

103

(Kittredge, & Lehrberger, 1982a) include the sublanguage of pharmacology reports (Sager, 1972), weather reports (Chevalier, as cited in Kittredge, & Lehrberger, 1982), technical manuals (Lehrberger, 1982), stock market reports (Kittredge, 1982), patient medical histories (Hirschman, & Sager, 1982), and the language of legal documents (Charrow, Crandall, & Charrow, 1982), among others. We have been involved in investigating the sublanguage properties of Navy messages about equipment failures. These messages are called CASREPs (casualty reports).

Recent work on sublanguage has concentrated on enumerating the syntactic and semantic properties of individual sublanguages. Although identifying differences in individual sublanguages is important for understanding how sublanguages differ from the language as a whole (Kittredge, 1982; Grishman, Nhan, Marsh, & Hirschman, 1984), it is equally important to compare particular sublanguages for usages held in common. Syntactic similarities that hold among sublanguages have been discussed in some detail (Kittredge, 1982; Marsh, 1983). However, the similarities in the semantic patterning of different sublanguages are often overlooked and rarely investigated.

In the course of our work on the equipment failure messages, it became clear that the equipment failures sublanguage and the medical history sublanguage were talking about different objects in the same manner. This paper describes in detail the semantic objects and relationships between objects found in the set of equipment failure messages. The semantic patterns in the equipment failure sublanguage and those in the patient medical histories being studied at New York University's Linguistic String Project (Friedman, this volume) will be compared. The similarities in the semantic patterns of the two sublanguages are substantial. As it happens, a subset of the semantic patterns in CASREPs also occurs in an artificial language, ATLAS, a programming language for test specifications. A set of general patterns is proposed to represent semantic patterns in the failures domain of discourse under which a set of sublanguages operates. The failures domain is more general than that of the individual sublanguages that comprise it and can be described by a hierarchical representation. Similarities in the semantic patterns of component sublanguages arise from their operating within a higher level domain. The location of sublanguages in the hierarchy explains why certain semantic patterns are shared and others are not.

CASREP CLASS OF MESSAGES

CASREPs (casualty reports) are a class of Navy operational reports about shipboard equipment failures. A CASREP is sent within 24 hours of the malfunction whenever an equipment malfunction cannot be repaired within 48 hours. It identifies the status of the equipment and the parts and assistance required. Its purpose is to provide explicit information about the equipment that failed and the Navy unit, usually a ship, that filed the report. CASREPs inform operational and support personnel about the equipment casualties that could affect a unit's ability to perform in a mission area, and they report the unit's need for technical assistance and for parts to correct the malfunction. In other words, they are useful to maintain units in a combat-ready status. Information in CASREPs is also used to gather data on the history of malfunctions and on ship readiness.

Like other operational reports, the text of a CASREP is highly formatted and consists of a sequence of data sets. Among other things the data sets specify an equipment identification code (EIC), an estimated time of repair, and an itinerary, all in accordance with format conventions. The data sets may also include narrative amplification and remarks in addition to the pro forma data. The amplification (AMPN) is used to amplify only the single, immediately preceding data set. The remarks (RMKS) section is used to amplify all or part of a message. In the RMKS section, the originator often describes a complete history of the casualty situation and the cause of the casualty, if known. Certain rules govern the structure of narrative text sets. These include restrictions on line length, on maximum length of the data set, and on termination symbols for the data set. The narrative text is usually explanatory and unformatted in nature but may contain information in any form. The inclusion of free text sets in a message is usually an option of the message originator.

The CASREPs can be categorized into separate subdomains, based on the type of EIC specified in the data set. The EIC consists of four alphanumeric symbols. The code specifically identifies the equipment being reported on, providing three levels of information: system, subsystem, and component. In this study, we have chosen to look at a set of CASREPs reporting on electronic equipment failure, specifically CASREPs concerning communications and data systems. These reports are identified by a Q as the first character in the EIC.

Figure 7.1 shows a portion of an example CASREP reporting on the failure of a whip antenna. The first data set in the text of Fig. 7.1 is labeled MSGID; it identifies the message as belonging to the CASREP class and the sender, here the ship name. The second data set labels the message as an INITIAL CASREP (the first CASREP sent in a series of reports), identifies the equipment that failed (a whip antenna), and rates the effect of the failure on ship readiness as CAT(egory) 2, substantially combat ready, with only minor deficiencies. The ESTIMATE data set gives the expected time when the repair will be completed; for this CASREP, value of the ESTIMATE data set is 3 OCT 1982, at 11:59 p.m. The ASSIST data set, with the value TENDER,

```
P 071540Z AUG 82
FM USS XXXX YYYY
TO . . .
BT
MSGID/CASREP/DD ### XXXX YYYY/164/
POSIT/2714N-05659E5/021400ZAUG82/
CASUALTY/INITIAL-82114/AFT TRUSSED 35FT WHIP ANTENNA/EIC:Q105/CAT:2/
ESTIMATE/032359ZOCT82/REPAIR OR REPLACEMENT OF ANTENNA/
ASSIST/TENDER/USS PUGET SOUND/
PARTSID/APL:NO APL LISTED/-/JCN:V52198-OC01-0624//
TECHPUB/NAVSHIPS 0956-166-3020/
RMKS/ANTENNA BROKE AWAY FROM BASE PLATE INSULATOR WELDS DUR-
ING NORMAL LOWERING FOR HELICOPTER OPERATIONS. BASE PLATE AND
INSULATOR BOTH DAMAGED IN FALL. ANTENNA MAYBE SERVICABLE. INSU-
LATOR IS UNUSABLE. ANTENNA WAS ONE OF TWO PRIMARY HF RECEIVE AN-
TENNAS. LOSS OF ANTENNA RENDERS SRA-50 COUPLER UNUSABLE. THIS IS
SECOND CASUALTY OF THIS TYPE TO ANTENNA IN PAST THREE MONTHS.
ORIGINAL ANTENNA REPLACED BY OUTSIDE CONTRACTOR THROUGH RSG
MAYPORT 7 JUN 82. BELIEVE PARTIAL CAUSE OF FAILURE IS DUE TO VIBRA-
TION. ANTENNA INSTALLATION IS ATOP MOUNT 52.
BT
#4007
```

FIG 7.1.   A Sample CASREP

indicates that the ship will need outside assistance to correct the problem. The RMKS section describes the equipment malfunction and its cause, if known.

Currently we are processing equipment failure messages with a system developed at the New York University Linguistic String Project (Sager, 1981). The system generates a tabular representation of message content, called an *information format,* that can be readily accessed and used by application systems. In simplest terms, an information format is a large table, with one column for each type of information that can occur in a class of texts and one row for each sentence or clause in the text. This approach uses an explicit grammar of English and a classification of the semantic relationships within the domain to derive the tabular representation of the information in a message narrative.

The characteristic property of CASREPs that makes it feasible to format them is that they report on situations in a restricted domain, made even more restricted by the ability to subcategorize the reports into failures about particular systems, here data and communications systems. In the course of this work, we have been required to investigate in some detail both the syntax and semantics of the equipment failure sublanguage. The syntactic constructions in the equipment failure sublanguage resemble those found in the medical sublanguage (Marsh, 1983; Grishman, 1984). A method for defining semantic patterns and the semantic patterns in the equipment failure sublanguage that were defined are described in the following section.

DEFINING SEMANTIC PATTERNS

Texts in a restricted domain talk about a limited number of classes of objects and express a limited number of relationships among these objects. The objects and relationships in a sublanguage can be derived using techniques of distributional analysis (Harris, 1968; Sager, 1975; Hirschman, 1982). this technique involves identifying the objects and relationships among objects in a sublanguage by looking at the co-occurrence properties of the words in the syntactic relations in which they occur in the texts. The words in the sublanguage that have similar co-occurrence patterns have similar informational standing in the domain. The recurring combinations that characterize this domain are used in determining a set of semantic patterns and their associated information format. By identifying these classes of objects and relationships, we can develop data structures, *information formats,* suitable for storing the information derived from the message narrative. The various classes of objects and relationships have their own "slots" in this data structure, so that information can be much more readily retrieved than from the original narrative (Sager, 1978).

A limited set of 26 equipment faiure messages has been analyzed using distributional analysis techniques to determine a preliminary set of semantic categories and semantic patterns. Word classes for this material were developed by examining and comparing sets of words occurring in particular syntactic environments and grouping together words that occur in the same context, e.g. as subjects of the same verb. For example, in the CASREPs we found that the noun phrases appearing as the subject of *repair* name personnel or organizations who operate or maintain the equipment, e.g. *technician* and *contractor.* Both serve as the subject of the verb *repair.* We then gave nouns that occur in the same context the semantic category ORG, for organization. Nouns that serve as objects of *repair,* such as *AN/URC-9, circuit card, antenna,* and *cable assembly,* are all pieces of equipment or parts. The semantic class PART was defined to include these elements.

The classes are extended by looking at similar subject-verb-object (SVO) class combinations. For example, *replace* has a distribution similar *to repair.* It occurs with *contractor* as subject and *antenna* as object. *Replace* also allows *APC* (automatic power control) as object. On the basis of these occurrences, it is possible to define a verb class REPAIR (containing *repair* and *replace*), whose members select ORG nouns as subject and PART nouns as object.

After collecting phases involving the same words or classes, for example, REPAIR, ORG, PART, we replaced the words by their classes to derive semantic patterns. For example, the semantic subject-verb-object (SVO) pattern derived above is ORG = REPAIR = PART. Such SVO patterns represent the argument structure for a single assertion in the sublanguage. Each assertion is represented by one SVO semantic pattern. When a sentence contains more than one assertion, for example when there is any conjoining, sentence subordination, or sentence connection (the words *cause, result in* which can connect two events), we represent each assertion separately to isolate its semantic pattern.

Distributional analysis may be complicated by co-occurrence patterns that are similar, but play different roles in the discourse structure of the sublanguage. The purely syntactic derivation of semantic patterns may not distinguish two semantic classes. For example, the verbs *investigate, examine,* and *troubleshoot* all have co-occurrence patterns similar to REPAIR class verbs. They take organizations as subjects and parts as objects. However, because CASREP discourse structure follows the pattern FAILURE INVESTIGATION DIAGNOSIS REPAIR, it is useful to assign the investigatory actions to a separate class INVEST and define a separate semantic pattern, ORG INVEST PART.

Semantic categories are not identified with any one syntactic category. For example, STATUS words can be nouns (*wear*), adjectives (*OK, inop*), verbs (*damaged*), and so on. These words, no matter what their syntactic categories, noun, adjective, or verb, are all operators and, as a result, have similar co-occurrence patterns. The semantic categories representing the objects and relationships in the equipment failure texts are presented in Table 7.1.[1]

Objects in CASREPs about electronic equipment include the equipment items and their component parts, the signals and data operated on by the equipment, the people and organizations who operate and maintain the equipment, and the documents involved in the maintenance process. Relationships include repair and investigatory actions on the equipment by organizations, actions of equipment on signals, etc. The various combinations of these classes reveal the semantic patterns discussed in the next section.

SUMMARY OF EQUIPMENT FAILURE SEMANTIC PATTERNS

In this section, we present a summary table of the semantic patterns defined for the equipment failure sublanguage and will discuss each pattern briefly. For more information, a detailed discussion of the semantic patterns identified for subject-verb-object and host-modifier constructions is provided in Appendix 7.1.

---

[1]Table 7.1 does not include two semantic categories: CONN and ENVENT. CONN is a connective word, such as *inhibit, cause, indicate.* ENVENT is a class representing environmental events such as *lightning strike.* The first has not been included because it is used in relating the semantic patterns to each other and not within the semantic patterns themselves. The second is not included because it was defined on the basis of only one instance.

TABLE 7.1
CASREP Semantic Categories and Modifiers of Categories

CASREP Semantic Categories

ADMIN	action or request for part, *forward, report, expedite*
FUNCTION	function performed by equipment *broadcast, communication, operate*
INVEST	investigative act, *check, isolate, troubleshooting*
MSG	message concerning part failure or request for part, *CASREP, message*
ORG	personnel or organization, *MOTU, ship, technical, originator, technician*
PART	equipment, subsystem, or part, *antenna, AN/URC-9, controller*
PROCESS	process performed by equipment on electrical signal, *encrypt, decrypt, cycle, deflection*
PROCURE	action to request, ship, receive, or hold part, *deliver, purchase, reorder*
PROPERTY	property of part, *allowance, clearance, sync, weight*
REPAIR	repair action, *repair, adjust, overhaul*
SIGNAL	electrical signal *current, band, voltage, UHF*
STASK	ship's task *arrival, assignment, transit*
STATUS	equipment status, *casualty, fault, malfunction, good*

Modifiers

TIME, LOC [location], QUANT [quantity, amount, value of property],
EFFORT [__man-hours], NEG [negation], MODAL [modality]

The sentence types that can occur in the sublanguage are, in some respects, application driven. For the dissemination and summarization applications we are working on at the Navy Center for Applied Research in Artificial Intelligence, information about assistance requests and equipment state are very important. These are assigned distinct sentence types. Assertions of these sentence types are associated with each other via connectives. Time information contained in modifiers is crucial for indicating the temporal relationships among the semantic patterns.

The general semantic patterns in the equipment failure sublanguage are presented in Table 7.2.[2] We identify the semantic patterns as events in the sublanguage. All of the category elements in a pattern need not be present for the pattern to be well formed. The list of semantic patterns is written in the same format as that of the patient medical history sublanguage presented in the next section; they can easily be compared there.

Pattern 1 includes general administrative functions of organizations, including administrative and procurement actions. The ADMIN and PRO-CURE categories have been grouped together because they both involve tasks that do not directly pertain to the description of a casualty. Examples of Pattern 1 include:

> *item listed on PARTSID APL; stock reqn shipped but not received; receipt NLT 7 OCT 82.*

Pattern 2 represents information about repair actions, basically indicating which organization is to do the repair and on what piece of equipment. Time information contained in modifiers is crucial for indicating the temporal relationships among the semantic patterns. Examples of Pattern 2 are:

> *original antenna replaced by outside contractor; multi-pin connector instl/repair; tube alignment.*

Pattern 3 represents information about investigative actions and may include information about the investigating organization and the part they are troubleshooting. A slot for status is included for text such as *casualty* in *troubleshooting the casualty.* In general, specific information about the status of the casualty is not given in these type of sentences. Pattern 3 describes such sentences as:

> *ships force is troubleshooting the system; ships force has examined the cable.*

Pattern 4 represents information about part status, including information about the status of equipment functions and information about specific properties of a piece of equipment:

> *upper half of antenna damaged beyond repair; SRA-50 coupler inop; inner oven operates erratically; no clearance.*

---

[2]For clarity of presentation, we have omitted the modifier semantic categories TIME, QUANT, LOC, EFFORT, NEG, MODAL from the table. These classes are generally associated with one of the VERB categories or with a STATUS specification.

TABLE 7.2
Equipment Failure Sublanguage Semantic Patterns

Sentence Type	No.	Pattern
General Administration	1	ORG PART VERB-ADMIN/PROCURE
Repair	2	ORG PART/STATUS VERB-REPAIR
Investigation	3	ORG PART/STATUS VERB-INVEST
Part State	4	PART FUNC PROP STATUS
Signal State	5	PART SIGNAL STATUS VERB-PROCESS
Assistance	6	ORG VERB-ASSIST
Ship Task	7	ORG VERB-STASK
Part Description	8	PART LOCATION ENVENT VERB

Pattern 5 is used to represent information about electrical signals. Because we are dealing with electronics casualty reports, it is useful to separate this information from status information about parts. Examples of Pattern 5 are:

current OK; unit will not decrypt/encrypt; low power output; large current surge.

Pattern 6 incorporates information about an assistance request, specifically whether technical or parts assistance is being requested:

MOTU TWELVE assist; msg tech assist.

Pattern 7 is used to present information concerning a ship's task. This information is included in the text to describe associated activities of the ship that could be used in determining the cause of the casualty. For example, in one messaage, an accident during the normal lowering of the ship's antenna resulted in a casualty. Other examples include:

in transit from Staten Island NY to Little Creek.

Pattern 8 provides general descriptive information, for example about a shipboard location of a part or general environmental events:

antenna installation is atop mount 52; large current surge from lightning strike.

COMPARISON OF NAVY AND MEDICAL SEMANTIC PATTERNS

The sublanguage of patient medical histories has been described in great detail by the researchers at the New York University Linguistic String Project. Friedman (this volume) has discussed six format types that characterize much of the information in the medical history sublanguage. Format types correspond to the types of semantic patterns and sentences found in that sublanguage. For clarity, the format types are presented again in Table 7.3; the numbers on the left (No.) correspond to the pattern numbers (ID.) of their correlates in the equipment failure messages. ID numbers in the third column of the table correspond to the format identification numbers assigned in the LSP system (Friedman, this volume). These format types can be compared with the equipment failure message semantic patterns on two levels: (a) the objects and actions represented in the semantic categories of the sublanguage and (b) the relationships that hold among the semantic categories.

The objects in the two sublanguages are quite different; they refer to two different worlds. In the medical documents, the objects of concern are the patient and things related to his hospital stay. These include the patient, hospital, and different types of tests and procedures. Descriptions include descriptions of tests (*test results*) and the patient (*patient status*). Actions in the medical sublanguage include medical management actions, testing actions, patient behavior, and treatment.

In the world of equipment failure messages, the objects of concern are the part that has failed and things related to the casualty. These include the part, organizations that repair parts, communications regarding the casualty, part properties and electrical signals. Descriptions include descriptions of the part status, part function, part properties and electrical signals. Actions include assistance, general administration, procurement, investigation, and repair.

Although the objects of the two sublanguages exist in different domains, the relationship among objects exhibited in the semantic patterns can be compared. The sublanguages seem to talk about different objects in the same

TABLE 7.3
Patient History Format Types

No.	Format type	ID.	Pattern
1	General Med. Management	1	INST PT VERB-MD VERB
2	Treatment (not medication)	2	INST PT VERB-TR VERB
3	Test & Result	4	TESTGROUP PROCEDURE BODYPART TESTYPE RESULT VERB
4	Patient State	5	PSTATE-SUBJ EXAMTEST TESTRES PT-STATE VERB
5	Patient Behavior	6	PT VERB-BEH
6	Medication	3	INST PT MED DOSE MANNER FREQ VERB-TR

way. This is evident from the similarities in the semantic patterns numbers (1)–(5) in the first column.

Pattern (1) from the CASREPs corresponds closely to Pattern (1) from the patient histories. Both patterns involve *general administration* actions by organizations (in the Navy messages, *ships, technicians, task groups,* and, in the medical histories, *doctors* and *hospitals*) on the casualty (in the Navy messages, the casualty is a piece of equipment; in the medical histories, it is the patient).

Pattern (2) corresponds to a remedy action in both sublanguages. In the equipment failure messages, the remedy action is a repair or replacement act; in the medical, it is some kind of treatment. Again, the agents are corresponding organizations, and the objects the casualties.

Pattern (3) in both sublanguages involves an investigative action. In the Navy texts, the investigative act is quite general because detailed testing information is not given in the casualty reports. The medical histories have a much richer range of objects involved in the investigative action; numerous test types and procedures are involved in the action.[3] However, in both instances, the action relates a test of a part (in the Navy messages, equipment part; in the medical histories, body part) with some finding. The finding in the Navy material is the status of the part; in the medical, it is some test result or observation.

Pattern (4) in both sublanguages corresponds to a description of the casualty's state. In the equipment failure messages, this may be the status of a property that the equipment has or of the piece of equipment itself. For the medical histories, the casualty can be a body part, in addition to the patient; or the status can describe a property of the patient, such as pulse or ability to swallow. Again there is much more detail in the medical patterns.

Pattern (5) in the two sublanguages does not correspond as closely as the other types. Yet there is some similarity. The action involves a description or specification of the behavior of the agent. In the Navy sublanguage, that action includes the behavior of a piece of equipment on a signal. In the medical sublanguage, it is patient behavior, such as eating or sleeping.

Five out of nine patterns are held in common in the two sublanguages. These common semantic patterns are shown in Table 7.4. Those patterns that do not overlap are specific to the individual sublanguages. For example, the medication pattern (the item specified by 6 in the first column of the patient histories table) does not exist in the equipment failure domain. This is understandable: the grammatical construction for the medication dose information is sublanguage specific, and the associated semantic pattern is also restricted. Patterns (6)–(8) of the CASREP semantic patterns are restricted to the equipment failure domain. These include semantic relations involving

---

[3]The Navy messages are written under time and length constraints, whereas the medical histories are not.

TABLE 7.4
General Semantic Patterns

	Pattern Type	Pattern
1.	General Administration	ORG CASUALTY VERB-ADMIN
2.	Remedy Action:	ORG CASUALTY VERB-REMEDY
3.	Investigation:	ORG CASUALTY TEST FINDING VERB-TEST
4.	Casualty State:	CASUALTY PROP STATUS
5.	Behavior Descriptor	PART BEHAVIOR

ship tasks and requests for assistance, as well as general descriptors. Patterns (6) and (7) reflect major concerns of the casualty reports; information about a ship's scheduled tasks and the type of assistance required are important in order for organizations to make arrangements for the receipt of parts and the scheduling of technical assistance.

The equipment failure domain involves a broad range of activities. As a result, we can expect a wide variety of semantic patterns. Actions such as procurement and administration not only pertain to the casualty, but also involve the general world of naval operations. The patient history domain, however, has fewer but more complex semantic patterns.

The similarities and differences in the two sublanguages can be explained if we consider them both to operate within a higher level generalized domain, the *domain of system failures* (hereafter called the *failures* domain). The common semantic patterns represent the kinds of information that are the concern of the failures domain. This information is more general than that contained in the sublanguage-specific semantic patterns. Casualty reports are subsumed under the general domain of failures: they concern equipment failures. The patient medical histories are also failure reports, but they are concerned with human system failures.[4]

We return to a discussion of the *failures domain* later.

ATLAS: A SPECIAL-PURPOSE PROGRAMMING
LANGUAGE AS A SUBLANGUAGE

Although sublanguage analysis has been performed on technical reports, textual material, and messages, it is also applicable to artifical languages such as programming languages, provided the domain of the programming lan-

---

[4]Another class of Navy operational reports, written with the same formatting conventions as the equipment failure messages is also produced. These are called personnel CASREPs, and they are filed when there has been a personnel injury.

guage is restricted. A set of semantic patterns can be derived for the artificial language, just as it is for natural language texts. One candidate for this type of sublanguage analysis is ATLAS. ATLAS is an artificial language used for preparing test requirements for automatic test equipment (IEEE, 1980, 1981). The objects of concern and the relationships between these objects are a subset of those found in the equipment failure messages.

The ATLAS test language was designed for both person-to-person and person-to-machine communications. It restricts itself to the statement of a problem and avoids specifying methods of solution for that problem. Test specifications for a particular unit, written in ATLAS, are translated into a test program to ensure the unit of operability and assist in its return to operation in the event that it failed. Like a sublanguage, ATLAS is domain specific, here, to the world of testing equipment. It serves the need for precise communication among members of the electronics troubleshooting and automatic test equipment community.

Atlas provides precise constructs, grammar, and terminology to communicate test requirements unambiguously and concisely, permitting the exact description of test procedures. It was designed to be translated into unambiguous test procedures. Its constructs are selected to be independent of particular solutions or equipment, allowing faithful implementation of an ATLAS test procedure in a variety of ways and on a variety of equipment.

In its grammar, ATLAS defines sets of words as nouns and modifiers. Each noun has a set of associated modifiers. Each modifier is defined to have particular numerical values depending on the piece of equipment under test. Table 7.5 illustrates some of the modifiers that are associated with the noun *DC Signal* (Direct Current Signal). DC Signal is defined in the user's manual as an unvarying electrical potential.

An example of ATLAS code follows (*IEEE,* 1980, p. 96);

```
REQUIRE, 'DC-POWER', SOURCE, DC SIGNAL,
    CONTROL, VOLTAGE RANGE 10V TO 14V BY 0.1V
    ERRLMT + - 05.V
    CAPABILITY, CURRENT MAX 750MA, LIMIT,
    AC-COMP MAX 50MV,
    CNX HI LO$
```

TABLE 7.5
ATLAS Modifiers

Modifier	Mnemonic	Dimension
Power	POWER	Watt
Voltage	VOLTAGE	Volt
DC Current	CURRENT	Ampere
AC Component Freq.	AC-COMP-FREQ	Hertz

NOTE. From *IEEE* (1981), pp.16–17. Adapted by permission.

Because ATLAS was designed as an unambiguous programming language, its syntax differs from that of English. However, it incorporates a subset of semantic patterns exhibited in the equipment failure sublanguage. The objects of concern in ATLAS are electrical signals and their attributes. For example, in the sample code, the host noun is *DC Signal.* Limits are set for the ranges of component signals, e.g., current, voltage, frequency; and values set for these ranges of signals are dependent on the unit under test. The status of a component is determined by the value of the signal being produced. In addition, the capability (*FUNCTION*) of a signal is indicated. All of these are defined as modifiers of the host noun.

It is possible to identify a set of semantic relations which hold among the nouns and their modifiers, just as was done with the equipment failure sublanguage. This is illustrated in Table 7.6.

These relationships are similar to those expressed in CASREP narrative, for example, *loss of plus or minus 20 V direct current on deflection amplifier board; APC-PPC voltages to T-827 IF stage are in excess of 10 volts*

In the first, a range is specified for the direct current on the deflection amplifier board. In the second, the status of a component *voltage* of a APC-PPC signal is being reported on. Currently, the distinction between signal and component signal is not made in the equipment failure sublanguage, largely because it has not been relevant to our applications. However, the distinction will be important when we begin to incorporate a richer model of the world of electronics failures.

The relationships expressed in the ATLAS test language are a subset of those represented by the relationships in the equipment failure sublanguage. ATLAS talks only about electrical signals and the parts, signals, and statuses associated with those signals. The equipment failure sublanguage, on the other hand, deals with a wider range of information than ATLAS does. Like ATLAS, it deals with information about signals, but it is also concerned with other properties of electronics equipment.

TABLE 7.6
ATLAS Semantic Relations

Component of Signal:	SIGNAL COMPONENT *DC signal, current; DC signal voltage;* *DC signal AC-COMP-FREQ*
Function of Signal:	SIGNAL FUNCTION *DC signal capability*
Status of Signal:	SIGNAL STATUS *current max 750MA;* *voltage range 10V to 14V by 0.1V;* *AC-COMP-FREQ range 1HZ to 2000HZ.*

SUBLANGUAGE SEMANTIC PATTERNS AND KNOWLEDGE REPRESENTATION

The Relationship of Semantic Patterns to Frames and Scripts

Sublanguage semantic patterns, which correlate with observed linguistic patterns and encode certain aspects of domain knowledge, are significant for representing the information found in texts. The semantic patterns state specific co-occurrence restrictions active in sublanguage sentences and reflect relations between objects. By identifying these sublanguage patterns, we can represent the knowledge in a domain; and, because semantic patterns represent stereotypical situations, they can be considered frame representations of the domain.

A frame is a general data-structure for representing a stereotyped situation through the identification of objects involved and the relations between objects (Minsky, 1975; Bobrow & Winograd, 1977; Stefik, 1980). In general, a frame contains a name, a reference to a prototype frame, and a set of slots. A frame's important substructures and its relations to other frames are defined in its slots. It typically describes a local pattern, although it represents a collection of information at many levels within the system. Larger semantic structures can be inferred from relations between frames, just as larger semantic patterns structures for an information format can be inferred by observing more global linguistic patterns.

Sublanguage semantic patterns can be considered to be frames. They describe typical instances of the concepts they represent. Defined by their occurrence in local constructions, semantic categories that make up the semantic patterns correspond to slots in the frame. Each pattern represents a class of objects that has been defined by its context, and each consists of a collection of slots describing relationships and various aspects of the objects. Patterns that are specific to individual sublanguages have a richer level of detail than the general semantic patterns enumerated in Table 7.4. Each element of the general pattern can be said to represent a class of categories in the specific pattern. Relations to other more specific categories are defined in the domain's more general categories. For example, the general category CASUALTY is related to a set of different objects, including patients, body parts, and body functions in the patient histories and pieces of equipment and their functions in the equipment failure messages.

As frames, the specific patterns can be useful for inferring unobserved facts about new situations. For example, both sublanguages are characterized by a large number of sentence fragments. Deletions from fragments can often be reconstructed on the basis of the semantic patterns that arise in full sentences (Marsh, 1983). In addition, semantic categories can be inferred for unassigned words by reference to the semantic pattern in which the word plays a role.

Scriptal knowledge (Schank & Abelson, 1977) about the domain can also be represented by sequences of semantic patterns and the relationships between them. Discourse structure can be represented by sequences of semantic patterns related to each other via *connectives,* including coordinating, subordinating, and causal connectives among others. For example, the discourse structure of the equipment failure message in Fig. 7.1 can be represented by a FAILURE-DIAGNOSIS-REPAIR script involving the sequence of several semantic patterns. First, several part states are described: the antenna broke away from the base plate insulator welds, it was damaged in the fall, it was possibly serviceable, but the insulator was unusable and so on. These correspond to a list of symptoms in the patient histories and describe the failure. The diagnosis involves investigatory actions, such as troubleshooting, and a hypothesis about the cause of the casualty. In the example message of Fig. 7.1, there is no troubleshooting action; the cause is hypothesized to be vibration, which is another part state. Throughout the discourse, semantic patterns are related by connectives or the progression of time in the narrative as signalled by time modifiers. In our example message, no repair is made of the current casualty, although the part was replaced earlier.

As with scripts, the sequence of semantic patterns and their related modifiers can be used in inferencing. The part state pattern may be related to another part state via a causal connective; in the message of Fig. 7.1, *render* relates the antenna's status to another casualty. From the relationship between the connective *render* and its associated part states, we can infer that the cause of the bad status of the SRA-50 coupler (*SRA-50 coupler is unusable*) is the loss of the antenna, which also has a bad status.

Being able to represent the information in the text as a sequence of related events focuses attention on the presence of unusual or missing events in the messages. It then becomes tractable to consider the problem of well-formedness and completeness in sublanguage texts. In the equipment failure messages, where a length limit is imposed, it is especially important to include as much quality information as possible in the limited amount of space allowed.

General Semantic Patterns and the Domain of Discourse

We have shown that general semantic patterns can be defined for different sublanguages. When two sublanguages share a set of semantic patterns, they share a *domain of discourse,* i.e., a generalized, higher-level domain type. In a shared domain of discourse, while the objects in the sublanguages are different, the relationships among objects are shared. The two sublanguages discussed peviously, electronics equipment failures and patient medical histories, are specific instances of the *failures* domain of discourse. The domains of discourse of the two sublanguages are viewed as sister nodes in a *generalization/specialization hierarchy* of discourse domains. The parent node represents the general *domain of failures.* The shared/different semantic patterns of the sublanguages correspond to the relative position of the sublanguages in this hierarchy. Figure 7.2 represents the failures domain.

Proposing a hierarchical structure for the failures domain allows us to formalize the relationships both between and within subdomains of a domain of discourse. The shared patterns are represented by the general failures domain; the different semantic patterns, specific to the sublanguange, are represented by daughter nodes. The electronics equipment failure domain is represented as a sister domain to propulsion equipment failures. Similarly, the subdomains of the personnel domain correspond to different classes of personnel failures: neurological, cardiac, and so on. The domain of discourse of the artificial language, the IEEE ATLAS programming language, can be considered a specialization of its parent domain, electronics equipment failures.

Within subdomains of the failures domain, objects discussed may not be the same, but relationships between the objects are often similar. For example, the patient histories discuss doctors and hospitals; the equipment failure messages discuss support personnel and naval organizations. In both sublanguages, these objects are agents in administrative and investigative actions. Similarly, the patient and the piece of equipment, respectively, are objects of these actions. The similarity in case relations among the objects makes it feasible to abstract the general failures domain of discourse.

This hierarchy supports differences between sublanguages. For example, there are semantic patterns that are specific to a particular sublanguage, such

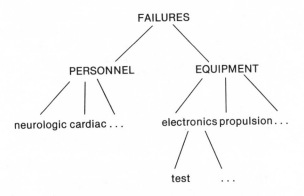

FIG 7.2.   The failures domain of discourse

as the medication format type in the medical histories. Moreover, we find that subdomains of sublanguages share these patterns, whereas others do not. For example, the personnel casualty reports and the patient histories may share the medication pattern since they are both subsumed under personnel failure.

CONCLUSIONS

A set of semantic patterns for the equipment failure sublanguage was defined using techniques of distributional analysis. These patterns were compared with those found in the patient history sublanguage, and substantial similarities were recognized in the relationships that hold between objects. It was shown that the ATLAS programming language, an artificial language for test specifications, exhibits a subset of the semantic patterns in the equipment failures sublanguage.

Sublanguage semantic patterns represent the knowledge expressed in the narrative in domain-specific texts. These sublanguage semantic patterns can be considered instances of a frame representation of the domain and are useful for representing scriptal knowledge in the sublanguage. Moreover, a set of common semantic patterns in different sublanguages permits us to define a general domain of discourse, the failures domain. Domains of discourse of the sublanguage domains are viewed as sister nodes in a generalization/specialization hierarchy, with the parent node representing the failures of domain of discourse. The distinctions and similarities in semantic patterns between the medical and equipment failures messages were shown to be related to the positions of the sublanguages in the failures hierarchy.

ACKNOWLEDGMENTS

This research was supported by the Office of Naval Research and the Office of Naval Technology PE-62721N. The author would like to thank Joan Bachenko and Dennis Perzanowski for comments on drafts of this paper and Richard Cantone for a rewarding discussion about domains of discourse.

APPENDIX 7.1: SEMANTIC PATTERNS IN THE EQUIPMENT FAILURE SUBLANGUAGE

The corpus of this study is a set of 26 equipment failure messages in the form described in the section, CASREP Class of Messages. The AMPN (amplification) and RMKs (remarks) sections of the text, which consist of narrative material, were analyzed using the techniques of distributional analysis described in the section, Defining Semantic Patterns. The whole corpus consists of 131 sentences. A prior analysis of a set of CASREPs (casualty reports) describing failures of propulsion systems was also performed to define semantic categories. The semantic patterns derived from them are not reported on here.

1. Subject-Verb-Object patterns

In the reports, we found 17 general co-occurrence patterns of the subject-verb-object (SVO) type, stated in terms of 11 participating word classes. The SVO patterns could be grouped into eight more general types. In the semantic patterns, the subject category is first, verb category second and the object category third. Examples are given below each pattern.

Part Procurement	1	ORG VERB-PROCURE PART/STATUS items not carried onboard; stock reqn shipped but not received.
Administration	2	ORG/MSG VERB-ADMIN PART STATUS item listed on PARTSID APL.
Investigation	3	ORG VERB-INVEST PART STATUS ship's force is troubleshooting the system; ship's force has examined cables.
Repair	4	ORG VERB-REPAIR PART STATUS original antenna replaced by outside contractor; previous issue to correct casualty.
Part Status	5	PART/FUNC/SIGNAL VERB-STATUS upper half of antenna damaged beyond repair; capabilities lost are as follows; SRA coupler inop; current OK.
Part Function	6	PART VERB-FUNC PART inner oven operates erratically; UYA-4 display system will not interface with the UYK-7 computer.
Part Process	7	PART VERB-PROCESS unit will not decrypt/encrypt; inner oven reads low on circit check meter.
Part Description	8	PART VERB LOCATION PLACE antenna installation is atop mount 52.

The SVO patterns describe a set of relationships between objects in the sublanguage. The objects of major concern in these SVO patterns are the equipment, the organizations that service the equipment, and signals produced by the equipment. The relationships between organizations and parts include actions on parts, such as repair and investigation, and general actions that do not relate directly to the equipment failure, such as administration and procurement actions as well as ship's tasks. Other relationships are reports on the status or functioning of a part. Thus, the SVO patterns describe functions of both parts (FUNCTION PROCESS) and organizations (ADMIN PROCURE INVEST). The world described by these patterns includes not only the immediate concerns of the equipment failure, but also objects that have affected these immediate concerns: weather, damage caused by ship's operations, problems with acquisition of supplies and so on.

Patterns 1–4 are actions; patterns 5–8 are descriptions of equipment status. Pattern 5 describes the equipment status directly. Patterns 6–7 describe equipment functions or processes. When these patterns are modified by negatives or amount adverbials, they indicate the status of the equipment. So, patterns 5–7 all indicate, in some manner, the status of a piece of equipment. Pattern 8 provides additional information about a piece of equipment, e.g. information about the location of the equipment on the ship. In the message in Fig. 7.1, this location information is useful in determining the cause of the problem.

2.   Modifier-Host Noun Patterns

Noun phrases in the equipment failure messages typically include numerous adjectival and noun modifiers on the head, and additional modifier types that are not so common in general English. The relationships expressed by this stacking are correspondingly complex. The sequences are highly descriptive, naming parts in terms of their function and relation to other parts and also describing the status of parts and other objects in the sublanguage.

2.1.   Possessive Modifiers.   The following chart specifies the available semantic patterns for possessive noun-host relationships.

Organizations:	ORG	ORG	ships force; originators TAD; ships technician.
	ORG	PROP	ships diesel exhaust.

This sublanguage characteristically permits only ORGs, such as ship and originator, to appear in possessive constructions. No other semantic category appears as a possessive noun. In addition, these possessive organizations are restricted to modifying personnel (here classified also as ORG). There was, however, one instance of an organization's modifying a property (ships diesel exhaust), which we have included in the semantic patterns for possessive constructions. The possessive construction does not appear elsewhere in the texts. Since all action described in the CASREP occurs on ship, it is not necessary to specify this relationship in the messages. Since these messages are instances of compact text, much information is shared between originator and the reader of the message and, therefore, is not expressed explicitly. ORG is a member of a distinguished set of classes that are often omitted from text but are implicitly understood.

2.2 Noun Modifiers. A comparison of two sublanguage grammars, the equipment failure messages discussed here and a set of patient medical histories, disclosed that the equipment failure messages had significantly more noun modifier constructions than the patient histories (Grishman et al., 1984; Marsh, 1984). The frequency of noun compounds was 2½ to 4 times higher in the equipment failure messages as in the medical histories.

The sequences of nouns represent complex semantic patterns. One set of patterns specifies the names of pieces of equipment, the second set of semantic patterns describe other types of relationships. The semantic patterns for part names are presented first.

Part-name on part:	PART PART	circuit diode; elastomer strip; antenna installation; demultiplexer cabinet; antenna coupler; system keyline; baseplate insulator welds.
Part names:	ID REPAIR FUNC/SIGNAL PART	CU-2007 antenna coupler; replacement antenna; deflection AMP; UYA-4 display system; HF XMIT antenna; primmary HF receive antennas.

Names for pieces of equipment are often stacked in this sublanguage. In the foregoing examples, the relationships between the part names indicate different levels of components. Assembly/component relationships are expressed. A diode is a component of a circuit; a coupler is a component of an antenna. Similarly, system/assembly levels are related in the example *system keyline.* As was mentioned previously, pieces of equipment are assigned an Equipment Identification Code (EIC) that uniquely specifies its component level. The levels (system, subsystem, and component) are important distinctions for our applications programs. Determining the level of a piece of equipment involves a large amount of world knowledge, but the relationships are indicated, however minimally, in the semantic patterning of the sublanguage classes.

Other sets of semantic relationships are also exhibited in part names, and there is a strict ordering of the nouns in part names. For example, identification numbers such as CU-2007 and UYA-4 are always first. The binding among the elements in these noun sequences gets stronger as they get closer to the host noun; UYA-4 is an identification number for the display system and not just for the display.

We have separated the part patterns from the others because they are names, and operate as such in the texts. The relationships expressed by the part name patterns are important for the proper bracketing of constitutents but do not play an important informational role except to identify a part uniquely. They act as a unit in the text. The semantic category PART represents the set of part name semantic patterns that we discuss.

The semantic patterns for the other noun sequences are presented here. The name on the left represents an event corresponding to the semantic pattern that follows. The modifier is given first; the host, second.

Repair event:	PART	REPAIR	multi-pin connector instl/ repair; tube alignment.
Assistance:	ORG MSG	ASSIST	MOTU 12 assistance; msg technical assistance
Task function:	PURP	TASK	helicopter operations; exercise CPX/DEFEX; rooftop trainer ops.
Func/Signal Description:	SIGNAL	PORT/FUNC	frequency output; VLF broadcast.
Place of signal origin:	PART	SIGNAL	driver current; PA current.

These noun sequence semantic patterns are similar to those of the SVO patterns. Here, instead of a verb operator, the operator is a noun. In the case of the repair, assistance, and function patterns, the host noun is frequently a nominalization. Nominalizations are very frequent in these texts. The noun to the right of the nominalization is sometimes the subject of the nominalization (e.g. in MOTU 12 assistance) and sometimes the object (e.g. in multi-pin connector instl/repair). The semantic relationships expressed are like those expressed in the SVO patterns. I return to a discussion of nominalizations in section 2.5 of this Appendix.

2.3. Adjective-Noun patterns. The semantic patterns expressed by adjective-noun constructions in the equipment failure sublanguage follow. Adjective-noun constructions are quite frequent, although not as frequent as noun-noun constructions. Illustrated are the function of the modifier-host construction, the semantic categories involved (in modifier-host order), and examples of the semantic pattern. Verbal right modifiers, such as *damaged* and *malfunctioning,* are taken to be similar to adjectives in this sublanguage because they express the same types of relationships as other adjectives. They are not taken as reduced passive clauses.

Part descriptions:	TIME	PART	original antenna.
	STATUS	PART	failed relay; broken diode; malfunctioning circuit card.
	LOC	PART	outside antenna; inner oven.
	FUNC	PART	remote KY-8; local key; interconnecting cable.
Property descriptions:	STATUS	PROP	poor sensitivity; proper sync.
	AMT	PROP/SIGNAL	excessive VSWR; low powerout.
Status descriptions:	TIME	STATUS	intermittent short
	AMT	STATUS	excessive wear; large current surge.
CONN descriptions:	AMT	CONN	minimal impact
	STATUS	CONN	negative results
Administration descriptions:	STATUS	STASK	normal lowering
Assist:	ORG	ASSIST	technical assistance
	ADMIN	ASSIST	expediting assistance

Some part descriptions, such as FUNC-PART, appear in noun-noun and SVO patterns also; other patterns occur only in adjective-noun combinations. These include locations of or on equipment (*inner oven, outside antenna*), and status of parts (*failed relay*), part properties (*proper sync*), and ship tasks (*normal lowering*).

2.4. Verb modifiers of nouns. The equipment failure sublanguage contains several instances of unmarked verb modifiers of nouns. These are not like the adjectival verbal modifiers because they are not attributive. This type of construction is found in standard English in noun compounds such as *turntable*.

Part:	FUNC	PART	transmit antenna; receive antenna.
Process:	FUNC	PROCESS	operate modes.
Property:	FUNC	PROP	receive sensitivity.
Status:	FUNC	STATUS	read/write error.

Verb modifiers have a very limited semantic usage in the equipment failure sublanguage. While the hosts fall into several semantic classes, verb modifiers are only members of the FUNCTION semantic category.

2.5. Prepositional Modifiers of Nouns. Prepositional modifiers of nouns are numerous in this sublanguage. In fact, the prepostional modifiers are almost twice as numerous in this sublanguage as in the medical (Grishman et al., 1984; Marsh, 1984). Many of these modifiers are arguments of nominalizations. The relationships among the arguments of the nominalized verb are similar to those in the SVO patterns. Nominalizations come from the ASSIST (assistance from MOTU 12 Mayport), REPAIR (installation of CR2), PROCURE (purchase from Miltrope), and STATUS (loss of antenna) classes of verbs.

The true prepositional modifier phrases (attributive ones) express very restricted semantic relations between the host and the object of the preposition. These are: time, geographic location (place), location on ship or equipment, and causal and partitive relations. Examples of these prepositional modifiers follow.

Time:	PROCURE/STASK	DATE	receipt NLT (not later than) 7 OCT 82; CPX/DEFEX 3-82.
Place:	STASK	PLACE	transit from Staten Island, NY to Little Creek; MOTU 12 Mayport.
	ORG	PLACE	
Location:	PART/LOC	PART	center of door; pin R in connector; strip on door.
Cause:	STATUS	ENEVENT	large current surge for lightning strike.
	STASK	STASK	lowering of antenna for logrep ops.
Partitive:	0	PART	2 of 3 antennas.

In these texts, prepositions are often omitted in place (*RSG Mayport*) and time phrases (*CPX/DEFEX 3-82*). The semantic categories of the nouns in these prepositionless phrases also appear in related prepositional phrases. By identifying the semantic classes of the noun in the object of the prepositionless phrase and that of its host, it is possible to automatically recognize these phrases in the text.

REFERENCES

Bobrow, D. G., & Winograd, T. (1977). An overview of KRL, a knowledge representation language. *Cognitive Science, 1,* 3–46.

Charrow, V., Crandall, J. A., & Charrow, R. (1982). Characteristics and functions of legal language. In R. Kittredge & J. Lehrberger (Eds.), *Sublanguage: Studies of language in restricted semantic domains* (pp. 175–190). New York: de Gruyter.

Grishman, R., Nhan, N. T., Marsh, E., & Hirschman, L. (1984, July). Automated determination of sublanguage syntactic using. *COLING-84 Abstracts: Proceedings of the Tenth International Conference on Computational Linguistics* (pp. 89–94), Stanford, CA.

Harris, Z. S. (1968). *Mathematical structures of language.* New York: Wiley (Interscience).

IEEE guide to the use of ATLAS. (1980). New York: Institute of Electrical and Electronics Engineers.

IEEE standard ATLAS test language. (1981). New York: Institute of Electrical and Electronics Engineers.

Hirschman, L., & Sager, N. (1982). Automatic information formatting of a medical sublanguage. In R. Kittredge & J. Lehrberger (Eds.), *Sublanguage: Studies of language in restricted semantic domains.* Berlin: de Gruyter.

Kittredge, R. (1982). Variation and homegeneity of sublanguages. In R. Kittredge & J. Lehrberger (Eds.), *Sublanguage: Studies of language in restricted semantic domains.* Berlin: de Gruyter.

Kittredge, R., & Lehrberger, J. (Eds.).(1982). *Sublanguage: Studies of language in restricted semantic domains.* New York & Berlin: de Gruyter.

Lehrberger, J. (1982). Automatic translation and the concept of sublanguage. In R. Kittredge & J. Lehrberger (Eds.), *Sublanguage: Studies of language in restricted semantic domains.* (pp. 81–106). Berlin: de Gruyter.

Marsh, E. (1983). Utilizing domain-specific information for processing compact text. *Proceedings of Conference on Applied Natural Language Processing* (pp. 99–103). Association for Computational Linguistics.

Marsh, E. (1984). A computational analysis of complex noun phrases in Navy Messages. *COLING-84 Abstracts: Proceedings of the Tenth International Conference on Computational Linguistics,* Stanford, CA.

Minsky, M. (1975). A framework for representing knowledge. In P. Winston (Ed.), *The psychology of computer vision* (pp. 211–277). New York: McGraw-Hill.

Sager, N. (1972). Syntactic formatting of scientific information. *Proceedings of the 1972 Fall Joint Computer Conference, AFIPS Computer Conference* (pp. 791–800). Montvale, NJ: AFIPS Press.

Sager, N. (1975). Computerized discovery of semantic word classes in scientific fields. *Directions in artificial intelligence: Natural language processing.* Courant Computer Science Report. No. 7 (pp. 27–48) New York University, Courant Institute of Mathematical Sciences.

Sager, N. (1978). Natural language information formatting: The automatic conversion of texts to a structured data base. In M. C. Yovits & M. Rubinoff (Eds.), *Advances in computers* (pp. 89–162). New York: Academic Press.

Sager, N. (1981). *Natural language information processing: A computer grammar of English and its applications.* Reading, MA: Addison-Wesley.

Schank, R., & Abelson, R. (1977). *Scripts, plans, goals and understanding.* Hillsdale, NJ: Lawrence Erlbaum Associates.

Stefik, N. (1980). *Planning with constraints.* (Rep. No. 784). Stanford University, Computer Science Department.

8
A Sublanguage for Reporting and Analysis of Space Events

Christine A. Montgomery
Bonnie C. Glover
Logicon, Inc.
Woodland Hills, California

ABSTRACT

This chapter describes a sublanguage used by space analysts for reporting and evaluation of space events — past, present, and future. The texts under investigation are observations, analyses, and predictions of space events in the form of temporally sequenced messages. The significant features of the space sublanguage are attributable to its dual function as a vehicle for conveying both factual reports about space events and evaluative commentary about the events. These functions are reflected in the two basic levels of discourse represented in the messages: an event reporting level and a meta level of commentary on the events. The lexical items and semantic structure for the two levels are quite distinct. The syntactic structure is also generally dissimilar, although there are some constructions that occur on both levels. Given these facts, does the space event language constitute a single sublanguage or two? This chapter examines the evidence on both sides of the issue and evaluates the current definition of a sublanguage in light of these data.

INTRODUCTION

Background

The space event reporting sublanguage functions as a reporting and evaluative vehicle for space event analysts, whose mission is to continuously assess the current situation in space and predict future space events. The sublanguage texts are space event observations, analyses, and predictions recorded as sequences of messages. These messages have been investigated in connection with the experimental development of an automated system for analyzing message text and synthesizing data elements to update a space events data base (Burge, Dwiggins, Glover, Kuhns, & Montgomery, 1982, 1983; Dwiggins & Silva, 1981; Kuhns, 1974; Kuhns & Montgomery, 1973; Silva, Dwiggins, & Kuhns, 1979; Silva & Montgomery, 1979). Most recently, the experimental system has been serving as a message understanding front end to a knowledge-based system for space situation assessment (Martins, Montgomery, Ruberti, & Burge, 1985; Montgomery & Ruspini, 1981).

A significant aspect of this space event reporting and commentary vehicle is the theoretical issues it raises concerning the definition of a sublanguage. As noted in Kittredge and Lehrberger (1982, in particular the chapters authored by the editors), the definition of a sublanguage is still in an evolutionary state. It appears that the space event sublanguage can play a role in increasing the precision of the sublanguage definition.

The interesting features of the space sublanguage derive from its dual function as a medium for communicating both factual reports about space events and analytical comments about the events. There are thus two basic[1] levels of discourse: an event reporting level and a meta level of commentary on the events. The lexicon and semantic structure for the two levels are quite distinct, and—although there is some overlap—the syntactic structures also tend to differ.

The meta level of commentary and evaluation applies to other semantic domains in the message traffic, as well as to some types of news articles and other texts combining events and analytical commentary. The latter class apparently includes Kittredge's weather synopses (Kittredge & Lehrberger, 1982), which he describes as having ". . . two distinct levels of text. The first is a sequence of observations and predictions about physical phenomena which constitute the essence of the synopsis . . . . The second level of text is found in the predicates which describe the act of observation itself or relate the observer to the phenomena . . . " (p. 117).

The question arises whether we are dealing with one sublanguage having two levels of discourse or with separate sublanguages. The following discussion is presented in the hope of illuminating this complex issue.

Summary

In the following sections, we describe the sublanguage structure and show how that structure reflects the sublanguage functions. We then examine functional variation within the sublanguage structure primarily between the

---

[1]As discussed later, there exist several levels of event reporting, any of which can have evaluative commentary.

reporting and analysis functions and the extent to which it violates sublanguage coherence – in other words, what determines sublanguage boundaries and whether such variation might better be captured as one sublanguage embedded in another. Finally, we illustrate how the information contained in the messages can be represented in terms of knowledge structures for automated computation, with particular attention to the more abstract predictive and evaluative information.

CORPUS

From a corpus of 25,000 words, a representative sample of 5000 words of message text comprising 44 messages has undergone detailed analysis. In addition, the larger corpus, comprising approximately 225 messages, has been partially analyzed for feature validation and discovery of additional significant features.

Each message consists of a title sentence followed by the body of the message, which ranges in length from a single sentence to three or four paragraphs. The messages are of different types corresponding to the stage in the event sequence that is being reported or analyzed. In addition, initial messages generally reflect uncertainty about the parameters of a given event. However, as time elapses more information becomes available, leading up to the detailed reports and analyses contained in later messages.

SEMANTIC DOMAIN

The semantic domain of space activities has been translated, for the purposes of this research, into a basic scenario involving two simulated nations, the Delta Confederation of the Atlantic States and the Epsilon Republic. Both nations have space programs, and each is interested in monitoring the technological progress of the other using various satellite and sensor resources. The corpus of messages contains reports of space launches and orbital activities of the Delta Confederation, which are being monitored and evaluated by the Epsilon Republic. The text of messages used in the scenario has the structure and format of the actual messages reporting on space activities, and, although the lexicon is substantially different, the general lexical categories have been preserved.

The messages report the various events in the life cycle of a space object or satellite. Although geosynchronous satellites do not orbit and additional events can occur with certain types of satellites (e.g., *dock*), the most common life cycle of a satellite consists of the major events of **launch, orbit, deorbit, impact,** and **recovery.** The life cycle of each satellite is characterized by a single launch event, as many orbit events as there are changes in orbit, and, in general, one deorbit, one impact, and one recovery event. (With the exception of a few messages from a demonstration scenario for the knowledge-based situation assessment system referred to above, no messages dealing with prelaunch events have been investigated to date.)

The semantic domain of the discourse level of evaluative commentary includes the foregoing factual event information, but, in addition, incorporates other features described in detail later. In general, these features involve evaluative commentary deriving from the space analyst's mission of identifying space objects and determining which space events are impending or in process, as well as the analyst's knowledge about the spacee event reporting system.

GENERAL FEATURES

Spatiotemporal Features

As previously described, the primary function of the space event reporting sublanguage is the identification of man-made objects detected in space and recording of the facts regarding their life cycle, particularly their location at a given time and their activities in space. The relation of a space object to a particular location at a particular point in time constitutes a *worldpoint* event. The set of *worldpoint* events described in the message traffic concerning a particular satellite comprises the *worldline* of that satellite (see Kuhns, 1974, for explication). In the context of the scenario described in the preceding section, the Epsilon Republic is attempting to monitor the status of the Deltas' space development program by reconstructing the *worldlines* of the Deltas' satellites through observations of *worldpoint* events staged by the Deltas.

Phrases containing temporal and locational information thus figure prominently in the message text, as seen in the following example:

(1) AN UNIDENTIFIED SATELLITE WAS LAUNCHED FROM THE HARRISBURG MISSILE AND SPACE COMPLEX (HMSC) AT 1831Z ON 22 AUGUST 2009.

Normally the time phrases are found at the beginning or end of the sentence, whereas the location phrases are more tightly embedded into the verb phrase. Time includes the "Z" or Zulu (i.e., Greenwich Mean Time) time and the date (day, month, and year); location may be a launchsite or impact location on the earth or an orbital location in space. Regarding the satellite in (1):

(2) THE BRO3 LAUNCH SYSTEM WAS USED TO PLACE THE SATELLITE INTO A 45-DEGREE ORBIT.

In addition to degree of inclination in (2), other orbital parameters measured in various units of distance and time define the location of an object in space.

Location and time as part of satellite identification are carried forward in subsequent messages reporting on further events in the satellite's life cycle, as in the following sentence, which is a later reference to the satellite in (1) and (2):

(3) SPACOID 4001, THE UNIDENTIFIED SATELLITE LAUNCHED FROM THE HARRISBURG MISSILE AND SPACE COMPLEX AT 1831Z ON 22 AUGUST 2009 HAS BEEN CONFIRMED IN ORBIT.

Identification of a satellite by place and time of launch is particularly important when a satellite is otherwise unidentified, as in the previous examples, inasmuch as it provides a description that can be linked with, or found not to be linked with, a later positive identification of a given space object, such as the following description of another satellite:

(4) TERREX 577, THE LOW DENSITY CROP ENHANCEMENT AGRICULTURAL SATELLITE LAUNCHED FROM THE HMSC ON 2 JANUARY, WAS DE-ORBITED ON REVOLUTION 498.

The spatiotemporal descriptions facilitate linking different referents for the same space object as well as providing a means for time sequencing of events within a given satellite *worldline* and between the *worldlines* of different satellites (a discussion of reference in the space event sublanguage is presented in a subsequent section). Except for a few abbreviations and acronyms, such as *lo-den* for low density, *agsat* for agricultural satellite, and *esv* for earth satellite vehicle, this sublanguage fully specifies objects, times, and locations to the point of redundancy, which has the effect of ensuring continuity in a discourse that is fragmented across messages.

Noun Phrases

The importance of space object identification and specification in the space event reports is reflected syntactically in the frequency of stacked noun phrases containing long strings of adjective, noun, noun-noun, and adjective-noun combinations such as:

(5) FIFTH GENERATION HIGH DENSITY CROP ENHANCEMENT AGRICULTURAL SATELLITE

Order variations are usually indicated by punctuation, evidenced in a comparison of the position of *fifth generation* in (5) with that of *first generation* in (6), marked by a slash to indicate its displacement:

(6) TERREX 492, A LOW DENSITY CROP ENHANCEMENT/FIRST GENERATION CORN AGRICULTURAL SATELLITE (BRO2X5)

Evaluative commentary can also be found in the NP, usually set off by commas:

(7) SPAC 4542, A CROP ENHANCEMENT AGRICULTURAL, POSSIBLE SOLAR RESOURCES, SATELLITE. . .

The stacked noun phrases, which are typical of many sublanguages dealing with technical, highly specified objects, describe the main focus of space event reporting, the space objects. The next section discusses the syntax of sentences containing these noun phrases.

Passivization in Space Object Sentences

In the reporting level of the sublanguage, the primary focus is on space objects rather than on the agents that control them (i.e., the Deltas). The underlying cause of this phenomenon appears to be that Delta control is so well known as to make explicit statement of it unnecessary. The real news concerns space objects and events. This focus is reflected in the frequent occurrence of agentless passive constructions such as (8):

(8) TERREX 492 WAS DEORBITED INTO THE DELTA CONFEDERATION EARLY ON REVOLUTION 85.

Sentences that have the agent as subject are rare in this sublanguage, although they do occur:

(9) AT APPROXIMATELY 1822 Z ON 10 AUGUST 2010, THE DELTAS DEORBITED TERREX 618, THE SOLAR RESOURCES CROP ENHANCEMENT SATELLITE LAUNCHED FROM HARRISBURG ON FEBRUARY 24.

The agents of the space activity are the Deltas, who **launch, orbit,** and **deorbit** satellites. The Epsilons **detect, identify,** and **confirm** the actions of the Deltas, based on Epsilon observations and Delta announcements. Table 8.1 shows the large number of passive constructions for the verbs in which the space object noun phrase has been promoted to subject, in contrast to the small number of active constructions conveying the same information. This is also shown for the verbs describing the naming of satellites by the Deltas and the number assignment by the Epsilons, for which verbs the space object name or number is frequently promoted to subject and the agent is not mentioned.

In addition to the functions described in Table 8.1, the Deltas and Epsilons engage in other specialized activities:

TABLE 8.1
Passivization with Primary Activity Verbs

Agent	Agentless Passive	Passive w/ By-phrase	Active
Deltas			
launch, orbit, deorbit	77	4	4
designate	2	0	0
Epsilons			
identify, detect, confirm	22	0	1
assign, give	14	1	0
Total	115	5	5

- the Deltas:
  announce space object events in the press,
  construct and maintain satellite programs, and perform various other
  activites in accordance with their space program development function.

- the Epsilons, in line with their monitoring function,
  depict space events in the message traffic,
  expect and assess space events.

Unlike the basic or **primitive** events of **launch, orbit**, and **deorbit** of satellites, the *announcement* of space events in the Delta press and the *depiction* of them in the Epsilon messages are *reporting events*, or *meta events*, as described later. Similarly, the *expectations* of the Epsilons regarding the Deltas *construction* and *maintenance* of space programs are not themselves primitive events, but rather speculations attributing the primitive events, **construct** and **maintain**, to the Deltas in certan instances. (They are essentially *meta comments* associated with the reporting meta events, as discussed in a subsequent section.)

Passivization, notable for these verbs (see Table 8.2), is less frequent than for the primary activity verbs shown in Table 8.1, except for the **expect/assess** class of verbs. This exception derives from the same source as was mentioned earlier for the agentless **launch, orbit**, and **deorbit** verbs describing Delta activities. The authors of the assessment activities are Epsilons; it is well known that assessment is their mission, so this is not news.

The data summarized in Tables 8.1 and 8.2 show that agentless passive constructions are favored in this sublanguage for reporting the major space events in which the agent is clearly the Delta Confederation, whereas the Delta Confederation retains its active role in the assessment context. On the other hand, in the assessment context, it is the Epsilons who are omitted as agents, since assessment is their mission. The *we* versus *they* aspects of the

TABLE 8.2
Passivization with Other Verbs

Agent	Agentless Passive	Passive w/ By-phrase	Active
Deltas			
announce	10	0	20
construct	4	1	14
Epsilons			
depict	0	0	4
expect	18	0	0
Total	32	1	38

underlying Delta/Epsilon scenario are clearly portrayed in the language of the messages. Passive voice can thus be viewed as a syntactic feature correlating with the sublanguage functions of reporting and analysis.

In a few instances the reporting event verb is intransitive. The primary example of this is *deorbit*, shown in the following:

(10) SKYLAB-34 LAUNCHED FROM THE VICKSBURG MISSILE TEST RANGE 06 SEPTEMBER 1134Z, DEORBITED ON THE EARLY PORTION OF REVOLUTION 235.

(11) SKYLAB-33 WITH THE SKYLAB-32 CREW IS EXPECTED TO DEORBIT WITHIN THE NEXT WEEK.

Although the verb *deorbit* is usually transitive, sentences like (10) and (11) are not uncommon. In a sense, a satellite can deorbit itself: it can fail or drift out of orbit. The typical message describing a *deorbit* event, however, refers to an intentional deorbit that is under automated or human control either from an on-board system or a remote agent. Also, satellites *orbit* by some agent (presumably a booster system); in addition, they *perform orbital maneuvers* and *have a maneuver capability*. Although these must be conrolled by some agent, the intransitive form is frequently used, implying the attribution of the action to the satellite.

An interesting and possibly related case which occurs in the corpus is that of the verb *launch*, which is also occasionally found to be intransitive:

(12) AT 1705Z, NYT – THE DELTA NEWS AGENCY – ANNOUNCED THE LAUNCH OF A HIGHFLYER-2 WHICH LAUNCHED FROM THE HARRISBURG MISSILE AND SPACE CENTER AT 1831 ON 22 AUGUST 2009.

In the text format of a **launch** rather than an **announce** type of message, the rather common feature of relative deletion creates a "garden path" situation, represented by (12a):

(12a) A HIGHFLYER-2 LAUNCHED FROM THE HARRISBURG MISSILE AND
SPACE CENTER AT 1831 ON 22 AUGUST 2009 FAILED TO ACHIEVE ORBIT

In some instances, the possible transitivity of *launch* would contribute to a
more complex ambiguity, as in the following sentence:

(13) AT 1657Z, NYT – THE DELTA NEWS AGENCY – ANNOUNCED THE LAUNCH
OF TERREX 558 AND TERREX 559, THE MAN RELATED SPACECRAFT
LAUNCHED FROM THE BOGOTA MISSILE TEST RANGE AT 0800Z ON 17
NOVEMBER.

Here the conjunction *and* could either link two satellite names (TERREX 558
and TERREX 559), one or both of which are the object of *launch*, or – if the
comma following TERREX 559 were missing (valid use of punctuation is not
necessarily a constant feature of these messages) – link two sentences, the
second of which has *Terrex 559* as the subject of an intransitive verb *launch*.
In this case, the construction would be ambiguous on the sentence level, but
not on the message level, since the remaining text of the message clarifies the
meaning:

(13a) THE ANNOUNCEMENT CONTAINED ROUTINE WORDING AND STATED
THE ESV'S WERE PLACED IN ORBIT BY A SINGLE CARRIER ROCKET. OR-
BITAL PARAMETERS CONTAINED IN THE ANNOUNCEMENT ARE . . .

DISCOURSE FEATURES

Discourse Structure: Message Types and Variations

The structure of the sublanguage reflects both its reporting and its analysis
functions. The reports are characterized by the importance of elements of
space object identification and by the prominent place accorded space object
noun phrases, particularly as subjects of passive verbs. The analytical function is reflected in the use of a greater variety of tenses, including present and
future, and the more frequent occurrence of active voice, evaluative expressions, and certain complex syntactic structures, such as comparatives.

The event reporting message sequence, described in Glover and Montgomery (1984) and shown in Fig. 8.1, for a given space object consists of a
series of **report messages** based on Epsilon observations of the major life cycle events of **launch, orbit,** and **deorbit.** These report messages are augmented by messages reporting Delta launch announcements from which key
elements of information related to space object identification may be
derived.

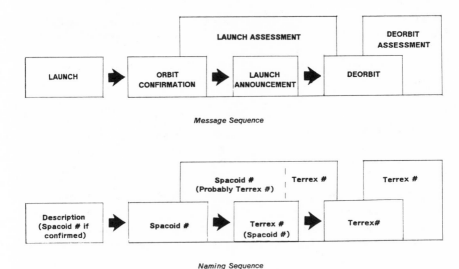

FIG. 8.1   Space object discourse sequence.

Supplementing the report messages are *assessment messages,* which contain report summaries followed by analysis and commentary concerning the mission of the space object, its role in the Delta space program and so on. The upper diagram in Fig. 8.1 illustrates the reporting message sequence and the assessment messages, which may focus on either the launch or the deorbit of the satellite. The launch assessment message may occur before or after the launch announcement message, whereas the deorbit assessment message comes in after the deorbit report. The lower diagram in Fig. 8.1 shows the evolution of satellite naming over the message sequence. This problem of satellite reference is further described in a later section.

Our approach to analysis of the discourse on the message level (sentence level features were discussed earlier) is based on the concept of **text grammar** originally defined in Propp (1958/1929), and later amplified by van Dijk (1972, 1980), and others. A text grammar is essentially a set of rules for generating or analyzing text conforming to the grammar. The knowledge bases for our experimental natural language understanding system thus include both a syntactic grammar and a text grammar, which generates the set of message **prototypes,** or characteristic discourse structures, of the various space event message types. These are described in detail in Glover and Montgomery (1984). Here we simply sketch the discourse boundaries of the sublanguage discourse levels under discussion.

A sample launch report message follows:

(14) UNIDENTIFIED SATELLITE LAUNCHED FROM HARRISBURG

AN UNIDENTIFIED SATELLITE WAS LAUNCHED FROM THE HARRIS-
BURG MISSILE AND SPACE COMPLEX (HMSC) AT 1831Z ON 22 AUGUST
2009. THE BRO3 LAUNCH SYSTEM WAS USED TO PLACE THE SATELLITE
INTO A 45 DEGREE ORBIT. WSJ OBJECT NUMBER 5009 HAS BEEN AS-
SIGNED TO THE PAYLOAD.

The report and assessment messages consist of a title sentence followed by the
body of the message. Message titles are distinguished syntactically from the
sentences in the message body by their lack of definite and indefinite articles,
prepositions in date expressions, and tense inflection. The verbs of the title
sentences appear as participles, nominalizations, or in the "tenseless" present
tense:

(15) DEORBIT OF TERREX 495, 24 OCTOBER 2009

(16) SKYLAB-34 DEORBITS 15 SEPTEMBER 2009

(17) SPACOID 4025 CONFIRMED IN ORBIT

The body of a report message consists of a description of the space object and
one or more events in which it was involved, including the significant facts
that identify the space object and its mission. Report messages may also contain a sentence describing the mission or capabilities of the spacecraft:

(18) THE MISSION OF THIS SATELLITE HAS NOT YET BEEN DETERMINED.

(19) A MANEUVER CAPABILITY IS ALSO ASSESSED FOR THIS TYPE
SPACECRAFT.

Additional examples of launch messages (see also 14) are the following:

(20) SKYLAB SPACECRAFT LAUNCHED FROM VICKSBURG, 06 SEPTEMBER
2009.

AT APPROXIMATELY 1134Z, A SKYLAB SPACECRAFT CARRYING TWO
ASTRONAUTS WAS LAUNCHED FROM THE VICKSBURG MISSILE TEST
RANGE BY THE BRO2 SPACE LAUNCH SYSTEM. IT WAS INJECTED INTO
AN ORBIT INCLINED 55 DEGREES TO THE EQUATOR. IF CONFIRMED IN
ORBIT, SPACOID NUMBER 502 WILL BE ASSIGNED. WSJ OBJECT NUMBER
5007 HAS BEEN GIVEN TO THE PAYLOAD.

(21) ESV LAUNCHED FROM BOGOTA, 17 BOGOTA, 17 NOVEMBER 2009.

AT APPROXIMATELY 1509Z, A NEW ESV WAS LAUNCHED FROM THE
BOGOTA MISSILE TEST RANGE BY THE BR-08 SPACE LAUNCH SYSTEM. IT

WAS INJECTED INTO AN ORBIT INCLINED 35 DEGREES TO THE EQUATOR. THIS SATELLITE IS A FIRST GENERATION VARIABLE DENSITY CROP EN-HANCEMENT SPACECRAFT.

IF CONFIRMED IN ORBIT, SPACOID NUMBER 4025 WILL BE ASSIGNED. WSJ OBJECT NUMBER 5171 HAS BEEN GIVEN TO THE PAYLOAD.

Figure 8.2 shows the prototypical launch message and variations specified by the text grammar.

T: SATELLITE TYPE launched from LAUNCHSITE, DATE.

1: A SATELLITE TYPE was launched from LAUNCHSITE at TIME on DATE.

2: The LAUNCH SYSTEM was used to place the satellite into ORBIT LOCATION.

3: [Comment].

4: If confirmed in orbit, SPACOID NUMBER will be assigned.

5: WSJ OBJECT NUMBER has been given to the payload.

Variant forms of the Title sentence (T):

T: a) SATELLITE TYPE launched, (from LAUNCHSITE) (on) DATE.

b) SATELLITE TYPE launch, DATE.

c) Launch of SATELLITE TYPE, DATE.

Variant forms of Sentences 1 and 2:

1 a) A SATELLITE TYPE was launched from LAUNCHSITE at TIME on DATE.

b) The LAUNCH SYSTEM was used to place the satellite into ORBIT LOCATION.

2 a) At TIME, a SATELLITE TYPE was launched from LAUNCHSITE by the LAUNCH SYSTEM.

b) It was injected into ORBIT LOCATION.

FIG. 8.2   Prototype launch message.

Assessment messages contain a report summary followed by commentary about the current state of the Delta space program and the role of the spacecraft in it. Typical of these messages are statements like:

(22) A REPLACEMENT OF THE INITIAL HIGHFLYER SATELLITE IN THE AURORA NETWORK CAN BE EXPECTED WITHIN THE NEXT THREE WEEKS.

(23) THE DELTAS CURRENTLY HAVE TWO CROP ENHANCEMENT SATELLITEES IN ORBIT: TERREX 495 AND TERREX 492, A LOW DENSITY/FIRST GENERATION AGRICULTURAL SATELLITE (BRO2X5) EXPECTED TO BE DEORBITED ON 8 OCTOBER.

(24) HOW LONG THE DELTAS WILL MAINTAIN THREE DISTINCT AGSAT PROGRAMS IS PRESENTLY UNCERTAIN.

The function of assessment and the artifacts of that function — assessment messages and comments — are discussed in detail in a later section.

Reference

As discussed earlier, the discourse contained in the message set under investigation concerns space objects and the events comprising the life cycle, or *worldline*, of these space objects. Two forms of reference are therefore particularly important in this discourse: object reference, deriving from the focus on object identification, and temporal reference, from the event orientation.[2] Although spatial reference is also of obvious importance, it is effectively subordinated to object and temporal reference. What is important is the location of a particular space object at a given point in time, and by extension, all the relations — past, actual, and potential — among the *worldlines* of the set of space objects.

Although the messages are discrete, bounded entities, there are typically several messages that refer to the same object at different times, describing different events in the *worldline* of that object. Moreover, because later messages may reference a previous space object or event (e.g., examples 8 and 12) as well as an anticipated future space object or event (e.g., examples 25 and 26), the space message traffic in its entirety can be considered as essentially a single, unbounded discourse, which may contain references to any previous (and in fact, any future) space object or event.

(25) A REPLACEMENT OF THE INITIAL HIGHFLYER SATELLITE IN THE AURORA NETWORK CAN BE EXPECTED WITHIN THE NEXT THREE WEEKS.

(26) HIGHFLYER 22 WAS LAUNCHED INTO NEARLY THE SAME PLANE AS HIGHFLYER 18, AND IS EVIDENTLY ITS REPLACEMENT.

---

[2]The problem of reference in the space event discourse is discussed in detail in Burge, Dwiggins, Glover, Kuhns, and Montgomery (1982, 1983).

Any space object or event can therefore potentially be discussed in the context of any other space object or event, and the relations obtaining among all such objects and events should be completely specifiable within the network of explicit object and spatiotemporal indices derived from the discourse. Thus, the resolution of references within the space event discourse is a pervasive and complex problem.

Object references may be direct (i.e., the proper name of the space object, such as "Terrex 549") or indirect (the combination of spatiotemporal referents comprising a unique description of the object — "the crop enhancement satellite launched from Vicksburg on 2 January"). Temporal references may be explicit, as in the immediately preceding example, or implicit in the tense of the verb and its relation to the tenses of other verbs, and ultimately to explicit times given in the body or header of the message.

In addition to the simpler forms of anaphoric reference given in (25) and (26), which are restricted to the context of a single message, there are a variety of indirect references that typically involve the larger context of the message traffic, as noted earlier. Indirect references, of course, do not necessarily involve the larger context but are ambiguous with respect to the domain over which they function. For example, (27) illustrates a type of reference that may operate within a single message or within the context of the total message traffic (the ambiguous referent *additional*).

(27) AN ADDITIONAL JOINT SCIENTIFIC EXPLORATION WAS ANNOUNCED.

The set of messages presented in Fig. 8.3 illustrates a range of reference problems, where the initial message creates an indirect reference to a satellite launched from HMSC at 1831Z on 22 August 2009, the type and mission of which are "unidentified." In the second message, a unique inventory number (a form of direct reference) is assigned to "the unidentified satellite launched from" HMSC at 1831Z on 22 August 2009, although the mission is still "unidentified." The press announcement quoted in the third message provides the proper name that identifies the space object and is used to refer to the satellite in subsequent messages. Fig. 8.1 shows the full sequence of direct satellite references for each message type. At each point where the reference changes, an attempt is made by the Epsilons to anticipate the new number or name in a previous message and so ensure continuity over the discourse.

THE REPORTING FUNCTION:
PRIMITIVE EVENTS AND META EVENTS

As discussed in the preceding sections, there are two basic levels of discourse in the space sublanguage: one is used for the reporting of events and the second for analysis and evaluation of those events. However, as indicated

MSG. 02 - 102   (8/22/09 1903Z)

UNIDENTIFIED SATELLITE LAUNCHED FROM HARRISBURG, 22 AUGUST 2009

AN UNIDENTIFIED SATELLITE WAS LAUNCHED FROM THE HARRISBURG
MISSILE AND SPACE COMPLEX (HMSC) AT 1831Z ON 22 AUGUST 1983.
THE BR03 LAUNCH SYSTEM WAS USED TO PLACE THE SATELLITE INTO
A 45 DEGREE ORBIT. WSJ OBJECT NUMBER 5009 HAS BEEN ASSIGNED
TO THE PAYLOAD.

MSG. 02 - 101   (8/22/83 2225Z)

SPAC01D 4001 CONFIRMED IN ORBIT, 22 AUGUST 1983

SPACOID 4001, THE UNIDENTIFIED SATELLITE LAUNCHED FROM THE
HARRISBURG MISSILE AND SPACE COMPLEX AT 1831Z ON 22 AUGUST 1983
HAS BEEN CONFIRMED IN ORBIT. THE MISSION OF THIS SATELLITE
HAS NOT BEEN IDENTIFIED.

MSG 02 - 100   (8/23/83 1810Z)

NYT ANNOUNCES LAUNCH OF HIGHFLYER-2/67

AT 1705Z, NYT-THE DELTA NEWS AGENCY-ANNOUNCED THE LAUNCH OF
A HIGHFLYER-2 WHICH LAUNCHED FROM THE HARRISBURG MISSILE AND SPACE
CENTER AT 1831Z ON 22 AUGUST 1983.

ORBITAL PARAMETERS AS CONTAINED IN THE ANNOUNCEMENT ARE:

APOGEE	_____	KILOMETERS
PERIGEE	_____	KILOMETERS
INCLINATION	_____	DEGREES
PERIOD	_____ HOURS	_____ MINUTES

FIG. 8.3   Example message sequence.

earlier, the discourse structure is more complex than this, being characterized
by several levels of event reporting, each of which has an associated level of
analytical commentary. These event reporting levels are described in detail in
Montgomery (1983), and are summarized in the following discussion.

The complexity of the discourse structure with respect to the event reporting function is due to the total process of event monitoring and reporting,
which includes several stages and involves activities of both the Deltas and
the Epsilons. The process is triggered by a Delta launch activity—**the primitive event**—where the booster ignition emits energy that may be detected by
an Epsilon sensor—**an observational event**—and generates a representation
of that observation.[3]

Epsilon space analysts then interpret the representation of that observation in terms of their knowledge of the total space context and the available

[3]These classes of events are derived from an earlier study of events reported in message traffic
(Kuhns & Montgomery, 1973).

particulars of the given space event, producing a report based on the observational event and the primitive event. This event does not involve a primitive action or an observation of such an action but is merely a reporting event, or **meta event** reporting on these basic **nonmeta events.** This type of report is the most frequent in our message corpus and is most basic to the message traffic. It is thus characterized as a **zeroth order meta event.**

While these activities are being carried out by the Epsilons, the Deltas are also producing their own reports about the event, which may eventually lead to an announcement in the Delta press (a report of a report; hence a **1st order meta event).** The Epsilon analyst then uses that announcement, together with what is known about the given space event (and the history of space events) to produce another report which is labeled a **2nd order meta event.** An example of this type of report is the third message in Fig. 8.3. Finally, there may be changes or updates to any of these reports; such changes constitute **3rd order meta events.**

There are thus four orders of meta events comprising the processes of the reporting function reflected in the space event sublanguage. Although this specification of the reporting process may seem baroque, it provides a framework within which to approach (a) sorting out which parts of a given message are attributable to which step in the reporting and analysis process, and (b) assigning to the various levels of information some indication of credibility and significance. This is crucial to the function of an automated language understanding system, whether it serves as front end to a conventional data base or to a knowledge-based system.

Information that is qualified in terms of where it is derived in the reporting process and how it is assessed cannot be sent as unqualified factual data to a data base or other downstream system. Rather, the qualifications must be identified and explicitly attached to the message contents to which they apply. The following section discusses types of qualification deriving from the evaluative or analytical level of discourse (which may be associated with any of the reporting levels described above), after which the representation of basic material and qualifications for our experimental natural language understanding system is described.

THE ASSESSMENT FUNCTION:
META EVENTS AND META COMMENTS

As noted earlier, associated with any of the meta events comprising the various levels of the space event reporting process is yet another level of meta information that represents the analytical function of the space event sublanguage.

To summarize,

- the **reporting events** constitute a meta level with respect to the primitive events of **launch, orbit, deorbit,** etc; they are thus referred to as **meta events;**
- the **analytical** or **assessment language** constitutes a meta level with respect to the **reporting language** — the basic language of the reports produced by reporting events; the assessment language reflects a variety of types of analytical judgments which are represented in terms of **meta comments** on objects and events described in the reporting language.

To understand the assessment function, it is useful to revisit the Delta/ Epsilon scenario described earlier. Driving the entities and events of the scenario are the plans of the Deltas to develop and maintain space programs of various sorts, and the corresponding plans of the Epsilons to monitor these developments. Wilensky (1981) has described the significance of plans in natural language story understanding and has illustrated how they can be exploited in the understanding process. However, we are at a disadvantage here inasmuch as our messages are reports produced by the Epsilons, who are essentially *attempting to determine what the Deltas' plans are,* based on whatever evidence can be collected through observation and analysis of Delta space activities, recounted in the reports.

The entire focus of Epsilon activity, then, is to identify space objects and reconstruct their *worldlines,* comparing them with the *worldlines* of other objects in space and time and predicting events comprising the *worldlines* where possible. The function of the **reporting language** is to report the observation and identification of space objects and events, while the function of the **analytical** or **assessment language** is to evaluate, amplify, and confirm what has been observed and identified and to speculate about the Deltas' plans — past, present, and future.

To satisfy these analytical functions, the assessment language contains a variety of predicates that specify different aspects of the given functions. Some of the most important of these are the set of predicates used to evaluate the credibility of information about space objects or events described in the reporting language, for example **possible, probable, apparent, unlikely, uncertain.** These meta comments reflect the reporter's degree of belief in the information reported in the message. Examples of meta expressions with these predicates are (7), (24), (26), (28).

(28) SPACOID 404, THE PROBABLE PILLAGE-4, WHICH WAS LAUNCHED FROM THE VICKSBURG MTC AT 0701Z ON 8 FEBRUARY HAS BEEN CONFIRMED IN ORBIT.

In addition to evaluation of credibility, a frequent type of evaluation occurring in the assessment language is evaluation of a given space event, object, or *worldline* in terms of comparable past events, objects, or *worldlines,* or aggregates of these representing a state of the space world at a given point in time. Predicates expressing such comparisons include **new, first, unusual, routine.** Examples (13a) and (29) show these predicates, for a 2nd order meta event and a zeroth order meta event, respectively.

(29) **AT APPROXIMATELY 0800Z, A NEW ESV WAS LAUNCHED FROM THE BOGOTA MISSILE TEST RANGE BY THE BR09 SPACE LAUNCH SYSTEM.**

An important class of assessment predicates involves prediction of future events. These predicates are limited mainly to **expect** and **assess** (relative to a future event, as distinct from the evaluative use of **assess**). Examples in (19). (30) and (31) illustrate prediction using these predicates.

(30) **THIS SATELLITE IS EXPECTED TO BE RECOVERED ON 31 OCTOBER.**

(31) **MISSION DURATION IS ASSESSED AS 14 DAYS.**

Another type of assessment predicate involves confirmation of activities previously reported with a qualification as to credibility, or of predicted next events in the *worldline* of a given space object. The most frequent of these are orbit confirmations, exemplified in (3), (17), (20), (21), and (28). Example (32) illustrates lack of confirmation of a particular payload.

(32) **AT PRESENT THERE IS NO CONFIRMATION OF THE PRESENCE OF THE SECONDARY SCIENTIFIC PAYLOAD.**

There are a variety of predicates used for identification of objects and activities and for speculations about plans and intentions. These include **identify, determine, indicate, suggest.** Fig. 8.3 illustrates a variety of identification problems; (18), (33), and (34) exemplify speculations about plans and intentions.

(33) **THE LAUNCHING OF TERREX 549 BY THE DELTAS INDICATES THAT THEY ARE STILL DEDICATED TO THE THREE-SATELLITE, FIRST-GENERATION TVSAT PROGRAM.**

(34) **IT IS TOO EARLY AT THIS TIME TO DETERMINE THE INTENT OF THE FOUR SHIPS WHICH WERE LOCATED IN THE GALVESTON AREA FOR THIS AGSAT LAUNCH EVENT.**

REPRESENTATION OF DISCOURSE LEVEL FEATURES

Representation of Objects and Events in the Reporting Language

As discussed earlier, the natural language understanding system for generating data base elements from the text of space event messages has provided the motivation and the support for investigation of this sublanguage. In this system (the Data Base Generator-DBG), knowledge about objects and events is represented by semantic structures called *templates* (Kuhns, 1974; Kuhns & Montgomery, 1973). Although they antedate Minsky's definition of frames, templates are essentially frame-based knowledge structures containing a number of slots describing attributes appropriate to the given object or event.

Templates are property lists that form the constant or intensional part of the domain knowledge; as the message is analyzed, templates are filled in or instantiated with the variable or extensional elements contained in the messages. Figure 8.4 illustrates the instantiated templates that form the output for the message presented. Basic templates comprising the *worldline* of a given space object are presented in Fig. 8.5.

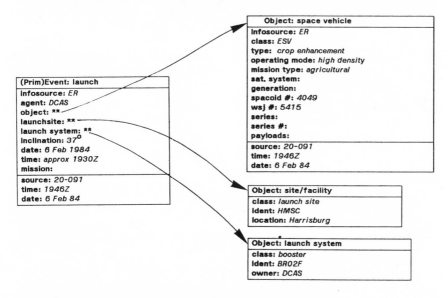

FIG. 8.4   Instantiated templates for message 20–091.

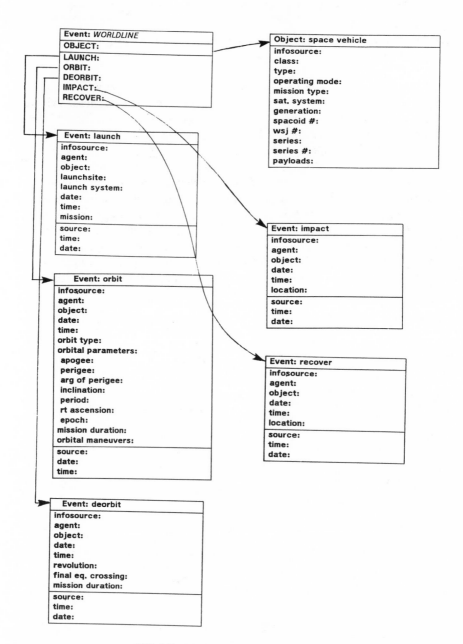

FIG. 8.5   Worldline of a space object.

TABLE 8.3
Orders of Meta Events

Meta event	Meta object	Definition
0	0	1st Epsilon report: observational event + primitive event
1	1	Delta Press announcement of primitive event
2	2	Epsilon report of announcement of primitive event
3	3	Epsilon changes to reports

Representation of Meta Objects and Events in the Reporting Language

As discussed earlier, the reporting language necessarily includes the concept of a reporting event as well as the object produced by that event. Both are meta events and meta objects with respect to the primitive events and objects they describe. The reporting process is complex, and the corresponding representation of reporting events and objects is inevitably complex. Recalling the orders of meta events for reporting, we see, in Table 8.3 the types of events and definitions.

Meta events (i.e., reporting events) and meta objects (reports) of this kind are represented by meta event and meta object templates. For example, Fig. 8.6 and 8.7 illustrate the several levels of reporting specified in Table 8.3.[4] Fig. 8.6 gives the interpretation of an *announce (meta-2)* type of report, exemplified by message 08–077. Each reporting event generates a meta-object (the report or message) at the given level. Thus the Epsilon meta-2 reporting event generates a meta-2 object which is a report of a meta-1 (Delta) announcement event that generates a meta-1 announcement object. This meta-1 object describes the launch (Event 1) and insertion into orbit (Event 2) of a space object designated Terrex 560. The remainder of the templates in the figure apply to the **analysis** rather than to the **reporting** level; these are described in the following section.

Figure 8.7 shows the effects of a **change** message. The change message first references the event report (Meta 0 level) produced for the launch of Terrex 540, which described not only the launch of Terrex 540 as Event 1 (which is apparently correct and will not be changed), but the launch of Terrex 529 as Event 2 in Paragraph 2. This part of the contents of the Meta 0 (basic) report will be changed to correct the **replacement** template. It had been previously thought that the replacement object (Terrex 529) was replacing the earlier satellite, Terrex 400, as opposed to Terrex 430, which now appears to be the case. Such changes are the result of the **analysis** process discussed later.

---

[4]The figures are intended as an illustration and explication of the relations involved in the levels of reporting and not as a representation of the internal form of the constituent templates in the computer.

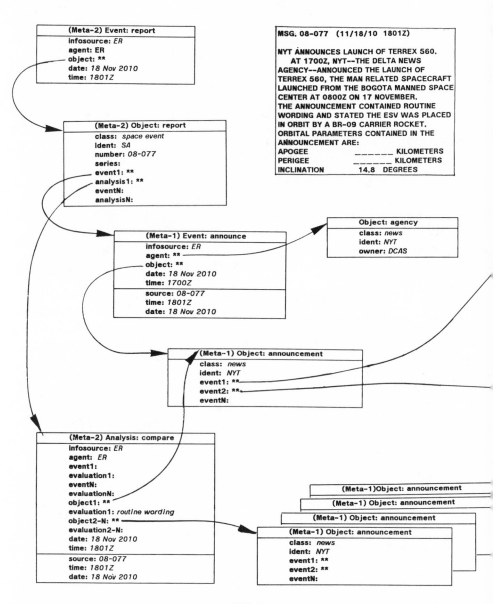

(Meta-2) Event: report
infosource: *ER*
agent: ER
object: **
date: *18 Nov 2010*
time: *1801Z*

MSG. 08-077 (11/18/10 1801Z)

NYT ÁNNOUNCES LAUNCH OF TERREX 560.
AT 1700Z, NYT--THE DELTA NEWS
AGENCY--ANNOUNCED THE LAUNCH OF
TERREX 560, THE MAN RELATED SPACECRAFT
LAUNCHED FROM THE BOGOTA MANNED SPACE
CENTER AT 0800Z ON 17 NOVEMBER.
THE ANNOUNCEMENT CONTAINED ROUTINE
WORDING AND STATED THE ESV WAS PLACED
IN ORBIT BY A BR-09 CARRIER ROCKET.
ORBITAL PARAMETERS CONTAINED IN THE
ANNOUNCEMENT ARE:
APOGEE _____ KILOMETERS
PERIGEE _____ KILOMETERS
INCLINATION 14.8 DEGREES

(Meta-2) Object: report
class: *space event*
ident: *SA*
number: *08-077*
series:
event1: **
analysis1: **
eventN:
analysisN:

Object: agency
class: *news*
ident: *NYT*
owner: *DCAS*

(Meta-1) Event: announce
infosource: *ER*
agent: **
object: **
date: *18 Nov 2010*
time: *1700Z*
source: *08-077*
time: *1801Z*
date: *18 Nov 2010*

(Meta-1) Object: announcement
class: *news*
ident: *NYT*
event1: **
event2: **
eventN:

(Meta-2) Analysis: compare
infosource: *ER*
agent: *ER*
event1:
evaluation1:
eventN:
evaluationN:
object1: **
evaluation1: *routine wording*
object2-N: **
evaluation2-N:
date: *18 Nov 2010*
time: *1801Z*
source: *08-077*
time: *1801Z*
date: *18 Nov 2010*

(Meta-1)Object: announcement

(Meta-1) Object: announcement

(Meta-1) Object: announcement

(Meta-1) Object: announcement
class: *news*
ident: *NYT*
event1: **
event2: **
eventN:

FIG. 8.6

150

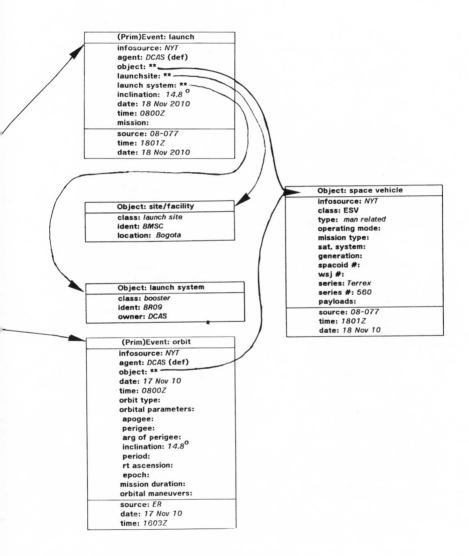

(Prim)Event: launch

infosource: *NYT*
agent: *DCAS* (def)
object: **
launchsite: **
launch system: **
inclination: *14.8 °*
date: *18 Nov 2010*
time: *0800Z*
mission:

source: *08-077*
time: *1801Z*
date: *18 Nov 2010*

Object: site/facility

class: *launch site*
ident: *BMSC*
location: *Bogota*

Object: launch system

class: *booster*
ident: *BR09*
owner: *DCAS*

(Prim)Event: orbit

infosource: *NYT*
agent: *DCAS* (def)
object: **
date: *17 Nov 10*
time: *0800Z*
orbit type:
orbital parameters:
 apogee:
 perigee:
 arg of perigee:
 inclination: *14.8°*
 period:
 rt ascension:
 epoch:
mission duration:
orbital maneuvers:

source: *ER*
date: *17 Nov 10*
time: *1603Z*

Object: space vehicle

infosource: *NYT*
class: ESV
type: *man related*
operating mode:
mission type:
sat. system:
generation:
spacoid #:
wsj #:
series: *Terrex*
series #: *560*
payloads:

source: *08-077*
time: *1801Z*
date: *18 Nov 10*

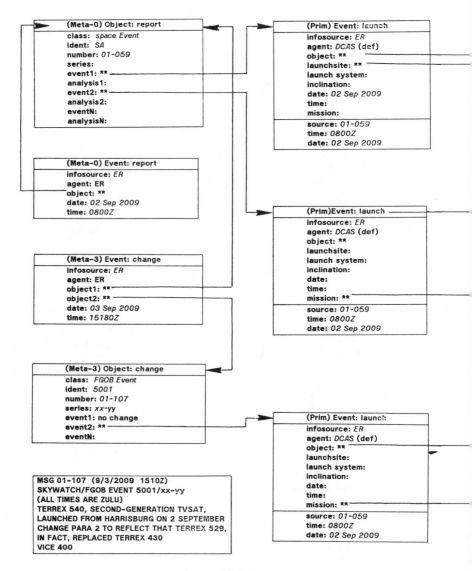

(Meta-0) Object: report

class: *space Event*
ident: *SA*
number: *01-059*
series:
event1: **
analysis1:
event2: **
analysis2:
eventN:
analysisN:

(Meta-0) Event: report

infosource: *ER*
agent: ER
object: **
date: *02 Sep 2009*
time: *0800Z*

(Meta-3) Event: change

Infosource: *ER*
agent: ER
object1: **
object2: **
date: *03 Sep 2009*
time: *15180Z*

(Meta-3) Object: change

class: *FGOB Event*
ident: *5001*
number: *01-107*
series: *xx-yy*
event1: no change
event2: **
eventN:

MSG 01-107 (9/3/2009 1510Z)
SKYWATCH/FGOB EVENT 5001/xx-yy
(ALL TIMES ARE ZULU)
TERREX 540, SECOND-GENERATION TVSAT,
LAUNCHED FROM HARRISBURG ON 2 SEPTEMBER
CHANGE PARA 2 TO REFLECT THAT TERREX 529,
IN FACT, REPLACED TERREX 430
VICE 400

(Prim) Event: launch

infosource: *ER*
agent: *DCAS* (def)
object: **
launchsite: **
launch system:
inclination:
date: *02 Sep 2009*
time:
mission:
source: *01-059*
time: *0800Z*
date: *02 Sep 2009*

(Prim)Event: launch

infosource: *ER*
agent: *DCAS* (def)
object: **
launchsite:
launch system:
inclination:
date:
time:
mission: **
source: *01-059*
time: *0800Z*
date: *02 Sep 2009*

(Prim) Event: launch

infosource: *ER*
agent: *DCAS* (def)
object: **
launchsite:
launch system:
inclination:
date:
time:
mission: **
source: *01-059*
time: *0800Z*
date: *02 Sep 2009*

FIG. 8.7

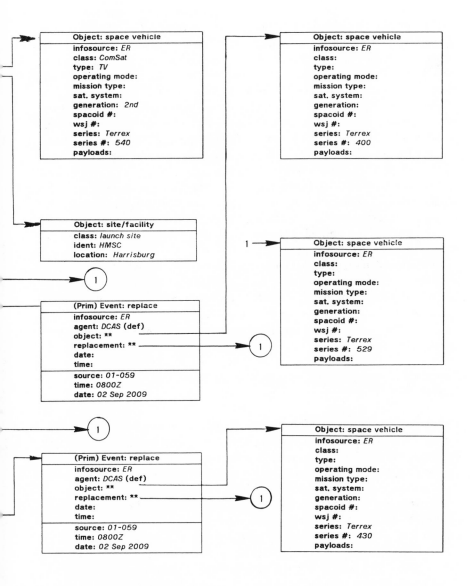

153

Representation of Meta Comments in the Analysis Language

Expressions in the analysis metalanguage are represented as meta templates labeled with the identifying term *analysis* and the meta report level with which they are associated. Figure 8.8 shows the basic set of templates that would be generated for a report describing the "impending launch of a High-flyer 6 communications satellite as a probable replacement for a current Highflyer 5." "Impending" falls under the generic **expect** predicate in the analysis metalanguage, as shown in the figure. The specific scope of "impending" — roughly, within the next 2 hours to the next 2 days, according to our space analyst informants — is represented as the time interval given in the template representing the expected launch event.

A degree of belief in the likelihood of the event shown as the mission of the launch event — a replacement of the current space object by the object to be launched — is expressed by the term *probable*. At present, our representation of degree of belief is limited to the five levels illustrated in Table 8.4 with exemplar expressions.

As discussed in previous sections, expressions in the analysis metalanguage may be associated with any level of meta event in the reporting language. Figure 8.6 contains a **compare** predicate at the Meta 2 level qualifying the language of the Meta 1 object — the NYT press announcement — by a statement that it contained "routine wording" in an implied comparison with previous press announcements.

Overview of the Natural Language Understanding System

Figure 8.9 presents a schematic of the experimental natural language understanding system for space event messages that is currently under development for the Air Force. This system is called the Data Base Generator (DBG); its primary application will be automated update of conventional space data bases and an expert system for space situation assessment.

The front end that feeds the natural language understanding component is an operational automated message handling (AMH) system. Based on interest profiles, which are ordered sets of key words and phrases connected by the boolean operators AND/OR/NOT as well as contiguity operators, the AMH system selects space event messages from other message traffic. (Profiles that match space event messages provide an initial indication of which message prototype should be used by the template instantiator.)

The automated system consists of three levels of processing with the following functions:

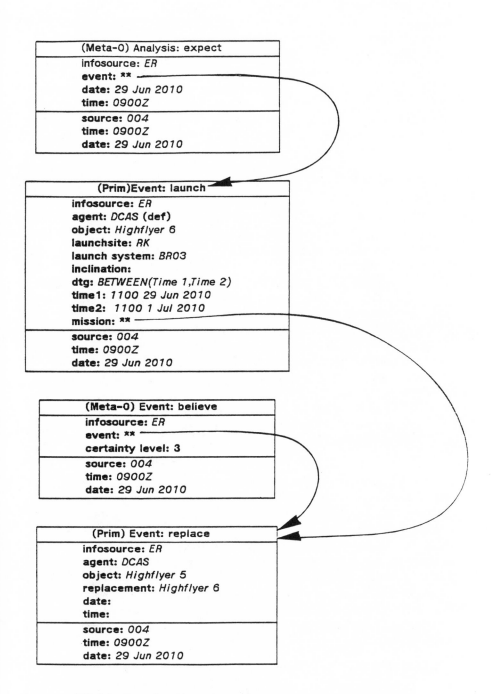

FIG. 8.8 Examples of instantiated templates for the analysis metalanguage.

TABLE 8.4
Representation of Certainty

CERTAINTY LEVELS FOR THE ANALYSIS METALANGUAGE				
0	*1*	*2*	*3*	*4*
impossible	improbable	possible	probable	certain
	unlikely	uncertain	likely	
	doubtful	may . . .	believed . . .	
		might . . .	assessed . . .	
		could . . .	suggests . . .	
		suspected		
		consistent with		

• *Character/Word Level Processing:* Segments the message into sentences, performs morphological analysis on inflectional suffixes, looks up words in the lexicon;

• *Sentence Level Processing:* Uses a Definite Clause Grammar (DCG) to parse the sentences of the message one at a time and generate a set of parse trees for input to message level processing;

• *Message Level Processing:* Uses the Text Grammar to perform semantic analysis of the entire message and generate output for downstream data bases or expert systems. This processing level includes several major processes:

  • searching the set of parse trees for appropriate fillers for slots of the set of templates predicted by the text grammar for the given message type;
  • resolving object and temporal references;
  • generating default slot fillers for attributes whose values are not explicitly stated in the message;
  • instantiating meta templates for reporting and analysis events.

The associated *knowledge bases* indicated in Fig. 8.9 include the lexicon, syntactic and text grammars, template inventory, and various rule sets for morphological analysis, reference resolution, generation of defaults, and other processes.

The *unexpected input modules* allow DBG to deal with inputs unknown to it; these may be ill formed — misspellings or grammatical errors — or well formed — new equipment designations, space object series, place names, and so on. One of the obvious problems is determining whether an item is new material or an error: e.g., a new facility name or a misspelling of a known facility name. There are four unexpected input modules, which perform the following functions:

1. A spelling corrector, which attempts to determine whether a word that does not match any item in the lexicon is a misspelling of any known lexical item.

2. A bottom-up parser which parses all sentences that would have or have caused the top-down parser to fail (i.e., sentences containing new words or unresolved spelling errors, or constructions not accounted for in the syntactic grammar).

3. A new input processor, which attempts to associate the partial trees and "leftover terminals" (unassociated items, which are either new words or uncorrected errors) with appropriate slots in the templates predicted by the text grammar for the given type of message.

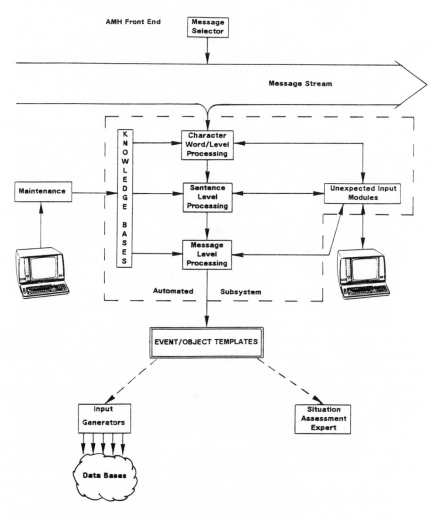

FIG. 8.9   Overview of the DBS system.

4. A self-evaluator, which takes account of the number of error hypotheses required for resolution of the unexpected inputs and develops figures of merit reflecting the system's degree of confidence in the analysis for each sentence, each template, and the complete message.

IN CONCLUSION: ONE SUBLANGUAGE OR TWO?

The issue raised in introduction is now worth re-examining in light of the previous discussion of this chapter. Concerning the definition of a sublanguage, where are we? Harris' (1968) criterion of closure seems to require more rigor than is realistic for a sublanguage, as Harris himself implied in a more recent article (Kittredge & Lehrberger, 1982, p. 235). Certainly, the space event sublanguage is a living language that is in the process of evolving, as illustrated by the discussion on interpreting agentless passives as inanimate agents. A grammatical construction that is not included in the sublanguage today, or that is currently interpreted as deviant, may be the standard of tomorrow — particularly with respect to a sublanguage like the space event reporting and analysis language, which is less formal and consequently more volatile than the language of scientific periodicals. One of the main reasons for the unexpected input component of the DBG system described earlier is to cope with this volatility, which will be exhibited in the syntactic and text grammar as well as in the obvious addition of new items to presumably infinite lists, such as place names, equipment designations, and the like.

Associated with this notion of limited, rather than absolute, closure is the concept of sublanguage overlap, which is also related to Harris' (1982) notion of the whole language as an envelope for its sublanguages. Clearly, a given sublanguage will never be totally distinct from other sublanguages in semantic domain and/or grammatical and discourse structure; some features will be shared by other related sublanguages. For example, the sublanguage of cookbooks and the sublanguages exemplified by other technical manuals such as aviation hydraulics share many grammatical and format features (Kittredge & Lehrberger, 1982), for they all involve the specification of procedures for carrying out tasks and require formats that are conceived of as optimal for communicating a procedural type of information. Similarly, the weather synopses described by Kittredge overlap in the semantic domain with the more telegraphic weather forecasts handled by METEO.

A comparison of the second paragraph of Kittredge and Lehrberger's (1982) weather synopsis example with the second paragraph of a space event assessment message shows some interesting parallels.

> Snow should fall at most localities for a few hours at least be-
> fore changing to rain. Over northern New-Brunswick however
> indications are that this change will not occur and that a size-
> able snowfall could result tonight and on Wednesday. It is
> however too early to make a reasonable estimate of these
> amounts.

---

2. THE LAUNCHING OF TERREX 549 BY THE DELTAS INDICATES
THAT THEY ARE STILL DEDICATED TO THE THREE-SATELLITE,
FIRST-GENERATION TVSAT PROGRAM. THIS IS IN ADDITION TO
THE CONTINUED MAINTENANCE OF THE SECOND-GEN-
ERATION TVSAT SERIES (BR-5X4) AND THE INCORPORATION
OF PRESUMABLY YET ANOTHER TVSAT PROGRAM (BR-5X5).
HOWEVER, THERE HAVE BEEN ONLY TWO LAUNCHES IN THE
LATTER PROGRAM (TERREX 420 AND 460) WHICH WAS BEGUN
IN OCTOBER 1979. HOW LONG THE DELTAS WILL MAINTAIN
THREE DISTINCT TVSAT SYSTEMS IS PRESENTLY UNCERTAIN.

For example, the use of the predicate 'indicate' is very similar in both texts:
the initial sentence of the space event message could be rewritten **INDICA-
TIONS ARE THAT THE DELTAS ARE STILL DEDICATED TO . . .**, the major difference being the mention of a specific indication (THE LAUNCHING OF
TERREX 549), which is lacking in the weather synopsis. The initial sentence
of the message could also be rewritten **INDICATIONS ARE THAT THE DELTAS
WILL MAINTAIN . . .**, showing a parallel use of the future tense, consistent
with the function of prediction, which is the motivation for both texts. Other
parallels are the use of the conjunction *however* (which does not occur in the
event reporting language), and the resemblance between the final sentence of
the weather synopsis and earlier example 34, both of which begin *It is too
early to . . .* In his discussion of the weather synopses, Kittredge (Kittredge &
Lehrberger, 1982) postulates two levels of text (see quote at beginning of
chapter), which are distinguished by the future tense, versus the present, as
in: *indications are . . . it is too early . . . ,* where the latter is embedded in the
former.

Unfortunately, if we applied this analysis to our case, we would have two
levels of analysis metalanguage on top of several levels of reporting language.
If these levels were considered candidates for separate sublanguages, this
would result in analyzing the space event language into a minimum of three
sublanguages, which is obviously undesirable for practical, if not for theoret-

ical, reasons. It seems best to deal with these levels as components of a particular sublanguage, keeping in mind that they might also be components of other sublanguages for other semantic domains. This approach allows each component to be treated separately where it is more efficient for automated language processing purposes (e.g., subsetting the grammar in terms of the given components), while maintaining the convenience of sublanguage segmentation along the lines of the semantic domain.

To summarize, we have seen differences in linguistic structure and the complementary distribution across messages of the reporting and analysis levels of discourse, and the additional level of meta information that the analytical function requires. However, we have also seen that both the reporting and the analytical functions are complex processes that necessitate the representation of meta events and meta objects. The similarity in representation of the underlying informational structure for these two discourse levels and the need to integrate the two types of information with one another in processing the text suggest the desirability of a unified sublanguage approach.

In conclusion, the disadvantages of insularity and resulting nontransportability of results cited by some critics of the sublanguage approach are offset by the idea of sublanguages as made up of transportable components. The analysis metalanguage is clearly transportable to other domains within the message traffic, as well as news reporting, and other texts involving event analysis. The concept of transportable components seems a productive area to pursue in future sublanguage studies.

ACKNOWLEDGMENTS

These projects have been carried out under the sponsorship of the Rome Air Development Center (RADC/IRDT), U.S. Air Force Systems Command, Griffiss Air Force Base, New York.

REFERENCES

Burge, J. W., Dwiggins, D. L., Glover, B. C., Kuhns, J. L., & Montgomery, C. A. (1982, 1983). *Automated data base generation.* Interim technical reports (U.S. Air Force Contract No. F30602-81-DC-0244, Rome Air Development Center), No. 1 May 1982, No. 3 June 1983. Woodland Hills, CA: Logicon, Inc., Operating Systems Division.

van Dijk, T. A. (1972). *Some aspects of text grammar.* The Hague: Mouton.

van Dijk, T. A. (1980). *Macrostructures.* Hillsdale, NJ: Lawrence Erlbaum Associates.

Dwiggins, D. L., & Silva, G. (1981). *AIS data base generation.* RADC-TR-81-43. Griffiss Air Force Base, NY: Rome Air Development Center.

Glover, B. C. & Montgomery, C. A. (1984). A text grammar for automated analysis of space C3I messages. *Proceedings of the Conference on Intelligent Systems and Machines.* Rochester, MI: Oakland University.

Harris, Z. S. (1968). *Mathematical structures of language.* New York: Wiley (Interscience).

Harris, Z. S. (1982). Discourse and Sublanguage. In R. Kittredge, & J. Lehrberger (Eds.), Sublanguage: Studies of language in restricted semantic domains (pp. 231–236). New York: de Gruyter.

Kittredge, R. (1982). Variation and homogeneity of sublanguages. In R. Kittredge & J. Lehrberger Eds.), *Sublanguage: Studies of language in restricted semantic domains* (pp. 108–137). New York: de Gruyter.

Kittredge, R. & Lehrberger, J. (Eds.). (1982). *Sublanguage: Studies of language in restricted semantic domains.* New York: de Gruyter.

Kuhns, J. L. (1974). *Synthesis of inference techniques: An interpreted syntax for the logical description of events.* N74-003. Woodland Hills, CA: Operating Systems.

Kuhns, J. L. & Montgomery, C. A. (1973). *Event record specification system concept: Preliminary notions.* N73-007. Woodland Hills, CA: Operating Systems.

Martins, G. R., Montgomery, C. A., Ruberti, R. N., & Burge, J. (1985). *A knowledge-based system for space threat warning.* Manuscript submitted for publication.

Montgomery, C. A. (1983). Distinguishing fact from opinion and events from meta-events. *Proceedings of the Conference on Applied Natural Language Processing* (pp. 55–61). Santa Monica, CA.

Montgomery, C. A., & Ruspini, E. H. (1981). The active information system: A data-driven system for the analysis of imprecise data. *Proceedings of the Seventh International Conference on Very Large Data Bases* (pp. 376–385). IEEE Computer Society Press.

Propp, V. (1958). *Morphology of the folk-tale.* Bloomington: Indiana University Press. (Original work published 1929.)

Silva, G., Dwiggins, D. L., Busby, S. G., & Kuhns, J. L. (1979). *A knowledge-based automated message understanding methodology for an advanced indications system.* (RADC-TR-79-133). Griffiss Air Force Base, NY: Rome Air Development Center.

Silva, G., & Montgomery, C. A. (1979). *Satellite and missile data generation for AIS.* (RADC-TR-79-314). Griffiss Air Force Base, NY: Rome Air Development Center.

Wilensky, R. (1981). Meta-planning: Representing and using knowledge about planning in problem solving and natural language understanding. *Cognitive Science, 5,* (3).

9 Constraining the Interpretation of Nominal Compounds in a Limited Context

Timothy W. Finin
Computer and Information Science
University of Pennsylvania

Nominal compounds are notoriously ambiguous. Syntactically, the number of parse trees of a nominal compound is exponential in the number of terms making up the compound. Worse, the semantic relationship between each term and its modifier has been deleted from the surface form and must be inferred. This makes nominal compounds even more highly ambiguous from a semantic point of view. The seemingly inherent ambiguity of nominal compounds might suggest that their utility is limited. On the contrary, they are very heavily used, especially in the context of a *sublanguage*.

In earlier work, we described a system that synthesized candidate semantic interpretations of nominal compounds from possible interpretations of their constituents. The candidates were partially ordered with respect to an appropriateness measure based on a number of syntactic, semantic and pragmatic factors. More recent work has examined the additional constraints that arise in the context of an extended dialogue. In addition, we discuss the use of nominal compounding as a short-term naming device in these two situations.

INTRODUCTION

In earlier work (Finin, 1980a, 1980b), we described UNCLE, a system that built semantic interpretations of nominal compounds — sequences of two or more nouns (or nominal adjectives) that function as a unit. Some examples of the kinds of nominal compounds dealt with are: *aircraft engine repairs, fuel pump float valve adjustments* and *January F105 maintenance data*. In the simplest case, where a compound contains only two nominals, the problem reduces to understanding the intended relationship between the concepts the nouns denote. For example, *engine repairs* might refer to events in which someone repaired an engine; *screwdriver repairs,* to events in which someone repaired something using a screwdriver; and *mechanic repairs,* to events in which someone who is a kind of mechanic repaired something.

As these examples show, there are typically more than one potential relationship between the modifier and modified nouns. Our initial system took the representations of the concepts making up the compound and synthesized a number of concepts which represented possible interpretations. Each candidate interpretation was then assigned an *appropriateness* measure based on a variety of factors.

One source of knowledge that was not used was the discourse context. Nominal compounding is often used as a naming device to refer to a concept already introduced, either directly or indirectly, into the discourse. For example, if one is fixing a broken screwdriver, then it is perfectly proper to refer to the activity as a *screwdriver repair.* If we are discussing the distant future in which we have robot automobile mechanics, then we may want to use the compound *mechanic repairs* to refer to the action of fixing a broken automobile repair robot.

Our current work in this area centers around three questions: (1) How can we effectively use discourse context as a primary source of evidence for both hypothesizing candidate interpretations (roughly in order of plausibility) and choosing a preferred interpretation from among them? (2) How much analysis is really required to do an adequate job of understanding nominal compounds used in discourse? We believe that many compound strings may require only a relatively shallow analysis. (3) When is it appropriate to use nominal compounds? We would like to formulate the conditions when a particular nominal compound is likely to be accurately and efficiently interpreted by a hearer.

In this chapter, we first describe the model developed in earlier work for understanding nominal compounds and then describe how it is being extended to account for the effects of discourse context.

BACKGROUND

The semantics of nominal compounds have been studied, either directly or indirectly by linguists and AI researchers. In an early study, Lees (1960) developed an impressive taxonomy of the forms. More recently, Levi (1979) and Downing (1977) attempted to capture the linguistic regularities evidenced by nominal compounding. Rhyne (1976) explored the problem of generating compounds from an underlying representation. Brachman (1978) used the problem of interpreting and representing nominal compounds as example domain in the development of his SI-Net representational formalism. Gershman (1977) and McDonald and Hayes-Roth (1978) attempt to handle noun-noun modification in the context of more general semantic systems.

Our own work on nominal compounds was done in the context of the natural language data base accessing system JETS (1979). UNCLE was designed to act as a specialist that, given a nominal compound, would produce its best guess at the most appropriate interpretation. In UNCLE, the interpretation of nominal compounds was divided into three intertwined subproblems: *lexical interpretation* (mapping words into concepts), *modifier parsing* (discovering the structure of compounds with more than two nominals), and *concept modification* (assigning an interpretation to the modification of one concept by another). The essential feature of this form of modification is that the underlying semantic relationship between the two concepts is not explicit. Moreover, a large number of relationships might, in principal, exist between the two concepts. The selection of the most appropriate one can depend, in general, on a host of semantic, pragmatic and contextual factors.

Let's restrict our attention for a moment to the simplest of compounds — those made up of just two nouns, both of which unambiguously refer to objects that we know and understand. What is the fundamental problem in interpreting the modificaton of the second noun by the first? The problem is to find the underlying relationship that the utterer intends to hold between the two concepts that the nouns denote. for example, in the compound "aircraft engine" the relationship is *part of*; in "meeting room" it is *location*; in "salt water" it is *dissolved in*.

There are several aspects that make this problem difficult. First, the relationship is not always evident in the surface form of the compound. What is it about the compound *GM cars* that suggests the relationship *made by*? The correct interpretation of this compound depends on our knowledge of several facts. We must know that GM is the name of an organization that manufactures things, in particular, automobiles. Another fact that strengthens this interpretation is that the identity of an artifact's manufacturer is a salient fact. It is even more important when the artifact is an automobile (as opposed to, say, a pencil).

A second source of difficulty is the general lack of syntactic clues to guide the interpretation process. The interpretation of clauses involves discovering and making explicit the relationships between the verb and its "arguments," for example, the subject, direct object, tense marker, aspect, etc. Clauses have well developed systems of syntactic clues and markers to guide interpretation. These include word order (e.g. the agent is usually expressed as the subject, which comes before an active verb); prepositions, which suggest case roles; and morphemic markers. None of these clues exists in the case of nominal compounds.

Third, even when the constituents are unambiguous, the result of compounding them may be multiply ambiguous. For example, *a woman doctor* may be a doctor who is a woman or a doctor whose patients are women. Similarly, *Chicago flights* may be those bound for Chicago, coming from Chicago, or even making a stop in Chicago.

A fourth aspect is that compounds exhibit a variable degree of lexicalization and idiomaticity. In general, the same compound form is used for lexical items (e.g. duck soup, hanger queen) and completely productive expression (e.g. engine maintenance, faculty meeting).

Finally, it is possible for any two nouns to be combined as a compound and be meaningful in some context. In fact, there can arbitrarily be many possible relationships between the two nouns, each relationship appropriate for a particular context.

INTERPRETATION RULES FOR NOMINAL COMPOUNDS

The UNCLE system uses three general classes of interpretation rules in the interpretation of nominal compounds. The first class contains *idiomatic rules* — rules in which the relationship created is totally dependent on the identity of the rule's constitutents. These rules typically match surface lexical items directly. Often, the compounds have an idiomatic or exocentric meaning.

The second class consists of *productive rules.* These rules attempt to capture forms of modification that are productive in the sense of defining a general pattern that can produce many instantiations. They are characterized by the semantic reltionships they create between the modifying and modified concepts. That is, the nature of the relationship is a property of the rule and not of the constituent concepts. The nature of the concepts determines only whether or not the rule applies and, perhaps, how strong the resulting interpretation is. For example, a rule for *dissolved in* could build interpretations of such compounds as "salt water" and "sugar water" and be triggered by compounds in which the head noun is a kind of liquid and the modifier is a kind chemical compound.

The third class contains the *structural rules.* These rules are characterized by the structural relationships they create between the modifying and modified concepts. The semantic nature of the relationship that a structural rule creates is a function of the concepts involved in the modification. Many of these rules are particularly useful for analyzing compounds which contain nominalized verbs.

Structural Rules

This class contains the most general semantic interpretation rules, those that help to achieve a degree of closure with respect to semantic coverage. Similar structural rules form the basis of the approaches of Brachman (1978) and McDonald and Hayes-Roth (1978). This section presents some of the structural rules we have catalogued. Each rule handles a compound with two constituents.

Role Value Modifies a Concept   The first structural rule is the most common. It interprets the modifying concept as specifying or filling one of the roles of the modified concept. Some examples of compounds that can be successfully interpreted by this rule are:

engine repair	(a to-repair with object = (an engine))
January flight	(a to-fly with time = (a January))
F4 flight	(a to-fly with vehicle = (an F4))
engine housing	(a housing with superpart = (an engine))
iron wheel	(a wheel with raw-material = (a iron))

Note that when the compound fits the form "subject + verb" or "object + verb," this works very nicely. The applicability of this rule is not limited to such compounds, however, as the last two examples demonstrate.

To apply this rule, we must be able to answer two questions. First, which of the modified concept's roles can the modifier fill? Obviously, some roles of the modified concept may be inappropriate. The concept for the to-repair event has many roles, such as an agent doing the repairing, an object being repaired, an instrument, a location, a time, etc. The concept representing an engine is clearly inappropriate as the filler for the agent and time roles, probably inappropriate as a filler for the location and instrument roles, and highly appropriate as the object's filler.

Second, given that we have found a set of roles that the modifier may fill, how do we select the best one? Moreover, is there a way to measure how well the modifier fits a role? Having such a figure of merit allows one to rate the overall interpretation. The process of determining which roles of a concept another may fill and assigning scores to the alternatives is called *role fitting*. This process returns a list of the roles that the modifier can fill and, for each, a measure of how "good" the fit is. Each possibility in this list represents one possible interpretation. Not all of the possibilities are worthy of becoming interpretations, however. A selection process is applied that takes into account the number of possible interpretations, their absolute scores, and their scores relative to each other. Making a role fit into an interpretations involves making a new instantiation of the modified concept and filling the appropriate role with modifier. Details of this process are presented in the next section.

Concept Modifies a Role Value   This rule is similar to the first, except that the concepts change places. In interpretations produced by this rule, the modified concept is seen as filling a role in the modifier concept. Note that the object referred to by the compound is still an instance of the modified concept. Some examples where this rule yields the most appropriate interpretation are:

drinking water	(a water which is (an object of (a to-drink)))
washing machine	(a machine which is (an instrument of (a to-wash)))
maintenance crew	(a crew which is (an agent of (a to-maintain)))

Again, the application of this rule is mediated by the *role fitting* process.

Concept Modifies a Role Nominal   This rule is applicable when the modified concept is in the class I call *role nominals,* nouns that refer to roles of other underlying concepts. English has but one productive system for naming role nominals: the agent of a verb can commonly be referenced by adding the -er or -or suffix to the verb stem. This should not hide the possibility of interpreting many concepts as referring to a *role* in another related concept. Some examples are:

a student is the *recipient* of a teaching,
a pipe is the *conduit* of a flowing,
a pump is the *instrument* of a pumping, and
a book is the *object* of a reading.

This rule tries to find an interpretation in which the modifier actually modifies the underlying concept to which the role nominal refers. For example, given *F4 Pilot*, the rule notes that *pilot* is a role nominal referring to the agent role of the to-fly event and attempts to find an interpretation in which *F4* modifies that to-fly event. The result is something like "an F4 pilot is the agent of a to-fly event in which the vehicle is an F4." Some other examples are:

cat food	(an object of (a to-eat with agent = (a cat)))
oil pump	(an instrument of (a to-pump with object = (an oil)))
dog house	(a location of (a to-dwell with agent = (a dog)))

Viewing a concept as a *role nominal* (e.g. food as the object of eating) ties the concept to a characteristic activity in which it participates. It is very much like a relative clause, except that the characteristic or habitual nature of the relationship is emphasized.

Role Nominal Modifies a Concept   This rule is similar to the previous one, except that it applies when the modifying concept is a role nominal. The action is to attempt an interpretation in which the modification is done, not by the first conept, but by the underlying concept to which it refers. For example, given the compound *pilot school*, we can derive the concept for "an organization that teaches people to fly." This is done by noting that pilot refers to the agent of a to-fly event and then trying to modify *school* by the *to-fly*. This, in turn, can be interpreted by the *Concept + Role Nominal* rule if school is defined as "an organization which is the agent of a to-teach." This leads to an attempt to interpret to-fly as modifying to-teach. The *Role Value + Concept* rule interprets to-fly as filling the object (or discipline) role of to-teach.

Some other examples of compounds that benefit from this interpretation rule are newspaper glasses (glasses used to read a newspaper), driver education (teaching people to drive), food bowl (a bowl used to eat food out of).

Other Structural Rules   Other structural interpretation rules that I have identified include *Specific + Generic*, which applies when the modifier is a specialization of the modified concept (e.g. F4 planes, boy child); *Generic + Specific*, which applies when the modifier is a generalization of the modified concept (e.g. Building NE43, the integer three); *Equivalence*, in which the resulting concept is descendant from both the modifier and modified concepts (e.g. woman doctor); and *Attribute Transfer*, in which a salient attribute of the modifier is transferred to the modified concept (e.g. iron will, crescent wrench.)

Role Fitting

The process of role fittng is one in which we are given two concepts, a *role Value* and a *Host*, and attempt to find appropriate roles in the Host concept in which the Role Value concept can be placed. Briefly, the steps carried out by the program are: (a) collect the local and inherited roles of the Host concept; (b) filter out any inappropriate ones (e.g. structural ones); (c) for each remaining role, compute a score for accepting the Role Value concept; (d) select the most appropriate role(s).

In the third step, the goodness-of-fit score is represented by a signed integer. Each role of a concept is divided into an arbitrary number of facets, each one representing a different aspect of the role. In computing the goodness of fit measure, each facet contributes to the overall score via a characteristic scoring function. The facets which participate include the following:

Requirements	descriptions candidate value *must* match.
Preferences	descriptions candidate value *should* match.
Default Value	a default value.
Typical Value	other very common values for this role.
Modality	one of Optional, Mandatory, Dependent or Prohibited.

Multiplicity   maximum and minimum number of values.
Salience   a measure of the role's importance with re-
                        spect to the concept.

For example, the scoring function for the *requirements* facet yields a score in-
crement of $+1$ for each requirement that the candidate value matches and a
negative infinity for any mismatch. For the *preferences* facet, we get a $+4$ for
each matching preference description and a -1 for each mismatching description. The *salience* facet holds a value from a 5-point scale (i.e. Very
Low, Low, Medium, High, Very High). Its scoring function maps these into
the integers $-1, 0, 2, 4, 8$.

DISCOURSE CONTEXT

The problem with this analysis is that it has ignored the discourse context as
a source of evidence for selecting appropriate interpretations of nominal
compounds. One can take a radical view that discourse should be the primary
source of evidence and treat most nominal compounds as referring expressions. Under this view, a compound's function is to select an object that has
been previously introduced into the discourse. Determining the correct interpretation of a nominal compound, then, is primarily a matter of finding the
proper referent.

Nominal Compounds as Referring Expressions

We can generalize our earlier approach to discover compounds whose interpretation is to be understood referentially. Consider a system that works in a
domain of discourse in which there are flights made by aircraft and which
have an origin, a destination, and sometimes a stopover location. The compound *Chicago flights* might well be used to describe flights coming from,
going to, or stopping at Chicago. Viewed in isolation, there is little evidence
in the compound to support one interpretation over another. In the context
of a particular discourse, there may be strong evidence for selecting one or
another of the candidate interpretations. Consider interpreting the compound *Chicago flights* in each of the following discourse fragments.

All of the flights coming from the midwest are delayed by the weather.
The *Chicago flights* are a full hour late.

I usually take a flight going through Chicago or St. Louis.
I prefer *Chicago flights*, sinnce they are usually shorter.

Last week I made trips to our Illinois and California offices.
The food on the *Chicago flight* was so bad I got sick.

As an example, consider a discourse containing the following text:

> All flights scheduled to stop at Chicago are being rerouted through Milwaukee. Flights scheduled to stop at St. Louis are being rerouted through Indianapolis. The *Chicago flights* will experience delays of up to one hour while the St. Louis flights will suffer little or no delays.

We want to account for the fact that, in this text, the compound *Chicago flights* is unambiguously interpreted as meaning "the flights that were to have stopped in Chicago."

The concept lattice can be seen as encoding all possible relationships between concepts. Finding candidate interpretations for nominal compounds composed of the nouns denoting CONCEPT1 and CONCEPT2 can then be described as:

> Candidate interpretations for a nominal compound with constituents denoting CONCEPT1 and CONCEPT2 can be found by considering all potential relationships between CONCEPT1 *and its generalizations* and CONCEPT2 *and its generalizations*.

For our example, the concept *flight* would be defined to include the source, destination, and stopovers roles:

```
(a movement-event is (an event) with
   . . .
   source matching (a location)
   modality = 1
   destination matching (a location)
   modality = 1
   . . .)

(a flight is (a movement-event) with
   . . .
   source typically (a city)
   destination typically (a city)
   stopovers typically (a city)
   modality > = 0
   . . .)
```

Chicago would be defined to be an instance of the concept CITY which, in turn, would be defined to be a subconcept of LOCATION. Thus, the strongest relationships are found between the concepts FLIGHT and CITY — those in which Chicago is seen as filling one of the three roles *source, destination,* and *stopovers.* The fact that the earlier text specifically mentioned flights that stopped in Chicago does not play a part in selecting or ranking the candidate interpretations.

A natural language understanding system using a representation system such as this would, in the course of processing the text of our example, add to the lattice a concept representing "flights stopping in Chicago." This concept might look something like the following:

(a flight32 is (a flight) with
stopOver = Chicago)

Adding this new concept to the lattice adds another connection between the concept FLIGHT and the concept CITY, namely, that there is a particular flight (FLIGHT32) that has a particular city (Chicago) as the filler for its *stopover* role. By changing the strategy for finding candidate interpretations slightly we can find this new connection:

Candidate interpretations for a nominal compound with constituents denoting CONCEPT1 and CONCEPT2 can be found by considering all potential relatinships between CONCEPT1 and its generalizations *and specializations* and CONCEPT2 and its generalization *and specializations.*

In order to work this into the scheme developed previously we need to cause such a match to be recognized and provide a method to assign a score to the match. This can be easily accomplished by adding a characteristic scoring function for the *value* facet. Furthermore, we can adjust this function to give more or less weight to the "discourse-bases" interpretations.

Generating Nominal Compounds

The system described in the foregoing can be adapted for use by a natural language generation system. We can use such a system as a critic for proposed nominal compounds. If the language generation system proposes to realize a constituent as a compound, then the proposed compound can be analyzed by the interpretation system. The result would be a list of all interpretations whose strength lay above the threshold. Criteria can be developed for deciding whether or not the proposed compound is appropriate. For example, we might choose to use it only if the meaning it as intended to convey is selected by the interpreter as the most likely one. Furthermore, we might require that the distance between its strength and the strength of the next best interpretation be greater than a certain threshold.

SUMMARY

This chapter discusses one approach to the task of interpreting nominal compounds. A nominal compound is a sequence of two or more nouns or nominal adjectives (i.e. nonpredicating) related through modification. The concepts denoted by the nouns (and the compound) are expressed in a frame-based representation system. The knowledge that drives the interpretation comes from the knowledge of the concepts themselves and from three classes of interpretation rules. Examples of the most general class of interpretation rules have been given. The basic approach can be extended slightly to take the discourse context into account.

REFERENCES

Brachman, R. A. (1978). *A structured paradigm for representing knowledge* (Tech. Rep. No. 3605). Cambridge, MA: Bolt Beranek & Newman.

Downing, P. (1977, December). On the creation and use of English compound nouns. *Language, 53* (4).

Finin, T., Goodman, B., & Tennant, H. (1979). JETS: Achieving completeness through coverage and closure. *Proceedings of the Sixth International Joint Conference on Artificial Intelligence.* Tokyo, Japan.

Finin, T. (1980a). *The semantic interpretation of compound nominals* (Tech. Rep. No. T–96). Champaign-Urbana: University of Illinois, Coordinated Science Laboratory.

Finin, T. (1980b). *The semantic interpretation of compound nominals.* Proceedings of the First National Conference on Artificial Intelligence. Stanford, CA: American Association of Artificial Intelligence.

Gershman, A. V. (1977). Conceptual analysis of noun groups in English. *Proceedings of the Fifth International Joint conference on Artificial Intelligence,* Cambridge, MA.

Grosz, B. (1982). Focusing and description in natural language dialogues. In Joshi, Webber (Eds.), *Elements of discourse understanding.* Cambrige, UK: Cambridge University Press.

Lees, R. B. (1960). *The grammar of English nominalizations.* Bloomington: Indiana University Press.

Levi, J. N. (1979). *The syntax and semantics of complex nominals.* New York: Academic Press.

McDonald, D. & Hayes-Roth, F. (1978). Inferential searches of knowledge networks as an approach to extensible language understanding systems. In Waterman & Hayes-Roth (Eds.), *Pattern-directed inference systems.* New York: Academic Press.

Rhyne, J. R. A lexical process model of nominal compounding in English (1976). *Computational Linguistics.*

Roberts, B. R. & Goldstein, I. P. (1977). *The FRL manual* (Tech. Rep.No. MIT-AI-409). Cambridge, MA: M. I. T., Artificial Intelligence Laboratory.

Waltz, D. (1978). An English language question answering system for a large relational data base. *Communications of the Association for Computational Machinery, 21,* 526–539.

10 The Role of Syntax in the Sublanguage of Medical Diagnostic Statements

George Dunham
Laboratory of Statistical and Mathematical Methodology
Division of Computer Research and Technology
National Institutes of Health
Washington, D.C.

ABSTRACT

The syntactic features of this sublanguage, consisting largely of complex noun phrases, are described. A semantic model used in semantic interpretation of medical diagnostic statements is presented. The chapter focuses on the role of syntax in the process of semantic interpretation in this sublanguage. A higher order predicate logic is used as the most perspicuous control structure for integrating the syntactic and semantic information in this process.

Although some syntactic forms such as the AN form do predict a predicative relationship between syntactic constitutents, the exact nature of this relationship is underdetermined by syntax (e.g., myocardial infarction, infarcted myocardium). A semantic model describing the predicative relationships among pragmatically based word and phrase clases is thus essential for semantic interpretation.

Syntactic information in this sublanguage is found to provide unreliable structure on which to perform componential semantic analysis, but it is used as a heuristic to restrict search in the semantic model.

INTRODUCTION

An account of the role of syntax in the semantic interpretation of the sublanguage of medical diagnostic statements is offered. These statements are complex noun phrases consisting principally of medical terms with accepted definitions and usage. They are used to summarize various parts or the whole of a patient's medical record and thus have considerable practical importance in epidemiological and other studies, as they are used both to categorize a case in a disease classification space and to record the particular spectrum of pathological findings and history, which can be used to index the case and compare it with others retrospectively.

That the sublanguage has syntactic formative rules is obvious. Partly because diagnostic statements used in medical records are sometimes only slightly elaborated transformations of terms found in standard disease nomenclatures and vocabularies such as ICD and SNOP (Cote, 1979; Manual of the International Statistical Classification of Diseases, 1977; Systematized Nomenclature of Pathology, 1965), and partly because true verbs (and therefore sentential forms of predication) are nearly absent, considerable work of practical value has been done with very limited use of syntactic analysis (Howell & Loy, 1968; Lamson, Glinsky, Hawthorne, Soutter, & Russell, 1965; Pacak & Dunham, 1979) [4,5,6], and the role of syntax in these statements has not been clarified.

Of course a generative grammar for this sublanguage in terms of conventional parts of speech is easy to write, but it was early noticed that the Fregean principle of componential semantic analysis, constructing a semantic interpretation by an interpretive process on semantic values of syntactic constituents (Frege, 1952; Knuth, 1968), which fairly suits languages in which predicates are syntactically explicit (Montague, 1970; Partee, 1975), seems to be invalid with high frequency in this sublanguage (examples are given later). The interesting question has always been: what role does syntax play in the structure and interpretation of this sublanguage?

A small fraction of diagnostic statements does require a syntactic analysis for proper semantic interpretation. This has been shown by further developing the techniques for multiple word dictionary entry matching reported in (Dunham, Pacak, & Pratt, 1978). These techniques use the same pragmatically based theory of discourse to be outlined. They handle anaphora and syntax by selecting an empirically determined segment of the utterance, based only loosely and heuristically on syntax and partly on distance, to match multiple word dictionary entries. In practice, this method provides matches of the relevant dictionary entries of the information language of the semantic model. Intersection techniques are used to weed the resulting crop of matches, and the dictionary entries are combined into statements in the information language using the discourse theory.

Full development of these techniques leaves a residue of problems in about 1-2% of surgical pathology diagnostic statements. These fall into two classes, both related to syntax: (a) highly discontinuous adjective and noun constituents that should in fact be matched together in a dictionary entry (example later) are not included in the same empirically determined segment of words to be matched (algorithm fails to match a relevant dictionary entry). Typically the noun term is matched, but only the less specific information in this constituent is then available for semantic representation. (b) an adjective that applies exclusively to one head noun matches with another head noun (algorithm erroneously matches an irrelevant dictionary entry). When the head nouns are of the same semantic category, no rule based solely on intersection of dictionary entry match sets can properly disassociate the adjective from the spurious head noun.

To define the role of syntax, it is necessary to provide independent accounts of semantic interpretation and anaphora resolution appropriate to the sublanguage.

The first section describes the phrase structure syntax of the sublanguage, emphasizing differences from the noun phrases of standard English. The prevalence of anaphora and the indeterminate nature of semantic relations among syntactically related constituents are demonstrated.

The second section describes a theory of semantic relations, that is, a formal information language, or Markerese, (Lewis, 1972) that can be used to represent the meaning of the medical diagnoses, for example, in a data base. The upper part of the hierarchy of this information language forms the basis of a theory of discourse for the natural language of medical diagnoses. A simple theory of intrastatement (intrasentential) anaphora is viewed as independent of the phrase structure component of syntax.

The third section shows how communication between these independent rule systems, for syntax, semantic information language, and anaphora via a higher order predicate logic, allows the systems' unification into a system for describing the role of syntax in semantic interpretation of the sublanguage.

SYNTAX

The medical record is written or dictated. Primarily, it is meant to be read, not understood by a listener. Secondly, diagnostic statements are intended to summarize and index the larger corpus of medical data accumulated during a patient's diagnosis and therapy. These two facts about the situational pragmatics of this sublanguage could be the basis of a psycholinguistic explanation of the syntactic features described below.

First, we will survey the morphological aspect of medical diagnostic statements. A prominent feature of the sublanguage is its use of greco-latin derivatives that dominate the vocabulary. Less frequently, fully latinized noun phrases such as *erythema annulare* are used, most often by dermatologists. Morphosyntactic analysis of this vocabulary (Pacak & Pratt, 1978; Pratt & Pacak, 1969) has permitted sufficiently reliable automatic part of speech identification and morphosyntactic information to allow transforms that accommodate the vagaries of paraphrase found in this sublanguage (Dunham, Pacak, & Pratt, 1978). For example:

bronchial adenoma
bronchial adenomata
bronchial adenomas
adenoma of bronchus

Most important for the present study, morphosyntactic analysis permits identification of part of speech, which, in turn, permits identification of the phrase structure patterns and syntactically based predicates discussed later. Morphosemantic analysis has established rules for semantic interpretation of selected groups of morphosemantic compound words such as:

pneumonitis—inflammation of the lung.
cholangectomy—surgical removal of bile duct.
granulopoiesis—production of granulocytes.

by analysis and interpretation rather than dictionary lookup of full word forms (Norton & Pacak, 1983; Pacak, Norton, & Dunham, 1980).

Lexicographically, the sublanguage is characterized by active formation of neologisms and abbreviations. Some are purposive and involve innovations of meaning; others are idiosyncratic or even sloppy. In a context of practical natural language processing, all consistent relationships between word and meaning must be dealt with on a more or less equal basis if an adequate data base is to be constructed. This makes some degree of continuous lexicographic ferment inevitable.

Turning to the phrase structure aspect of syntax, we note that these staements are characteristically complex noun phrases rather than sentences. Sometimes, the verb to-be is explicit, creating a sentence. When this does occur, the sentence usually hedges a diagnosis or adds further information using nonmedical vocabulary. Other sentential verbs are extremely rare or absent.

The comma is much used as a link or a separator in this sublanguage. It occurs with about two thirds the frequency of nouns. In addition to uses common in general English, such as demarcating list items and certain phrase types, it links terms in a way suggestive of a role as vestigial indication of some deleted constituent: for example, for the preposition IN in *inflammation, liver* or for the verb *to be* in the postposed adjective phrase type described later. The duality of its roles as link and separator necessitates interpretation of the comma (and likewise colons) in the context of the patterns of surrounding parts of speech and the semantic categories of words. Commas and a few other delimiters frame the phrase structure patterns discussed next.

The following are types of phrase structure found in the sublanguage with some of their characteristics. We do not list each quantitative variant of a pattern e.g. A N vs. A A N, nor all of the hybrids and recursive embedding of types.

A. The basic English noun phrase containing adjectives and noun in conventional order (A N) is frequently found. Infrequently it is preceeded by a determiner or associated with a quantifying expression such as 50 *ml*.

It is with this common form that problems of semantic interpretation of syntactic constituents most often arise. Normally, as in *left lung*, a semantic interpretive rule or medical dictionary lookup operates on the immediate constituents of the NP. However exceptions arise in this sublanguage with considerable frequency. Consider:

(1) *cortical cyst of the kidney*
(2) *stomach: chronic ulceration, mucosal hyperplasia.*

Cortical and *mucosal* are adjectives in NPs of the A N form. *Cortical* cannot be interpreted apart from the noun *kidney*. Its coconstituent cyst comes in many descriptive varieties, for example, *sebaceous cyst*; but the adjective *cortical* simply further specifies the site *kidney* in which *cyst* is found. In this case, one might invent a transformational rule in the sense of Syntactic Structures (Chomsky, 1957) to show paraphrase with, for example, *cyst of the cortex of the kidney.*

Similarly, *mucosal* in (2) refers to the gastric mucous membrane, but this interpretation cannot be made without establishing a connection with *stomach*. In contrast to (1), there is no rule of syntax that justifies making such a connection. *Mucosal* and *stomach* are discontinuous constituents of a virtual NP that does not exist in (2), but which we may hypothesize on the basis of a detailed model of medical facts.

B. Noun noun forms, (N N), are found in medical diagnostic terminology as they are in most contemporary jargons: *heart disease, lymph node,* and so on. The constituent nouns are contiguous or are related to the contiguous form by basic transformations, for example, *disease of heart* and thus, when the lexicon models medical usage at this level, present no problem for semantic interpretation via immediate constituents.

C. The postposed adjective (N, A) is a syntactic form not found in general English, but which occurs frequently in this sublanguage. A comma invariably occurs in this pattern *inflammation, chronic.* There is a temptation here to interpret the comma as a place holder for the verb *to be* and *chronic* as a predicate adjective, presupposing that N, A is the result of transformation from N is A, but this interpretation is not necessary. Indeed, the constituents may be highly discontinuous:

inflammation with mesothelial reaction, visceral
pleura of left lung, chronic.

D. Syntactic forms in which one constituent is a coconstituent with each of a list of constituents take a variety of forms:

(a) N, A_1, A_2
inflammation, chronic, necrotizing
to be interpreted as A_1 N and A_2 N.

(b) A_1, A_2, and A_3 N
celiac, ileocolic, and iliac lymph nodes
to be interpreted as A_1 N and A_2 N and A_3 N.

(c) A N_1 and N_2
focal fibrosis and calcification
to be interpreted as A N_1 and A N_2.

We term these *distributive syntactic structures*. Although identifying these structures as a whole and applying the distributive rule across the list is troublesome, it can be done efficiently. Distributive structures, recognized on the basis of syntax alone, predict quite well the constituents that must be associated for semantic interpretation.

Ambiguity introduced by the writer can occur:

focal ulceration and fibrosis.

In these cases our local decision is to assume a distributive structure, and the *focal fibrosis* interpretation is recorded if it occurs in the model of medical facts.

E. Latin noun phrases occur embedded in statements of the sublanguage. These may have the form of N A, such as *lupus erythematosus*. As in the N N phrases, the word order is fixed; no transformations are possible. These noun phrases are essentially lexical items consisting of an ordered string of words, reducing semantic interpretation for them to lexical lookup.

F. Certain nouns, such as *cell,* can combine with adjectives to form a constituent that serves as a modifier to a head noun, A N_1 N_2:

squamous cell carcinoma
carcinoma, squamous cell type

The constituent *squamous cell, A N_1*, is quite real: *cell carcinoma* is not. The exact nature of this constituent is not resolved.

It may be transformationally related to a prepositional phrase construction. In a study of translation of nomenclature terms from English to Spanish, (Garcia-Hidalgo & Dunham, 1981) these constituents mapped to prepositional phrases:

squamous cell carcinoma
carcinoma de cellulas escamosas

An N_1 noun like *cell* was called a nonprinciple nominal. A generative semantic approach following Levi (1978) would derive squamous cell from something like *squamous being cell,* and the whole phrase from something like {*squamous cell*}-*having carcinoma* by predicate (*being, having*) deletion.

Another approach is to note that within the sublanguage, nonprinciple nominals, although morphologically nouns, are less noun-like (Ross, 1972) than other nouns and many adjectives. They can be viewed as qualifiers or specifiers of the relation between the adjective and the head noun:

? *squamous cellular carcinoma.*

They thus assume, along with deverbals, the role of explicit predicates in medical diagnoses.

Whatever the linguistic generation process is that produces them, it operates almost exclusively when the full term is thought to have diagnostic or prognostic significance. In diagnostic nomenclatures *squamous cell,* the descriptive specifier of *carcinoma,* is not listed independently. The full term is listed, thus making semantic interpretation straightforward in practice.

G. Prepositional phrases are found as components of diagnostic noun phrases. Although commonly used, they are most frequently seen in situations in which they merely corroborate default rules of discourse that are determined from the semantic categories of noun phrases (see section on Semantic Discourse Models): *carcinoma in right lung. Of,* in particular, is an all purpose preposition whose distribution overlaps considerably with the comma.

carcinoma of left lower lobe of lung
carcinoma, left lower lobe, lung

Prepositions do carry information that is not also a default of the discourse rules. They are never used to demarcate list items within a list. Therefore, when some relation that is not a default of the discourse rules between two noun phrases of the same category must be expressed, a preposition may be used. *Adrenal gland; tumor with necrosis,* carries different information from *Adrenal gland: tumor and necrosis.*

H. Constructions involving deverbal adjectives and nouns are common in this sublanguage. Adjectives unrelated to a verb, for example, *due* in *due to,* are known to form this construction. Prepositions are frequently involved. We interpret these constructions as the surface manifestations of binary predicates, having a role analogous to that of the explicit verb in a sentence. For example:

*arteries **narrowed by** plaques*
*liver infarcts **secondary to** vascular occlusion*
*fibrosis **involving** aortic arch*
*carcinoma **arising in** severe actinic keratosis*

*ovarian tumor **with extension into** adnexal soft tissues*
*ovarian tumor **extending into** adnexal soft tissues*
*erosion **with overgrowth of** bacilli, colon.*
*vascular **occlusion by** tumor*

Theoretical objections have been made from the transformationalist standpoint to parallelisms between noun phrases and sentences in general English (Williams, 1982). Nonetheless, in a language lacking in verbs, it is inevitable that deverbal constructions and prepositions occurring in settings relating two noun phrases should be seen as predicates, when consideration moves beyond syntax to the question of semantic interpretation.

SEMANTIC AND DISCOURSE MODELS

The purpose of this section is to briefly describe a model of medical facts or, loosely, a semantic model for describing the role of syntax in medical diagnostic statements. The model is independent of syntax in that deductions can be made from it without dependence on predicates referring to the syntax of the natural language of the sublanguage. In addition, it underlies a simple model of discourse.

The model presented here may be taken as an abstract account of the SNOP dictionary (Systematized Nomenclature of Pathology, 1965; Cote, 1979; Pratt, 1973), errors, blemishes, and committee parenthood aside. Although not a state of the art model of its type (categorized nomenclature [Dunham, Henson & Pacak, 1984]) it suffices to define the relationship of syntax to this type of semantic model.

A model Δ consists of a set of lexical entries or nomenclature terms $\{e_i\}$ hierarchically organized, more general terms dominating more specific ones. That is $\{e_i\}$ is the node set of a tree graph. A node e_0 is the root node which dominates all others. A binary relation R^* of reachability is defined on Δ by: $<e_j,e_k> \in R^*$ if there is a path in tree Δ from e_j to e_k.

In the process of providing an interpretation for an utterance, the dictionary entries e_i are interpreted as unary predicates on subsets of its words. Interpreting the e_i as predicates on the diagnostic statement or the medical case record is widespread in existing data bases. Of great utility in both applications is the binary relation of predicate entailment, $\rightarrow$, for which we will use infix notation. e_j predicate entails e_k or $e_j \rightarrow e_k \iff <e_k,e_j> \in R^*$.

The diagram (fig. 1) shows e_0 as the root node in the tree. At the first level below the root, the nomenclature terms are divided into categories, topographic site, and so on. Integrated with the tree model in this way, the category names are seen to be of the same type as other lexical entries. However, they play a special role in a model of discourse for the sublanguage. Moving down (leafward) in the tree leads to entries of greater specificity of description. Consider the lexical entry *apex of right lung*. If it can be truly predicated of some object, say a syntactic unit, then those entries that it predicate-entails, such as *lung* and *topographic site*, may also be truly predicated of the same object.

Just below the root node in Fig. 10.1 are dictionary entries *topographic site* (T), *morphologic alteration* (M), *etiological agent* (E). These are names of semantic categories. The semantic category T consists of exactly those dictionary entries that predicate entail T, and so forth.

Semantic categories at this level are the linguistic reflection of classes of acts or behavior by physicians in the process of making and describing a diagnosis. Although we have described them in formal terms as entries within a dictionary, they are derived from the pragmatics of medical practice. The terms in each category answer a specific question which it is the purpose of a diagnosis to answer to the extent possible. Answering these questions is the sine qua non of diagnosis.

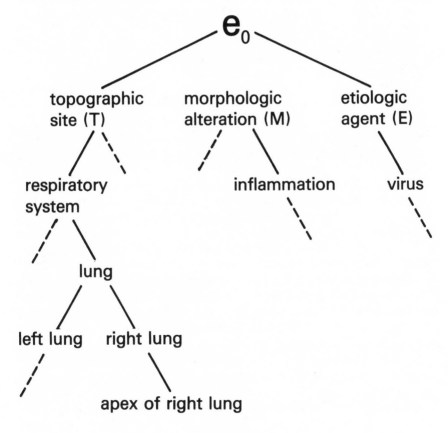

FIG. 10.1

How is disease localized in the patient? (T)
What abnormal alterations are observed? (M)
What is the causative agent? (E)

The discourse of medical diagnostic statements is composed of answers to these questions as its vocabulary is partitioned by them. Therefore, the pragmatically based model of discourse is, for the present discussion, an unordered triple of categories (T,M,E).

This simple model of diagnostic discourse is used throughout processing of the sublanguage. First, because it models the set of answers that constitute a diagnosis, it determines the elementary form for coding a diagnosis in a data base of medical diagnoses.

Focusing on a representation for diagnosis in an artificial information language, the model provides a syntax for the representation if an order is imposed on the T,M,E triple:

elementary diagnosis → t m e.
$t \in \{e_i: e_i \rightarrow T\}$.
$m \in \{e_i: e_i \rightarrow M\}$.
$e \in \{e_i: e_i \rightarrow E\}$.

The discourse model is used when syntax rules fail to show any relation between words in an utterance, as between *stomach* and *mucosal* in the aforementioned (2). The term *mucosal* itself corresponds to no categorized entry in Δ. It does, however, occur within a number of dictionary entries e_i, which predicate entail T. When this fact is lexically associated with *mucosal* and dictionary search for *mucosal* with syntactically associated words does not yield one of the e_i sought, simple discourse level strategies greatly narrow further lexicographic search.

For example: presuming the anaphora to be resolvable within the diagnostic statement (not the only case in medical diagnoses), look for a word to the left, matching a lexical entry that predicate entails T (*stomach*). If found, reuse this word as key with *mucosal* to find the desired match. If such a word is not found to the left, preserve *mucosal* to be added to the list of syntactically associated words to be matched with a word to the right as key, at the time when that word is known to match an entry which predicate entails T.

For present purposes, we state the problem of interpreting an utterance as follows, using the pragmatically derived model: Determine the set of elementary diagnoses entailed by the utterance, and write them into the data base.

Known problems with the models just sketched include:

1. The inadequacy of the tree as a mathematical model for the dictionary. The partially ordered set, including trees is preferred (Dunham et al., 1984).

2. The medical incompleteness of all existing categorized nomenclatures for diagnosis (although this is due, in part, to the distorting effect of representing them as trees).

3. Incompletely understood distinctions between categories representing diseased and normal states: morphological alteration, disease, syndrome, physiological function and dysfunction. M has done duty for all of these in our exposition.

4. The existence of utterances that express predication between several elementary diagnoses, or a relation other than elementary diagnosis between dictionary entries of one or more categories. These relations include: time, cause, spatial relations; but the list of particular relations may be quite large or unclosed. The rules of paraphrase among them are complex. These were touched upon in connection with prepositions and deverbals above.

*necrosis **in** tumor*   spatial, causal?
*tumor **with** necrosis*   spatial, causal?

*scarring **in** smallpox*   causal-secondary
*scarring **from** smallpos*   causal-secondary

*axillary lymph nodes, **metastatic** carcinoma **from** breast*   spatial, causal, temporal

*duct cell carcinoma **of** the breast, **metastatic to** axillary lymph nodes*   spatial, causal, temporal

*hernia **from** pelvic cavity*   spatial
*hernia **into** pelvic cavity*   spatial

*allergy **to** pollens*   causal-agent
*allergy **from** age 4.*   temporal

We believe that a discourse model that defines an adequate data base representation for these utterances will be difficult to describe. These utterances are infrequent in diagnostic statements, though they are of high frequency in important medical narrative such as clinical summaries.

THE ROLE OF SYNTAX

In the previous section, the informal term *semantic interpretation of a diagnostic statement* was defined as determining the exact set of elementary diagnoses entailed by the utterance. What does syntax analysis contribute to this process?

One task that must be performed for semantic interpretation of each utterance is finding the set of dictionary entries that match to subsets of utterance words. This information is most conveniently represented by a list of unary predicates having the same name as dictionary entries e_i, on a domain of variables having subsets of utterance words (the supporting set of a dictionary entry) as values. For example in the case of (2):

$$\underset{w_1}{Stomach} \quad \underset{w_2}{:} \quad \underset{w_3}{chronic} \quad \underset{w_4}{ulceration} \quad \underset{w_5}{,} \quad \underset{w_6}{mucosal} \quad \underset{w_7}{hyperplasia} \quad \underset{w_8}{}$$

and the relevant portion of the dictionary being:

$e_1 = stomach$
$e_2 = gastric\ mucous\ membrane$
$e_3 = chronic\ ulceration$
$e_4 = hyperplasia$

$e_1 \rightarrow T, e_2 \rightarrow T, e_3 \rightarrow M, e_4 \rightarrow M.$

we have the set of lexical predicates:

$e_1(\{w_1\}), e_2(\{w_1,w_6\}), e_3(\{w_3,w_4\}), e_4(\{w_7\}).$

Another essential task or group of tasks is to eradicate spurious matches, if any; identify and eliminate redundancy; and determine which elementary diagnoses among those combinatorially possible are actually entailed by the utterance. For example:

e_1e_3 paraphrased by *chronic ulceration of the stomach;*
e_2e_4 paraphrased by *hyperplasia of gastric mucous membrane*

The supporting set of an elementary diagnosis is the union of the supporting sets of its constituent dictionary predicates.

Let us look at a characteristic syntactic pattern in diagnostic utterances...A N_1 , N_2...to see how the information in it can be used. This is the pattern of

(3) *left lung, emphysema*
(4) *epidermoid carcinoma, lung*
(5) *cortical cyst, kidney*
(6) *..., right lung, kidney,...*

The relation between A and N_1 is quite strong, as our intuitions of syntax would dictate. This intuition is confirmed by the discourse model, in which A and N_1 always co-occur in the set of utterance words supporting an elementary diagnosis for (3-6).

When syntax predicts that two words of an utterance will either co-occur or be absent in the supporting set of each of the elementary diagnoses that are its interpretation, we call the syntactic relation between the words *necessary*.

In general terms, we could say that A is predicatively related (here called syntactically necessary) to N_1, but not more. Predicate and arguments are not distinguished. *Cirrhotic liver* is found as well as *hepatic cirrhosis*. Semantic categories will determine the details of interpretation for these noun phrases. Syntax tells us only that the adjective and noun will be interpreted together.

Consider the relation exemplified between A and N_2. Examples (3-5) fulfill the criteria for a necessary syntactic relation, but A and N_2 will not co-occur in the supporting set of an elementary diagnosis for (6). When syntax predicts that the defining criterion for a necessary syntactic relation will sometimes but not always be fulfilled between a pair of words, we call the syntactic relation between them *possible*. Possible syntactic relations are generated when simple noun phrases are separated by a comma or the preposition *with* inter alia.

A third, unnamed syntactic relation is defined when syntax is unable to make any prediction about two syntactically unrelated words. This does not mean that syntactically unrelated words cannot co-occur in the supporting set of an elementary diagnosis, for example, *stomach* and *mucosal* in (2), simply that syntax does not predict a necessary or possible relation between them.

Let us see how syntactic predicates having the three values necessary, possible, and syntactically unrelated, can be used in semantic interpretation.

We have seen that two syntactically unrelated words may nonetheless co-occur in the supporting set of a dictionary entry and a fortiori in the supporting set of an elementary diagnosis. This places a constraint on our use of syntactic information as a heuristic. We cannot use absence of syntactic relation to forclose the possibility of two words' supporting the same elementary diagnosis or the same dictionary entry.

A syntactically possible pair of words is omnipotential. The words may be unrelated in semantic interpretation or related at the lexical or discourse level. From syntactically possible relations, which one must explore at the lexical level prior to obtaining semantic category information, come the majority of the false paths which must be pursued in computing a semantic interpretation for an utterance. The nonspecific comma linking two noun phrases plays a major role in creating this kind of syntactic relation.

A syntactically necessary pair of words predicts a relation at the discourse level as previously defined but, like the syntactically possible relation, leaves the question of relation at the lexical level to be tested by dictionary search. The A N_1 relation is verified lexically in (3,4, and 6), but not in (5). For necessary syntactic relations, however, failure to find a categorized lexical predicate supported by the pair assures us that the necessary syntactic relation is utilized on the discourse level. It then tells us that lexical entries supported by one of the pair are to be combined with lexical entries supported by the other in forming elementary diagnoses. Here is a use of syntax of the kind usually supposed to be useful for semantic interpretation of language.

A curious fact about positive syntactic information, necessary or possible, is that it never specifies whether it will be applicable in the task of determining lexical predicates or in the task of constructing elementary diagnoses, yet it is never useful in both tasks. If a necessary syntactic relation between two words is verified by lexical lookup, then the relation between these two words has lost all value for determining an elementary diagnosis. The converse is true. A necessary syntactic relation like that in *cortical cyst,* which will be useful in determining an elementary diagnosis, will never be verified at the lexicographic level.

Two consequences follow from this.

1. Syntactic relations cannot provide a continuous stable framework during the semantic interpretation of an utterance.

2. In the task of identifying lexical predicates, possible and necessary syntactic relations are heuristically indistinguishable. They narrow search to the same degree.

In summary, syntax in this sublanguage provides somewhat weak heuristic guidance for lexical search. In practice, more than double the number of paths must be explored than will result in verified lexical predicates. Syntax does not reveal the point in a semantic interpretation process at which the most definite syntactic information (necessary) can be applied. Syntax seems to play a supporting rather than a central role in semantic interpretation of an utterance. Syntax provides well-formed noun phrases for the sublanguage, but little definite information that parallels or is redundant to discourse rules and lexical predicates.

These three types of syntactic information—necessary, possible, and unrelated—are fundamental to the medical diagnosis sublanguage in the following sense. Consider the following hypothetical sublanguage: (a) the vocabulary of medical diagnosis, minus prepositions and deverbals; (b) syntax features are those described in the Syntax, minus preposition and deverbals.

Roughly one third of medical diagnostic statements are entirely within this sublanguage. Any elementary diagnosis can be expressed in it. It seems to be the central core of the medical diagnostic sublanguage. Therefore, we have first described the role of syntax for this core sublanguage in the conviction that processes required for semantic interpretation in the presence of barely useful syntactic information are fundamental to the diagnosis sublanguage and will be required to some degree in interpreting "superlanguages" of the diagnostic core.

The further removed a syntactic pattern is from the standard English noun phrase pattern, A N, the more likely it is to provide relatively solid syntactic information in this sublanguage. Distributive forms, such as *left lung and pleura,* postposed adjective forms, and Latin N A forms all generate fewer spurious syntactic relations with neighboring noun phrases than simple A N forms and identify only the necessary syntactic relations within their own structures.

Reintroducing prepositions and deverbals provides more opportunities for the use of syntax. This information is not strictly syntactic but is (loosely) semantic in nature. It makes predictions about the semantic categories of neighboring noun phrases. These predictions are necessarily framed in the language of syntax.

In diagnostic statements, much of this information is confirmatory of information derivable from the semantic categories of lexical predicates and from the discourse model. There is no difference in semantic interpretation between *inflammation of lung; inflammation in lung; inflammation, lung;* or *pulmonary inflammation.* This accounts in part for the reported practical successes in semantic interpretation of this sublanguage without processing of syntax. Moreover, some deverbals have nominalized representations in the dictionary and are semantically interpreted via the lexicon in the manner of adjectives, for example, *calcifying* interpreted as *calcification.*

Only after the set of correct lexical predicates has been established and related to their supporting sets of utterance words, and problems of anaphora among nominal and adjectival elements are resolved, does the use of syntax in semantic interpretation become truly productive.

To address the increased information introduced by prepositions and deverbals in diagnostic statements and the accompanying increase in utility of syntactic information, it is convenient to formalize further and unify the sublanguage and its models in a higher order logic. By quantifying over predicates, we sweep aside important issues concerning the algorithmic process of semantic interpretation. This demystifies the role of syntax by focusing us on the issue of what information is present in an utterance, rather than the means of representing it internally via an algorithm. By explicit representation of the presence or absence of syntactic information, its ambiguities, and the deductions obtainable from it, its use in semantic interpretation is described.

In a problem of semantic interpretation for an utterance, there is a sequence of words $\{w_1, w_2, \ldots, w_n\}$ in the utterance. Each logical formula in the following text is taken to be universally quantified for each free occurrence of a letter subscripted variable over utterance words. Supporting sets of words for lexical predicates and higher levels of representation for semantic interpretation are represented by variables over subsets from the utterance word sequence. These variables are represented by lower case letters a,b, etc. Each logical formula in the following text is taken to be universally quantified for each free supporting set variable it contains. Lexical predicates on supporting sets are represented by the symbols e_i, names of the node set of the dictionary tree as described in the previous section.

Necessary syntactic relationships and possible syntactic relationships between words are represented by the predicates N and P on pairs of words. By extension, syntactic relationships will be applied to supporting sets, that is:

$$N(a,b) \Longleftrightarrow \exists w_i,w_j(N(w_i,w_j) \wedge w_i \in a \wedge w_j \in b).$$

We define a postulate:

$$L(a) \equiv \exists e_i(e_i \in \triangle \wedge e_i(a)),$$

meaning roughly that a lexical predicate is supported by set a.

More than one lexical predicate can be supported by a set of words (cf morphosemantic analysis in the syntax section). In addition, all predicate entailments of these dictionary entries are entailed by $L(a)$. Thus we may say that $L(a) \Longrightarrow Q(a)$, where

$$Q(a) \equiv \{e_k : \exists e_j(e_j \in \triangle \wedge e_j(a) \wedge e_j \rightarrow e_k)\}.$$

A category naming function $\varkappa'$ is defined on $\{e_i\}$ the node set of $\triangle$. The value $\varkappa' (e_i)$ is the category name predicate entailed by e_i.

A function $\varkappa''$ can be defined on sets of words, taking sets of category names as its values. The value of $\varkappa''(a)$ is the set of lexical predicate names in $Q(a)$ which are category names.

Finally, a function $\varkappa$ can be defined on sets of words. $\varkappa(a)$ is defined when $\varkappa''(a)$ has exactly one member, to be the category name in $Q(a)$. Otherwise $\varkappa(a)$ is undefined.

The task of determining the set of lexical predicates for an utterance, with its syntactically based heuristics, can be described. Define:

$$\overline{N}(w_j) \equiv \{w_k : N(w_j,w_k)\}$$
$$\overline{P}(w_j) \equiv \overline{N}(w_j) \cup \{w_k : w_i \in \overline{N}(w_j) \wedge P(w_i,w_k)\}$$
$$\overset{o}{P}(w_j) \equiv \overline{P}(w_j) \cup \{w_k : \exists \ w_i(w_k \in \overline{P}(w_i) \wedge w_i \in \overline{P}(w_j) \wedge$$
$$\overline{P}(w_j) \subseteq \overline{P}(w_i))\}.$$

For each distinct set $\overset{o}{P}(w_j)$, determine all non-empty $Q(a)$ where $a \subseteq \overset{o}{P}(w_j)$. This corresponds to the dictionary search task.

If $Q(\{w_j\})$ for a single word has exactly one member, necessarily a category name, then no specific dictionary entry has been matched. This case can occur when there is no syntactic relation between two members of the supporting set of a lexical predicate (previous section). Finding a more specific dictionary entry, if one exists, is done by searching for w_k such that

$$\neg \, (N(w_i, w_k) \vee P(w_i, w_k)) \wedge \varkappa(\{w_k\}) = \varkappa(\{w_j\})$$

and then determining $Q(\{w_i w_k\})$.

The following useful axiom, incorporating both syntactic and semantic conditions, places a type of dictionary mismatch in contradiction, for example, that between *chronic* and *inflammation* in:

chronic   ulceration   ,   focal   inflammation
w_1 w_2 w_3 w_4 w_5

the relevant portion of the dictionary being:

e_1 = *ulceration*
e_2 = *chronic ulceration*
e_3 = *inflammation*
e_4 = *focal inflammation*
e_5 = *chronic inflammation*

$e_1, e_2, e_3, e_4, e_5 \rightarrow M.$

$$(N(w_i, w_j) \wedge \exists \, a(w_i, w_j \in a \wedge L(a)) \wedge P(w_i, w_k) \wedge \varkappa(\{w_j\}) = \varkappa(\{w_k\}))$$

$$\Rightarrow \quad \neg \; \exists \, b(w_i, w_k \in b \wedge L(b))$$
Read with i = 1, j = 2, k = 5.

The following meaning postulate defines D a predicate on pairs of supporting sets. When D(a,b) is satisfied, then the union of a and b will be a supporting set of some elementary diagnosis.

$$D(a,b) \equiv \varkappa(a) \neq \varkappa(b) \wedge$$
$$(\; \exists \, c,d(c \neq d \wedge \varkappa(c) = \varkappa(b) \wedge N(a,c) \wedge \varkappa(d) = \varkappa(a) \wedge N(b,d))$$
$$\Rightarrow \quad N(a,b))$$

Loosely, this says that two lexical predicates of different categories will be combined into an elementary diagnosis if they do not each have distinct competitive lexical predicates of the appropriate category necessarily related or if they are in necessary syntactic relation to each other. This expression states the relationship between the necessary syntactic relation and the model of discourse, and the condition under which pragmatically based discourse rules are applied in default of necessary syntactic relations between supporting sets.

CONCLUSIONS

It is a common assumption in processing sublanguages with verbal predication or general English that knowledge of syntax provides the essential framework for semantic interpretation, with only a few anaphoric phenomena, such as pronomial reference, evading neat syntactic treatment. We have described a sublanguage in which, on the contrary, anaphora is prominent, and syntax plays the weak sister of pragmatically based discourse rules in computing a semantic interpretation.

In a sublanguage where the correlation between syntactic form and semantic interpretation is weak, variable, and ambiguous, as in medical diagnostic noun phrases, pragmatically based discourse rules supply information needed for semantic interpretation. The converse is revealing: In a sublanguage serving communication governed by strong but limited pragmatic conventions, the role of syntax in semantic interpretation diminishes without loss of sureness of communication.

The heavy nominalization and classification of nominals observed in this sublanguage may be a side effect of social structures in a medical faculty created by the need for specialization. Each category has its own warden: the anatomist (T), the pathologist (M), the microbiologist et al. (E). Nominalization is required for the classification needed to give the subject area overall coherence for the student.

Psycholinguistic and sociolinguistic research on sublanguages to account for the differing sets of syntax rules found in them would be interesting and useful to specialists in practical applications of sublanguage text.

The core sublanguage of the previous section is not fundamental to the natural language of diagnostic statements in an important sense. It has a very low level of informational redundancy, lower than usually characterizes natural sublanguages. Therefore, one would not expect it to be learnable from its own text. In the absence of conventional order syntax associated with semantic categories or explicit forms of copula and predication, it is not to be expected that semantic categorical information could be induced from the core by distributional analysis (Harris, 1952).

When the pragmatics of a sublanguage is well fixed and easily formalizable (never quite the case), then isolating or constructing a simple core sublanguage having no more syntactic richness than is required for the pretense of being a medium of communication may be a useful step in developing a strategy of semantic interpretation. For an interpretation strategy for the core must fully exploit the pragmatically based discourse rules, and they may be discovered and defined by this exercise.

Syntax rules are then added to accommodate the full existing sublanguage, but, once the default rules of discourse have been defined, they can be brought into play whenever syntactically guided algorithms come to a dead end. This methodology offers the pleasant experience of seeing each added syntax rule reduce the uncertainty of interpretation, rather than increasing the complexity of the problem posed for a semantic interpreter, as when the classical Fregean view of semantic interpretation is adopted.

With regard to utterances that express predication between several elementary diagnoses, we have at present the capability of creating a data base from these utterances in which the language cues for the discourse relations have been identified, and semantic typing at all levels of embedding is achieved. Moreover, relations of importance in diagnosis, such as negation (Barnhard, Jacobson & Nance, 1974) and metastatic tumor sites (Systematized Nomenclature of Pathology, 1965; Dunham et al., 1978), have practical ad hoc solutions in existing data bases. However, in the absence of a model of discourse comprehending this class of utterances, no general claim can be made that putting the structures so identified from text into a data base will allow good recall of the information contained in the original utterance.

Thus, over and above information conforming to basic discourse models such as that presented here, we are currently able to reproducibly extract considerable "data" from sublanguage text, the uses and application of which we do not fully understand. As we proceed, we need to distinguish two classes of data extracted from sublanguage text. (a) data for which we have a discourse theory providing a canonical representation of the information it carries; and (b) data for which a satisfactory theory of paraphrase is currently unavailable. A method is needed in sublanguage studies to describe the boundary between the two for each sublanguage and each state of the art as precisely as possible.

REFERENCES

Barnhard, H. J., Jacobson, H. G., & Nance, J. W. (1974). Diagnostic Radiology Information System (DRIS). *Radiologe, 14,* 314–319.

Chomsky, N. (1957). *Syntactic Structures.* 's-Gravenhage: Mouton.

Cote, R. A. (Ed.), (1979). *Systematized nomenclature of medicine* (SNOMED) (2nd ed.). Skokie, IL: College of American Pathologists.

Dunham, G. S., Henson, D. E., & Pacak, M. G. (1984). Three solutions to problems of categorized medical nomenclatures. *Methods of Information in Medicine, 23,* 87–95.

Dunham, G. S., Pacak, M. G., & Pratt, A. W. (1978). Automatic indexing of pathology data. *Journal of the American Society for Information Science, 29*(2), 81–90.

Frege, G. (1952). P. Geach, & M. Black (Eds.), *Translations from the philosophical writings of Gottlob Frege,* Oxford: Basic Blackwell.

Garcia-Hidalgo, I., & Dunham,, G. (1981). An experiment in English-Spanish automatic translation of medical language data. *Methods of Information in Medicine, 20,* 38–46.

Harris, Z. S. (1952). Discourse analysis. *Language, 28*(1), 1–30.

Howell, R. W., & Loy, R. M. (1968). Disease coding by computer: The "Fruit Machine" method. *British Journal of Preventive and Social Medicine, 22,* 178–181.

Knuth, D. E. (1968). Semantics of context free languages. *Mathematical Systems Theory*, 2(2), 127–145.

Lamson, B. G., Glinsky, B. C., Hawthorne, G. S., Soutter, J. C., & Russell, W. S. (1965, October). Storage and retrieval of uncoded tissue pathology diagnoses in the original English free-text form. *Proceedings of the Seventh IBM Medical Symposium*, Poughkeepsie, NY, 411–426.

Levi, J. N. (1978). *The syntax and semantics of complex nominals*. New York: Academic Press.

Lewis, D. (1972). General Semantics. In D. Davidson & G. Harman (Eds.), *Semantics of natural language* (pp. 169–218). Dordrecht: D. Reidel.

Manual of the international statistical classification of diseases, injuries, and causes of death; Ninth revision of the international classification of diseases (ICD) (1977). Geneva: World Health Organization.

Montague, R. (1970). The proper treatment of quantification in ordinary English. In R. H. Thomason (Ed.), *Formal philosophy: Selected papers of Richard Montague* (1974), New Haven, CT: Yale University Press.

Norton, L. M., & Pacak, M. G. (1983). Morphosemantic analysis of compound word forms denoting surgical procedures. *Methods of Information in Medicine, 22,* 29–36.

Pacak, M. G., & Dunham, G. S. (1979). Computers and medical language. *Medical Informatics, 4,* 13–27.

Pacak, M. G., Norton, L. M., & Dunham, G. S. (1980). Morphosemantic analysis of -ITIS forms in medical language. *Methods of Information in Medicine, 19,* 99–105.

Pacack, M. G., & Pratt, A. W. (1978). Identification and transformation of terminal morphemes in medical English Part II. *Methods of Information in Medicine, 17,* 95–100.

Partee, B. (1975). Montague grammar and transformational grammar. *Linguistic Inquiry, 6,* 203–300.

Pratt, A. W. (1973). Medicine, computers, and linguistics. In J. H. U. Brown & J. F. Dickson III (Eds.), *Advances in Biomedical Engineering, 3* (pp. 97–140), New York: Academic Press.

Pratt, A. W., & Pacak, M. (1969). Identification and transformation of terminal morphemes in medical English. *Methods of Information in Medice, 8,* 84–90.

Ross, J. R. (1972). The category squish: Endstation Hauptwort. In P. M. Peranteau, J. N. Levi, & G. C. Phares (Eds.), *Papers from the Eighth Regional Meeting Chicago Linguistic Society* (pp. 316–328). Chicago: Chicago Linguistic Society.

Systematized nomenclature of pathology (SNOP) (1965). Skokie, IL: College of American Pathologists.

Williams, E. S. (1982). The NP cycle. *Linguistic Inquiry, 13*, 277–295.

11 How One Might Automatically Identify and Adapt to a Sublanguage: An Initial Exploration

Jonathan Slocum
*Microelectronics and Computer Technology Corporation
and The University of Texas*

ABSTRACT

This chapter presents the results of the first study of sublanguages carried out at the Linguistics Research Center of the University of Texas as part of the Machine Translation project. Our goal is the improvement of both the efficiency and the quality of automated grammatical analysis of texts. We believe that the issues of speed and quality are closely related in ways that are explained later. Our approach here is to discover ways in which texts within a single sublanguage resemble each other and how texts in different sublanguages differ. We then propose a means for (semi) automatically identifying the sublanguage of a new text and optimizing a Natural Language Processing system for that text, so that overall performance may be improved.

The questions we most directly address, then, are these: Are there predictable characteristics of texts said to lie within a single sublanguage, and differences between texts said to be in different sublanguages (i.e., Is there such a phenomenon as sublanguage)? If so, how can these characteristics be described, and can the sublanguage of a text be automatically identified? If the sublanguage of a text can be identified, how does one contruct a system that can quickly, automatically, and on-the-fly, optimize its performance for that text (sublanguage)?

We begin with a very brief overview of some of the relevant properties of the LRC Machine Translation system (Lehmann et al., 1981), so that our means of gathering data and our conclusions about how one might structure an adaptive system will be apparent to the reader. Afterwards, we describe the experimental setup in which we gathered our data, present and comment on the data, discuss the significance of our findings, and conclude with answers to the questions raised earlier, along with some commentary on the questions raised by the workshop organizers.

OVERVIEW OF **METAL**

The LRC Machine Translation system is a collection of programs and data designed to automate the complete process of translating technical texts from one natural language into another. Programs include a relational database management system and several human interfaces to it (for maintaining dictionaries and grammar rules), a rule validation module (to check the syntactic integrity of all grammar rules and dictionary entries), a text-processsng system (for automatically extracting from a formatted text the "sentences" to be translated and reformatting the translation like the original), and METAL, which is the central translation engine.

METAL is composed of a set of dictionary and grammar rule definition modules, plus the linguistic rule interpreter, which effects the analysis and translation of input sentence units (Slocum & Bennett, 1982). For the purposes of this chapter, the main points of interest are the METAL parser, and the use of subject area ("provenience") tags in the dictionary entries.

The Parser

The METAL parser has evolved over a number of years, as dictated by experience in attempting the analysis and translation of large volumes of (primarily German) text: approximately 1,000 pages in the past 4 years. Based on experiments begun at SRI International in 1978 and continued at the Linguistics Research Center (Slocum, 1980, 1981), we used a simple, unadorned, all-paths Cocke-Kasami-Younger algorithm (Aho & Ullman, 1972), later augmented by top-down filtering (Pratt, 1973), and then a Left-Corner algorithm (Chester, 1980) similarly augmented (which resulted in its strongly resembling — if not actually being equivalent to — the Earley (1970) algorithm). Each step was taken only after large-scale experiments on real texts indicated that a significant efficiency gain would result.

Our latest steps took us out of the realm of purely all-paths parsers. In the fall of 1983, we began using a scheduler based on a static partial-ordering of the grammar rules: we have a stratified grammar, where all rules of a lower level are applied before any rules of a higher level and where the parser ceases to apply any rules when the application of those on a given level has resulted in one or more analyses of the input sentence. Thus, we have a "some paths" parser, and our linguists tune the grammar rules (by means of leveling) so that, if all goes well, the "correct" parse is highly likely to be among the first interpretations found. The intent, obviously, is to avoid the production of many extraneous analyses. This technique resembles that of Wotschke (1975), though there are some important operational differences, notably the lack of any "control graph" over the subgrammars. Our experience to date has amply demonstrated the effectiveness of this technique when coupled with other heuristic tools enabled by static rule ordering.

Late in 1983, we supplanted the *static scheduler* (based strictly on rule level) with a *dynamic scheduler* (based on arbitrary heuristics, which currently include both static rule level and plausibility scores [Robinson, 1974, 1975]). In this way, we aimed to have a system that can be tuned in accordance with experience, so as to apply the most likely rules first and achieve analysis, on the average, much more efficiently. It is always possible that some sentences will cause the parser to thrash, but if overall average performance is improved we will have achieved our goal.

Provenience Tags

The METAL system has always assumed the existence of *tags*, which indicate the subject-area(s) for which a given word or idiom is applicable. This is critical in our application, where the meaning (translation) of a term depends greatly on the technical area in which it is used. As it turns out, *technical area* is part of the semantics of the topic of this volume: Sublanguage. It should be no surprise when, later, we indicate how our tag scheme can be used to adapt the higher level behavior of the METAL system to the analysis of specific sublanguages. (METAL has been adapting its dictionary behavior for many years, on the basis of provenience tags.)

THE EXPERIMENTAL SETUP

In order for us to gather data for this study, the METAL parser was instrumented to record the application of all grammar rules; this was made trivial by the fact that the evaluation of all rules is carried out by a single METAL subroutine. In addition, a special data analysis program was written to summarize and present the data thus gathered. Data points included the number of attempted applications of each individual grammar rule, the number of successes/failures that resulted (conditioned on subcategorization features, including semantic tests), and the number of times that the phrase (parse tree node) built by a sucessful rule actually appeared in a sentence-level parse tree.

We then searched our files for a set of four texts of approximately equal size, two each in what were presumed to be two different sublanguages. No attempt was made to equate the sizes of the texts because, for one thing, it is not obvious what criteria one might use without risking distortion of the results. The goal was to perform a factor analysis measuring the similarities of texts supposedly in the same sublanguage, and at the same time the differences between texts supposedly in different sublanguages. We found four such texts: two are extracts from operating/maintenance manuals for a Siemens digital telephone switching system, and the other two are essentially sales brochures from Computer Gesellschaft Konstanz of West Germany (a Siemens OEM subsidiary), describing and promoting certain Siemens computer systems that CGK deals in.

Even a brief glance at the texts reveals gross differences. The two manuals are primarily directive, whereas the two computer system sales brochures are descriptive in nature. All four German texts were analyzed and translated into English by METAL, without human intervention. Table 11.1 presents data about the sizes of the texts, their average "sentence" length, the portion actually parsed by METAL, the number of resulting interpretations, and for general information the total runtime (in real time) on a Symbolics LM-2 Lisp Machine. The four test runs were made under as close to identical condi-

TABLE 11.1
A Comparison of the 4 Texts Used For Data Acquisition

	SIEMAR	*SIEAPR*	*CGKMAR*	*CGKAPR*
#Words	1112	1157	1685	1243
#Pages @250 W/P	4.45	4.63	6.74	4.97
#Sentences	284	281	144	105
#Words/Sentences	3.9	4.1	11.7	11.8
#S's Parsed	236	258	105	80
(pct)	83%	92%	73%	76%
#Parses	461	481	703	534
#Parses/Parsed-S	1.95	1.86	6.70	6.68
Run Time	1h29m55s	1h18m33s	2h07m54s	2h20m50s
(sec)	5395	4713	7674	8450
#Sec/Word	4.85	4.07	4.55	6.80

SIEMAR: a digital telephone system op/maint manual from Siemens, Mar. '83
SIEAPR: a digital telephone system op/maint manual from Siemens, Apr. '83
CGKMAR: a computer system description (sales mat'l) from CGK, Mar. '83
CGKAPR: a computer system description (sales mat'l) from CGK, Apr. '83

#Words: the number of words in the text (as sent from the sponsor for testing)
#Pages: the approximate size of the text, at 250 Words/Page
#Sentences: the exact number of sentences (or "sentence units") in the text
#Words/Sent: the average number of words per sentence
#Parsed: the number of sentences that resulted in one or more interpretations
    (pct): the percentage of the "sentences" in the text that were parsed
#Parses: the total number of readings (interpretations) derived by the grammar
#Parses/S: the average number of readings/sentence, given that it was parsed
Run Time: the elapsed (real) time for the complete TRANSLATION of the text
#Sec/Word: the averaged number of (real time) seconds expended per word, for the
    complete translation run

tions as was possible; in particular, the identical system image was used. That is, the grammar rules, dictionary entries, and so forth were all the same.

It is clear from Table 11.1 that the sentences in the CGK texts average about three times the length of the sentences in the Siemens texts. Because the texts were chosen for their approximately equal number of words, the number of sentences in the Siemens texts greatly exceeds the number of sentences in the CGK texts. (In point of fact, "sentence" must be taken figuratively, as technical texts frequently employ sentence units of simple phrases or even single words. The Siemens manuals are especially notable for this.)

THE EXPERIMENTAL DATA

Tables 11.2–11.5 summarize the data by grammatical category, for each of the four German texts. Each table presents a complete accounting of every grammar rule called (organized by Left-Hand-Side category), and the outcome of the attempt (in terms of the numbers of local successes [phrases built], failures [rules rejected for violating subcategorization conditions], and the number of phrases which eventually appeared in S-level interpretations [parse trees]). The latter number can exceed the number of phrases accepted due to sharing of nodes among multiple parse trees.

A brief review of the data reveals what one would expect: the CGK texts seem to be richer, with more of everything in the way of syntactic variety. For example, by looking in each successive table at the categories ADJ, ADV, NN (NouN), and VB — which with other constituents build to the higher level categories NP, PP, CLS (CLauSe, including main, RELative, and SUBordinate varieties) — one can see that the CGK texts exhibit more syntactic phenomena than the Siemens texts. With a little closer study, it also becomes clear that the texts do fall into two categories: the two CGK texts lie in one sublanguage (as defined by syntactic characteristics), whereas the two Siemens texts fall into another. Table 11.6 eases this comparison; alternate columns represent the absolute and rank-order (w.r.t. appearances in S readings) frequencies of occurrence of phrases in the various categories.

It also becomes clear, even at this superficial level, that the syntactic phenomena in the Siemens texts are *not* simply a subset of those in the CGK texts. Most obviously, there are constructs in the one that are entirely unrepresented in the other: parenthetical phrases of various kinds, and "ZU CLauses" (characteristic of the German equivalent of the English "in order to" construct). Thus, the language in the Siemens texts is not a subset of the language in the CGK texts. (Prescriptive inspection also reveals that the Siemens texts are not a subset of acceptable German, either, though the CGK texts appear to be so — perhaps because the former were written by engineeers, whereas the latter were presumably written by sales personnel.)

TABLE 11.2
Summary of Rule Applications for the text SIEMAR

Cat	#Calls	#Succs	pct	#Fails	pct	#Apps	#C/#A
ADJ	2094	462	22	1632	77	176	11
ADJ-LCL	1695	699	41	996	58	25	67
ADV	1163	55	4	1108	95	29	40
AST	363	5	1	358	98	1	363
AST-LCL	542	71	13	471	86	25	21
CLS	4325	670	15	3655	84	190	22
CLS-REL	2484	435	17	2049	82	3	828
CLS-SUB	2666	30	1	2636	98	4	666
COMP	719	392	54	327	45	3	239
CON	8	3	37	5	62	0	99999
CONJ	97	0	0	97	100	0	99999
DEG	1	1	100	0	0	0	99999
DET	46	0	0	46	100	0	99999
HYPHCLS	24	0	0	24	100	0	99999
HYPHNP	12	0	0	12	100	0	99999
HYPHPP	4	0	0	4	100	0	99999
LCL	1336	1218	91	118	8	18	74
NFCL	674	574	85	100	14	369	1
NFPRED	610	178	29	432	70	152	4
NN	2125	663	31	1462	68	879	2
NO	1450	915	63	535	36	1057	1
NP	18830	2798	14	16032	85	1220	15
NPMOD	3	1	33	2	66	0	99999
NST	338	46	13	292	86	14	24
PARADJ	4	4	100	0	0	2	2
PARAV	5	5	100	0	0	0	99999
PARCLS	7	5	71	2	28	0	99999
PARNP	10	10	100	0	0	12	0
PP	672	216	32	456	67	207	3
PRED	586	227	38	359	61	45	13
PREP	3	0	0	3	100	0	99999
PRFX	353	104	29	249	70	6	58
PRN	167	88	52	79	47	13	12
PRT	3	0	0	3	100	0	99999
RCL	1780	882	49	898	50	159	11
S	831	509	61	322	38	461	1
VB	15585	528	3	15057	96	244	63
VBMOD	1	1	100	0	0	0	99999
ZUCL	721	156	21	565	78	12	60

Cat: the grammatical category (of a set of 1 + PS rules)
#Calls: the number of applications of rules attempted by the parser
#Succs: the number of rules successfully applied
#Fails: the number of rules rejected on sub-categorization grounds
#Apps: the number of appearances of the phrase-type in S readings
#C/#A: the ratio of #Calls to #Appearances (a measure of utility) (99999 = "infinite")

TABLE 11.3
Summary of Rule Applications for the text SIEAPR

Cat	#Calls	#Succs	pct	#Fails	pct	#Apps	#C/#A
ADJ	2270	427	18	1843	81	184	12
ADJ-LCL	284	110	38	174	61	38	7
ADV	771	26	3	745	96	10	77
AST	274	3	1	271	98	4	68
AST-LCL	545	68	12	477	87	36	15
CLS	3786	1501	39	2285	60	212	17
CLS-REL	1653	1091	66	562	33	13	127
CLS-SUB	2217	8	0	2209	99	8	277
COMP	666	320	48	346	51	13	51
CON	12	7	58	5	41	0	99999
CONJ	65	2	3	63	96	0	99999
DEG	1	1	100	0	0	0	99999
DET	76	0	0	76	100	0	99999
HYPHCLS	18	0	0	18	100	0	99999
HYPHNP	7	0	0	7	100	0	99999
HYPHPP	3	0	0	3	100	0	99999
LCL	2313	1518	65	795	34	44	52
NFCL	845	548	64	297	35	279	3
NFPRED	647	202	31	445	68	173	3
NN	2512	696	27	1816	72	786	3
NO	1424	974	68	450	31	1084	1
NP	10616	2156	20	8460	79	1116	9
NPMOD	3	1	33	2	66	0	99999
NST	174	27	15	147	84	41	4
PARCLS	5	3	60	2	40	20	0
PARNP	12	12	100	0	0	14	99999
PP	879	345	39	534	60	199	4
PRED	614	244	39	370	60	79	7
PRFX	344	104	30	240	69	4	86
PRN	100	45	45	55	55	18	5
PRT	8	0	0	8	100	0	99999
RCL	948	570	60	378	39	229	4
S	832	504	60	328	39	481	1
VB	15251	538	3	14713	96	311	49
VBMOD	1	1	100	0	0	0	99999
ZUCL	596	63	10	533	89	40	14

A deeper analysis of the full data set reveals some even more interesting findings. Table 11.7 is a breakdown of some selected individual grammar rules, from which it is possible to discern not only what categories of phrases were built, but also how they were built (i.e., with what constituent structure). We have chosen clauses, nouns, and noun phrases for this illustration.

The rule CLS = (NP RCL) takes a Right-branching CLause (in German, a portion of a sentence with a finite verb/auxiliary at the front) and adds a

TABLE 11.4
Summary of Rule Applications for the text CGKMAR

Cat	#Calls	#Succs	pct	#Fails	pct	#Apps	#C/#A
ADJ	2409	799	33	1610	66	843	2
ADJ-LCL	393	254	64	139	35	189	2
ADV	814	101	12	713	87	169	4
AST	529	24	4	505	95	21	25
AST-LCL	725	79	10	646	89	111	6
CLS	21570	5163	23	16407	76	1071	20
CLS-REL	568	467	82	101	17	185	3
CLS-SUB	3136	147	4	2989	95	246	12
COMP	1684	717	42	967	57	193	8
CON	16	2	12	14	87	36	0
CONJ	210	9	4	201	95	8	26
DEG	1	1	100	0	0	0	99999
DET	249	8	3	241	96	0	99999
HYPHCLS	28	0	0	28	100	0	99999
HYPHNP	27	0	0	27	100	0	99999
HYPHPP	1	0	0	1	100	0	99999
LCL	3057	2650	86	407	13	1280	2
NFCL	2246	1785	79	461	20	1072	2
NFPRED	928	271	29	657	70	514	1
NN	2533	668	26	1865	73	3080	0
NO	1644	910	55	734	44	3847	0
NP	11595	1827	15	9768	84	4535	2
NPMOD	13	3	23	10	76	0	99999
NST	440	38	8	402	91	14	31
PP	1253	445	35	808	64	1272	0
PRED	814	287	35	527	64	812	1
PREP	6	2	33	4	66	0	99999
PRFX	567	395	69	172	30	29	19
PRN	332	159	47	173	52	54	6
RCL	3022	1650	54	1372	45	1399	2
S	754	742	98	12	1	703	1
VB	10706	717	6	9989	93	1272	8
VBMOD	6	0	0	6	100	0	99999
ZUCL	765	37	4	728	95	0	99999

complement NP (e.g., a subject or direct object) to it. This is the most frequently represented CLS rule in three of the four texts (clauses are usually finite and have subjects, and most have direct objects as well; it is much more
prevalent in the CGK texts because so many "sentences" in the Siemens texts
are just nouns or noun phrases. However, the rule that adds a PP complement is far more obviously common in the CGK texts than in the Siemens
texts, because the longer CGK sentences have many more complements to
add.

The rule CLS = (NFCL) appears more often in the Siemens texts (indeed,
it appears only once in the two CGK texts combined) because this construct

(in our grammar) is characteristic of an imperative — much more likely to occur in an operating/maintenance manual.

The rule CLS = (CLS PNT REL) adds a relative clause (actually modifying one of the constituents of the CLS) which has been separated from its modificand. (A transformation in the body of this PS rule produces a phrase structure representing the proper association.) The CGK texts have many more relative clauses than do the Siemens texts.

The NN rules indicate that the relative order of noun types (stems, inflected forms, and acronyms) is the same in all texts, but the relative number

TABLE 11.5
Summary of Rule Applications for the text CGKAPR

Cat	#Calls	#Succs	pct	#Fails	pct	#Apps	#C/#A
ADJ	1303	268	20	1035	79	372	3
ADJ-LCL	791	331	41	460	58	124	6
ADV	364	42	11	322	88	89	4
AST	208	10	4	198	95	62	3
AST-LCL	573	91	15	482	84	106	5
CLS	31700	10155	32	21545	67	511	62
CLS-REL	1652	1330	80	322	19	91	18
CLS-SUB	5384	193	3	5191	96	306	17
COMP	1213	678	55	535	44	94	12
CON	4	0	0	4	100	0	99999
CONJ	151	1	0	150	99	0	99999
DEG	1	1	100	0	0	6	0
DET	64	3	4	61	95	0	99999
HYPHCLS	30	0	0	30	100	0	99999
HYPHNP	25	0	0	25	100	0	99999
HYPHPP	54	0	0	54	100	0	99999
LCL	5528	4134	74	1394	25	1107	4
NFCL	2391	1696	70	695	29	580	4
NFPRED	833	198	23	635	76	688	1
NN	1428	431	30	997	69	2111	0
NO	848	579	68	269	31	2831	0
NP	23888	1911	7	21977	92	3600	6
NPMOD	15	0	0	15	100	0	99999
NST	377	21	5	356	94	8	47
PP	1300	631	48	669	51	1019	1
PRED	967	305	31	662	68	574	1
PREP	8	0	0	8	100	0	99999
PRFX	845	691	81	154	18	67	12
PRN	234	118	50	116	49	16	14
PRT	3	0	0	3	100	0	99999
RCL	3237	1704	52	1533	47	1009	3
S	660	559	84	101	15	534	1
VB	15815	564	3	15251	96	1072	14
VBMOD	3	0	0	3	100	0	99999
ZUCL	1171	462	39	709	60	0	99999

TABLE 11.6
Absolute and Relative # Appearances of grammatical phrases in S interpretations

Category	SIEMAR #App	SIEMAR #App/#S-Int	SIEAPR #App	SIEAPR #App/#S-Int	CGKMAR #App	CGKMAR #App/#S-Int	CGKAPR #App	CGKAPR #App/#S-Int
S	461	1.0	481	1.0	703	1.0	534	1.0
ADJ	176	.3817787	184	.3825364	843	1.199147	372	.6966292
ADJ-LCL	25	.05422993	38	.07900208	189	.2688478	124	.2322097
ADV	29	.06290672	10	.02079002	169	.2403983	89	.1666667
AST	1	.002169197	4	.008316008	21	.02987198	62	.1161049
AST-LCL	25	.05422993	36	.07484407	111	.1578947	106	.1985019
CLS	190	.4121475	212	.4407484	1071	1.523471	511	.9569288
CLS-REL	3	.006507592	13	.02702703	185	.2631579	91	.170412
CLS-SUB	4	.00867679	8	.01663202	246	.3499289	306	.5730337
COMP	3	.006507592	13	.022702703	193	.2745377	94	.17603
CON	0		0		36	.05112091	0	
CONJ	0		0		8	.0113798		
DEG	0		0		0		6	.01123596
DET	0		0		0		0	
HYPHCLS	0		0		0		0	
HYPHNP	0		0		0		0	
HYPHPP	0		0		0		0	
LCL	18	.03904555	44	.09147609	1280	1.820768	1107	2.073034
NFCL	369	.8004338	279	.5800416	1072	1.524893	580	1.086142
NFPRED	152	.329718	173	.3596674	514	.7311522	688	1.28839
NN	879	1.906725	786	1.634096	3080	4.381223	2111	3.953184
NO	1057	2.292842	1084	2.253638	3847	5.472262	2831	5.301498

	#App	#App/S	#App	#App/S	#App	#App/S	#App	#App/S
NP	1220	2.646421	1116	2.320166	4535	6.450925	3600	6.741573
NPMOD	0		0		0		0	
NST	14	.03036876	41	.08523909	14	.01991465	8	.01498127
PARADJ	2	.00438395	0		0		0	
PARAV	0		0		0		0	
PARCLS	0		20	.04158004	0		0	
PARNP	12	.02603037	14	.02910603	0		0	
PP	207	.4490239	199	.4137214	1272	1.809388	1019	1.90824
PRED	45	.09761388	79	.1642412	812	1.15505	574	1.074906
PREP	0		0		0		0	
PRFX	6	.01301518	4	.008316008	29	.04125178	67	.1254682
PRN	13	.02819957	18	.03742204	54	.0768136	16	.02996255
PRT	0		0		0		0	
RCL	159	.3449024	229	.4760915	1399	1.990043	1009	1.889513
VB	244	.5292842	311	.6465696	1272	1.809388	1072	2.007491
VBMOD	0		0		0		0	
ZUCL	12	.02603037	40	.08316008	0		0	

#App: the total number of appearances of a phrase of the given category in all interpretations of the sentences actually parsed

#App/S: the average number of appearances of a phrase of the given category per sentence interpretation

TABLE 11.7
Breakdown of Selected PS Rules appearing in final parse trees

Syntax Rules		Number (and Relative Frequency) of Appearances in Texts			
LHS	RHS	SIEMAR	SIEAPR	CGKMAR	CGKAPR
CLS	(NP RCL)	83(1)	43(1)	464(1)	133(2)
CLS	(PP RCL)	7(4)	23(3)	192(2)	157(1)
CLS	(RCL)	17(3)	35(2)	0(*)	36(3)
CLS	(NFCL)	59(2)	10(8)	0(*)	1(*)
CLS	(CLS PCT REL)	3(*)	11(7)	144(3)	31(5)
NN	(NST)	486(1)	528(1)	1982(1)	1648(1)
NN	(NST N-FLEX)	216(2)	164(2)	1082(2)	375(2)
NN	(ACRON)	176(3)	93(3)	15(3)	87(3)
NP	(NO)	510(1)	544(1)	969(2)	1043(2)
NP	(DET NO)	347(2)	234(2)	2039(1)	1245(1)
NP	(NP PP)	105(4)	115(3)	446(3)	340(3)
NP	(NP NP)	164(3)	111(4)	263(5)	335(4)
NP	(NP CONJ NP)	1(*)	10(*)	231(6)	158(5)
NP	(PRN)	16(5)	21(6)	284(4)	107(6)

CLS:	[main] CLause
NFCL:	Non-Finite CLause
RCL:	Right-branching CLause
REL:	RELative clause
NP:	Noun Phrase
PP:	Prepositional Phrase
NO:	NOminal (e.g., a NouN plus modifying adjectives)
NN:	NouN (built from a stem and an [optional] inflectional ending)
ACRON:	ACRONym
CONJ:	CONJunction
DET:	DETerminer
NST:	Noun STem
PCT:	PunCTuation (e.g., a comma)
PRN:	ProNoun
N-FLEX:	a noun inflectional ending

of acronyms in the Siemens texts is much higher than in the CGK texts. (Engineers love acronyms.)

The NP rules reveal a striking reversal of NP types: whereas the CGK texts display the usual pattern of German whereby nouns are very likely to have determiners (even when English would not), the Siemens texts indicate that engineers writing manuals prefer to drop the determiners (as they tend to drop most words they consider not absolutely essential). Similarly, the CGK salesmen like to modify NP's with PP's; the engineers do not. Likewise, CGK salesmen are more likely to employ appositive (NP NP) constructs and conjoined NP's. Finally, the CGK texts display a far higher incidence of pronouns than do the Siemens texts. Thus, for example, pronominal resolution is likely to be a much more severe problem in the sales domain than in that of operating/maintenance manuals.

DISCUSSION

Knowing about the existence of sublanguages is of little value unless one can take advantage of this knowledge in some fashion. Here we discuss how one might detect the existence of a particular sublanguage and consequently adjust parameters that optimize the system for that sublanguage.

Detection

There are two obvious, not necessarily mutually exclusive, means for identifying the sublanguage of a new text. First, the system can ask the user about the text — probably through a menu-type of interface — in terms that are easy to comprehend and respond to reliably (e.g., "Is this a manual?"; "What technical subject area does this text cover?"). Second, the system could scan the text, looking up the words in its dictionary and determining from relative frequencies of pre-stored subject-area tags what the most likely topic of the text is. (Walker & Amsler, this volume, discuss such a technique.) This might not suffice to identify the type of text (e.g., a manual), but then this is not yet known to be the case. One might, for example, compare the number of determiners with the number of nouns and/or consider the relative incidence of acronyms.

The METAL system always employed subject-area tag coding in dictionary entries for translation purposes (and also for idiom analysis). We should be able to make use of these tags to identify automatically the subject-area of any text at hand, as long as it lies in one of the areas covered by the system dictionary. (If the text lies outside the METAL's lexical domain, the system cannot be used effectively in any case.) Thus, a completely automatic determination of the provenience area of any text in the areas covered by the dictionary seems feasible.

Deriving Advantage

Again, knowing what sublanguage is in use is not by itself valuable. One must be able to take beneficial action based on such knowledge. We recall the new METAL dynamic scheduler (invented for reasons entirely independent of the existence of sublanguage). The grammar rules are manually stratified (assigned to one of a number of static levels) by the LRC linguists. In its static form, the scheduler caused the parser to invoke all possible lower level rules before any higher level ones; in its new, dynamic form, the parser schedules rule application by a combination of static level and a plausibility factor (a "weight" attached to each phrase satisfying a rule constituent). That is, certain phrase readings are naturally preferred over others (we use the weights at the S level to select "the best" analysis for translation), and the dynamic scheduler attempts to alter the parser's activity by using these weights to bias the otherwise static rule stratification.

The experimental data presented here indicate that there are significant differences in the syntactic rule sets and consequently in their optimal application order, vis-à-vis the particular sublanguage. Findings like these are supported by other workers in the field (e.g., Kittredge & Lehrberger, 1982). The METAL dynamic scheduler can easily be modified so that the rule selection strategy is biased by the identification of the sublanguage of the text at hand. We intend to perform this modification and carry out further experiments along this vein in the near future.

CONCLUSIONS

We have independently determined that sublanguages do indeed appear to exist (i.e., that there seem to be reliable and measurable differences), and furthermore that sublanguages can be described on syntactic grounds (among others). We have adduced two simple, inexpensive techniques for automatically identifying the sublanguage of a text. We have described how at least one NLP system (METAL) can be modified to take advantage of sublanguage identification (even more than it does now) using tools already present in the system. What remains to be seen—and what we will address in future experiments—is whether, and to what extent, the advantage gained will be significant. We have reason to believe that such modification not only will enhance the runtime performance of our Machine Translation system by reducing the number of grammar rules applied (currently the limiting performance factor in METAL [Slocum, 1983]), but also will improve the quality of its translations by further reducing the number of incorrect readings that compete for translation attention.

Regarding some of the questions raised by the workshop organizers, we can make the following comments based on our experience (including the experiment reported herein). We are not aware of any sublanguages for which any NLP system is currently able to obtain correct sentence analyses with high reliability. However, the data we present here (and our in-house examination of the translation results produced by these runs) indicate that the

METAL system now appears to perform in the 80% range for documents like the Siemens texts used here. Furthermore, based on our history of continual quality improvement (Slocum, 1983), we see no reason why a 90% accuracy figure for such manuals could not be attained with current technology. (In our particular situation, unfortunately, Siemens has recently directed us away from the telephone manuals toward other, much more difficult types of material, such as the CGK sales brochures used here. Thus, we ourselves do not expect to attain 90% reliability in the foreseeable future. Our conjecture must therefore be taken with the proper dose of salt.)

It is certainly the case that, for ultimate understanding in ANY domain, an NLP system will have to be augmented with a wide variety of powerful tools for syntactic, semantic, and pragmatic analysis. For appropriate response at the 90% level within some sublanguages, this may not be necessary. We certainly hope that such powerful tools are not necessary, inasmuch as it is obvious that they will not exist for quite some time — probably not in this century. For example, little if anything is known about discourse structures that can be used in an NLP system with even minimal reliability (50%?) in large-scale application. Indeed, exceptionally few NLP workers have made a serious attempt at large-scale application of the techniques they espouse.

As for the question of the representation and utilization of sublanguage characteristics, there seems to be no objective evidence whatever that one school of thought is necessarily superior to any other. No one has tried to come up with empirical evidence bearing on these arguments, and such questions as are raised about sufficiency in application are banished to the rarely trod ("uninteresting") realm of "implementation details." In such a climate, objective arguments are difficult to muster.

Accordingly, little information about sublanguage characteristics can be discovered in an automatic or semiautomatic fashion for a new domain. But it does seem that the type of data we present here can be used to tune a grammar automatically for syntactic reliability. Whether this is ultimately beneficial has yet to be determined.

REFERENCES

Aho, A. V., & Ullman, J. D. (1972). *The theory of parsing, translation, and compiling, Vol. 1.* Englewood Cliffs, NJ: Prentice Hall.

Chester, D. (1980). A parsing algorithm that extends phrases. *American Journal of Computational Linguistics, 6* (2), 71–86.

Earley, J. An efficient context-free parsing algorithm. *Communications of the Association for Computing Machinery, 13*(2), 94–102.

Kittredge, R., & Lehrberger, J. (1982). *Sublanguage: Studies of language in restricted semantic domains.* New York: de Gruyter.

Lehmann, W. P., Bennett, W. S., Slocum, J., Smith, H., Pfluger, S. M. V., & Eveland, S. A. (1981). *The METAL system,* (Final Technical Report RADC-TR-80-374). Griffis AFB, NY:

Rome Air Development Center. (Available as Report AO-97896, National Technical Information Service, U. S. Department of Commerce, Springfield, VA.)

Pratt, V. R. (1973, August). A linguistics oriented programming language. *Proceedings of the Third International Joint Conference on Artificial Intelligence* (pp. 372–381). Stanford University, CA.

Robinson, J. J. (1974, April). Performance grammars. *Proceedings of the IEEE Speech Symposium,* Carnegie-Mellon University, Pittsburgh, PA.

Robinson, J. J. (1975, October-November). *A tuneable performance grammar.* Paper presented at the Thirteenth Annual Meeting of the Association for Computational Linguistics. Boston, MA.

Slocum, J. (1980, June). An experiment in machine translation. *Coling-80 Abstracts: Proceedings of the 18th Annual Meeting of the Association for Computational Linguistics,* (pp. 163-167). Philadelphia.

Slocum, J. (1981). A practical comparison of parsing strategies for machine translation and other natural language processing purposes [microfilm]. Ann Arbor, MI: University Microfilms International.

Slocum, J. (1983, February). A status report on the LRC Machine translation system. *Proceedings of the ACL Conference on Applied Natural Language Processing,* Santa Monica, CA.

Slocum, J. & Bennett, W. S. (1982, July). The LRC machine translation system: An application of state-of-the-art text and natural language processing techniques to the translation of technical manuals. (Working Paper LRC-82-1) Linguistics Research Center, University of Texas.

Wotschke, E. M. (1975). *Ordered grammars with equivalence classes: Some formal and linguistic aspects.* Unpublished doctoral dissertation, University of California, Los Angeles.

12 Discovering Sublanguage Structures

Lynette Hirschman
Research and Development Division
SDC — A Burroughs Company
Paoli, Pennsylvania

ABSTRACT

To date, automatic language processing has been possible only within the tightly constrained context of a sublanguage. The generality of the sublanguage approach is dependent on an ability to adapt (or port) existing systems to new domains (sublanguages). Successful portability requires the definition of a restricted set of semantic relations adequate for natural language processing and the rapid, cost-effective acquisition of these relations for each new domain. This chapter explores a specific approach that identifies a limited set of relations for language processing and discusses the techniques available to automate the acquisition of this information.

The approach is based on the Linguistic String Project system, which uses a domain-independent grammar, augmented by a very limited set of domain-specific relations. The kinds of domain-specific relations include a set of distributionally based semantic classes and the relations between these semantic classes. These relations form the basis for stating allowable subject-verb-object and host-modifier combinations of classes, used to eliminate incorrect parses. The basis for automating the discovery procedure is the distributional hypothesis: words containing similar kinds of information will appear in similar syntactic environments.

The chapter summarizes the results from a series of experiments on the automatic generation of sublanguage semantic classes and sublanguage semantic patterns. It discusses the problems of omitted material and the phenomenon of phrasal attributes, and how both of these affect distributional data. It concludes with some possible ways to approach the circularity inherent in the distributional approach, where obtaining good distributional data depends on a correct syntactic analysis, but the correct syntactic analysis depends on having available the semantic classes and patterns of classes for the particular domain.

211

INTRODUCTION

To date, natural language text processing has been limited primarily to restricted domains that constitute sublanguages. The success of this approach depends on the *robustness,* or accuracy, of the processing system and on its *portability,* in the sense of adaptability of a system to new sublanguages. Both robustness and portability rely on rapid, cost-effective acquisition of the sublanguage semantics. This chapter describes an approach to a portable discovery procedure for sublanguage semantics, based on a domain-independent syntactic analysis. Underlying this approach is Harris' (1947, 1968) distributional hypothesis and Sager's (1972, 1978, 1981) computational framework for processing sublanguage texts.

Automatic discovery of sublanguage structures is an extremely ambitious goal. It has resisted solution for well over 10 years. However, pursuit of this goal has produced important results along the way: a more sophisticated understanding of sublanguage structure and its relation to the language as a whole; a principled approach to domain-dependent semantic description; and an approach to the interaction of syntax and semantics. Once we are able to tailor a general description of the syntax and semantics of a language to a particular domain without the intervention of a trained linguist (and preferably with limited intervention from a subject matter expert), then we will have achieved an extremely important technological breakthrough: a portable natural language processing system.

The research described in this chapter is the result of some 10 year's work investigating automatic generation of sublanguage classes and patterns. The bulk of the work (1973–1981) was performed at the Linguistic String Project at New York University. The remainder has been carried out at SDC, but in close contact and collaboration with the research at NYU. These experiments are the result of collaboration with a number of people: Naomi Sager, Ralph Grishman, Carol Friedman, Elaine Marsh and Ngo Thanh Nhan. Many of the experimental results have not been published, except in research reports on supporting grants. This is because, individually, each experiment addressed a particular problem, only to turn up a different problem that still prevented us from reliably automating discovery procedures for sublanguage structures. Taken collectively, however, these experiments have contributed to our understanding of the structure of sublanguage grammars and the possibilities of automating their discovery.

SUBLANGUAGE AND SEMANTICS

Most natural language processing systems have a *semantic* component that produces a representation of the meaning of the input. In addition to producing a meaning representation, the semantic component is also responsible for ruling out incorrect analyses of the input. That is, the semantic component requires a (limited) model of the domain in order to interpret and screen its input. The restriction of processing to a sublanguage is one way to narrow the domain sufficiently to provide an adequate semantics. In this respect, the success of the sublanguage approach in natural language processing is analogous to the success of expert systems applications in tightly constrained problem domains.

Even within a restricted domain, the development of a suitable semantic component is problematic. What information belongs in a semantic component — how deep should the model be? How is the semantic component integrated with other components, for instance, the syntax? And finally, can an acquisition procedure be defined, so that the system can be ported to different domains?

In natural language, the definition of a semantic component has been approached from two directions: either the semantic component has been developed independently of the syntactic component, or it has been derived from the syntactic component. Certain applications, such as data base query applications, come with a limited domain model already specified, namely, the data base schema. The INTELLECT system (Harris, 1978), for example, relies heavily on the data base schema to define its semantic component. Some systems have created their semantics to interface with the data base schema, as in the TEAM system (Grosz, 1983), or the ASK system (Thompson & Thompson, 1983). These systems provide a user interface to facilitate the acquisition of domain-specific information from the user. However, these approaches still require substantial time from the subject matter expert and depend heavily on the expert's reliability, linguistic consistency, and, often, linguistic sophistication.

In applications not involving a data base, there is no predetermined model of the domain. In this case, some researchers have focused on modeling the domain largely independent of linguistic considerations (Schank & Abelson, 1977). Such systems have difficulty in bounding the acquisition of semantic information — it is very difficult to determine when the semantic model is finished. A second problem is the definition of a mapping between syntactic structures and the independently derived semantic structures.

The approach described in this chapter is the derivation of a (shallow) semantic model from the analysis of a sample of texts in the domain. The approach is based on Harris' (1968) *distributional hypothesis*, which relates syntactic distribution of words (called *entities*) to their informational content: "...the meaning of entities, and the meaning of grammatical relations among them, is related to the restriction of combinations of these entities relative to other entities" (p. 12). The distributional hypothesis, coupled with the concept of a sublanguage, provides the basis for a portable natural language processing system. According to Harris, a sublanguage grammar shares its syntax with that of the general language and is distinguished from the general language by special co-occurrence patterns of word classes that differ from those of the general language. Because for Harris co-occurrence patterns reflect what is expressible in a sublanguage (its semantics), his claim is that syntax is general to a language as a whole and hence is completely portable;[1] therefore the semantics can be derived by a study of the words that occur in given syntactic patterns (i.e., which kinds of subjects can go with what verbs, or which adjectives can modify what nouns). The derivation of the semantic information draws on the domain-independent syntax, thus ensuring that the tools to derive the semantics are themselves portable.

THE DOMAIN INFORMATION SCHEMA

As mentioned earlier, the two functions of a semantic component are (a) to generate a meaning representation of the input, and (b) to rule out incorrect interpretations of the input. This second function is partially filled by a semantic selection mechanism, which accepts or rejects syntactic constructions, based on semantic compatibility between predicate and arguments (e.g., allowable subject-verb-object combinations) or between head and modifiers (e.g., noun-adjective combinations). To maintain portability of the entire system, it is essential to devise a domain-independent selection mechanism that accepts sublanguage-specific patterns as data to drive semantic selection. To create a general framework for expressing semantic information, we have developed the concept of a Domain Information Schema (DIS) (Grishman, Hirschman & Friedman, 1982, 1983).

The relations in the Domain Information Schema consist of:

1. semantic word classes specific to the sublanguage;
2. predicate-argument relations stated in terms of allowable co-occurrence of semantic classes;
3. modifier-host relations (also in terms of semantic classes), including adjective-noun, noun-noun, and prepositional phrase-host combinations;
4. limited kinds of other semantic relations, including conjunctional equivalence classes, classes causing phrasal attributes differing from the head noun, and functional dependencies among certain semantic classes.

---

[1]In certain cases, the syntax of the general language may need augmentations, e.g., for telegraphic style (Marsh & Sager, 1982). For efficiency purposes, it may also prove desirable to remove those syntactic constructions not needed in the particular sublanguage (Grishman, Nhan, Marsh, & Hirschman, 1984). Nonetheless, the expectation is that the syntactic description remains relatively sublanguage independent.

A general mechanism draws on the domain-specific information in the DIS, in order to enforce semantic selection for a particular domain. Our claim is that the Domain Information Schema is an adequate semantics for certain types of natural language processing. The DIS underlies meaning representations in terms of an information format (Hirschman & Sager, 1982), a relational database schema (Chi, Sager, Tick, & Lyman, 1983), and a predicate calculus expression (Grishman & Hirschman, 1978).

DISCOVERING THE DOMAIN INFORMATION SCHEMA

The distributional hypothesis forms the basis for a discovery procedure for elements of the Domain Information Schema: words that share syntactic environments will also share similarities in their information content, that is, will belong to the same informational class. Thus, a distributional analysis of words in their syntactic environments will yield the set of semantic classes for a sublanguage. Once the classes have been established, the patterns of classes (the relations between classes) can be obtained by substituting class names for words in the syntactic analysis of sentences of the corpus.

Over the past 10 years, we have performed a number of experiments to test the distributional hypothesis and the associated discovery procedure. In theory, the procedure is simple:

- Select a sample corpus of the sublanguage.
- Obtain the sublanguage semantic classes by grouping together into a class those words occurring in similar syntactic environments; these are the semantic classes for the sublanguage.
- For each syntactic relation of interest, collect the patterns of semantic classes found occurring in that relation (e.g., subject-verb-object) in the sample corpus; these patterns (using class names instead of individual words) are the sets of predicate-argument and modifier-host relations for the Domain Information Schema.

In practice, of course, there are many complications. Our experiments, aimed at carrying out this program, have raised a number of problems, which are discussed in the remainder of this chapter.

Validity   There is the question of whether the distributional hypothesis is valid: Is it possible to define valid (and useful) semantic classes based on distributional criteria?

Refinements to Remove Noise   Not all syntactic environments are equally good for obtaining coherent semantic classes. Certain operators (particularly prepositions) have too wide a distribution, which causes some "noise" or blurring of the patterns. In other cases, contextually redundant material has been omitted or zeroed, causing peculiar patterns in the distribution. Also, certain phrases have a distribution different from that of the head of the phrase. This is the phrasal attribute problem: *stiff neck* is not a kind of neck, but a condition. This is another source of noise in the statistical analysis.

Classification of Individual Words   If statistical techniques are used, these will be effective only for the frequently occurring cases. How do we capture infrequently occurring words, or new words as they appear?

Domain-Independent Semantic Mechanism   For the semantic component to rule out incorrect interpretations, it requires domain-specific semantic information. However, to preserve portability, the semantic mechanism must be domain-independent. Can the DIS serve as data to a general semantic mechanism?

Circularity   There is some hidden circularity in the procedure outlined earlier. To obtain the semantic classes, we group together words occurring in similar syntactic environments, for example, as subject of the same predicate or modifier of the same host. However, this presupposes that those syntactic relations are available. But, as noted earlier, the correct parsing of sublanguage text requires that we have the sublanguage classes and patterns of classes, hence the circularity.

VERIFYING THE DISTRIBUTIONAL HYPOTHESIS

Our first series of experiments was directed at verification of the distributional hypothesis. The goal was to use statistical clustering techniques to group together words occurring in the same syntactic environment, based on a syntactic analysis of a sample corpus. We worked with two different sublanguages. One was a corpus of six pharmacology articles on digitalis (400 sentences) (Hirschman, Grishman, & Sager, 1975); the second was a corpus of follow-up radiology reports on 19 cancer patients (350 sentences).

Table 12.1 shows a sample of the radiology material, namely, all 31 occurrences of the verb *show*. Inspection of the occurrences shows a fairly regular pattern: the most common type of subject is some kind of test (*film, x-ray, examination, plate, scan, series, urinalysis* account for all but four occurrences). We would expect our automatic procedure to group these words together. In the object position, there is more variation: some objects record some kind of normal finding (*clearing, improvement, finding*), abnormal finding (*abnormality, scarring, thickening, infiltration, clouding, lesion,*

TABLE 12.1
Occurrences of the verb *show*

SUBJECT	VERB	OBJECT
hilar apex and area	show	no abnormalities
chest	shows	evidence of metastatic disease
examination	shows	the same findings
examination	shows	some scarring and thickening
lung field	shows	some increase in their markings
chest films	show	essential changes
chest films	show	no change
chest film	shows	same infiltration
repeat film	shows	some changes in left apex
chest film	shows	clouding
chest film	shows	no evidence of fluid, metastases or cardiomegaly
films of chest, spine and pelvis	show	no evidence of metastatic disease
films of chest, spine and pelvis	show	no evidence of metastatic disease
films of chest and shoulder	show	no callus formation
chest film	shows	no improvement
flat plate of abdomen	shows	lumbar spine to be riddled with metastatic areas
brain scan	shows	midline lesion
metastatic series	shows	osteolytic metastases
the dorsal spine	shows	degenerative changes
urinalysis	shows	1% proteinuria
chest x-ray	showed	no change
chest x-ray	showed	no change
x-rays of spine	showed	extreme arthritic change
chest x-ray	showed	no metastatic disease
chest x-ray	showed	no evidence of metastasis
chest x-ray	showed	no evidence of metastatic disease
chest x-ray	showed	no evidence of active disease
chest x-ray	showed	radiation fibrosis
x-ray	shows	fracture of right clavicle
chest x-ray	shows	lungs to be within normal limits
chest x-ray	showed	marked reactions

metastasis, proteinuria, fibrosis, fracture), or *change* (six occurrences), or *evidence* (seven occurrences). Inasmuch as there appear to be at least 4 distinct classes here, we would hope that the automatic word class generation procedure would distinguish these classes on the basis of other environments.

The automatic word class generation involved a number of steps. First, we needed a syntactic analysis of the sentences. The simplest approach (used in our initial experiments) was to analyze the sentences manually into verb-argument and host-modifier relations; thus, only the correct syntactic analysis was recorded for each sentence. These relations were then input into a series of programs that record each word and its syntactic relations to the other words. Several such relational tuples are shown in Table 12.2, corresponding to the first three sentences in Table 12.1. Note the morphological regularization that has taken place in generating the relations: singular and plural affixes have been removed and adjectival forms have been reduced to their noun form (e.g., *hilar = > hilum*). Note also that prepositions are treated as operators similar to verbs, with the prepositional object as first argument and the host as the second argument.

A second program took the operator-argument tuples and automatically generated three-place relations consisting of the name of a syntactic relation and a pair of words in that relation. Some sample tuples are shown in Table 12.3. For example, the operator-argument tuple *show apex abnormality* gives rise to three new tuples:

VERB-SUBJ	*SHOW*	*APEX*
VERB-OBJ	*SHOW*	*ABNORMALITY*
SUBJ-OBJ	*APEX*	*ABNORMALITY*

These tuples form the input for an automatic clustering program. This program compares all words in the corpus pairwise and assigns a non-zero similarity coefficient to any pair of words occurring in the same syntactic environment. Two words occur in the same environment if they occur in tuples differing only by the two words being compared. Using the examples from Table 12.3, the words *apex* and *area* would receive a non-zero similarity coefficient because they both occur as the third element in the relation *VERB-SUBJ show_____*; likewise, *abnormality* and *evidence* would receive a non-zero similarity coefficient (on the basis of occurrence in *VERB-OBJ show _____*). The value of the similarity coefficient for a pair of words is related to the number of common environments they occur in and to the frequency

TABLE 12.2
Tuples generated from first three sentences in
Table 1

OPERATOR	*ARG1*	*ARG2*
show	apex	abnormality
show	area	abnormality
show	chest	evidence
of	disease	evidence
host-adjunct	disease	metastatis
host-adjunct	apex	hilum
host-adjunct	abnormality	no
show	examination	finding
host-adjunct	finding	same
host-adjunct	finding	the

TABLE 12.3
Relations used in automatic clustering (from Table 12.2)

RELATION TYPE	ELEMENT1	ELEMENT2
VERB-SUBJ	show	apex
VERB-OBJ	show	abnormality
SUBJ-OBJ	apex	abnormality
VERB-SUBJ	show	area
VERB-OBJ	show	abnormality
SUBJ-OBJ	area	abnormality
HOST-ADJUNCT	apex	hilum
HOST-ADJUNCT	abnormality	no
VERB-SUBJ	show	chest
VERB-OBJ	show	evidence
SUBJ-OBJ	chest	evidence
VERB-SUBJ	of	disease
VERB-OBJ	of	evidence
SUBJ-OBJ	disease	evidence
HOST-ADJUNCT	disease	metastasis
VERB-SUBJ	show	examination
VERB-OBJ	show	finding
SUBJ-OBJ	examination	finding
HOST-ADJUNCT	finding	same
HOST-ADJUNCT	finding	the

of occurrence of each word in the common environment. The similarity coefficients are then used as input into a clustering program which groups together words whose average similarity coefficient exceeds a threshold value. The threshold value is chosen to give the "best" clusters, that is, clusters that are both the most homogeneous and capture the largest number of words.

The results of this processing for the pharmacology material are described in the work of (Hirschman et al., 1975). In general, the automated clustering algorithm produced word classes that corresponded to the major classes identified by a manual sublanguage analysis of the material. Because of the statistical nature of the program, it identified only frequently occurring words and classes. The results for the radiology corpus were similar to those obtained for the pharmacology material: in general, the program identified the most frequently occurring members of the major classes.

A third experiment used a set of automatically generated syntactic analyses of the radiology material. These analyses were produced by the LSP English Grammar, specialized for use with a telegraphic style and medical sublanguage (Hirschman, Grishman & Sager, 1976; Sager et al., 1980). The set of syntactic analyses consisted of the first parse generated by the English Grammar for each of the 350 sentences. The results of the automatic clustering at two thresholds are shown in Tables 12.4 and 12.5. Note that the out-

TABLE 12.4
Clusters generated at a threshold of .300

8 CLUSTERS OF 2 WORDS GENERATED	
EVIDENCE	*{BAD CLASS: EVIDENCE SHOULD BE TRANSPARENT}*
FOR	*{FOR SHOULD NOT BE USED IN CLUSTERING}*
X-RAY	*{TEST CLASS}*
FILM	
DISEASE	*{INDIC(ator) CLASS}*
LESION	
LUMBAR	*{ADJSPINE CLASS}*
LUMBODORSAL	
EXAM	*{VISIT CLASS}*
EXAMINATION	
1 CLUSTERS OF 3 WORDS GENERATED	
PELVIS	
SPINE	*{BODY-PART CLASS}*
CHEST	
0 CLUSTERS OF 4 WORDS GENERATED	

put from the clustering program shows only classes not subsumed by a larger class. Thus, Table 12.4 reports 8 two-word classes, but shows only the 5 classes that are not subsets of the three-word class.

REFINEMENTS TO AUTOMATED DISTRIBUTIONAL ANALYSIS

We performed the experiments just described in order to test the validity of the distributional hypothesis. Analysis of the preliminary results showed that the hypothesis was reasonable, but that our implementation required certain adjustments and refinements. Many of these refinements were incorporated into the programs that eventually produced Tables 12.4 and 12.5 as output; a few other refinements required such major changes that they were not implemented.

First, the decision to use pairs of words in a given syntactic relation (e.g., VERB-SUBJECT or VERB-OBJECT, as shown in Table 12.3) caused problems that could have been avoided had we used the full environment (e.g., VERB-SUBJECT-OBJECT). The reason for using pairs was to maximize the number of occurrences of each pair. There clearly would have been many fewer occurrences of words with identical full environments. Although we recognized this as a problem, we did not revise the implementation to use full environments, partly because this would have drastically reduced the number of occurrences available for clustering. In hindsight, however, this approach may well have given more accurate results. As discussed later, the fact that we did not use full environments caused us to make certain other refinements.

One refinement that was implemented was to discard certain "noisy" operators. Certain operators have too wide a distribution, especially when the full environment is not preserved in a single relation. These include operators consisting of certain commonly occurring prepositions (*of, in, on,* etc.); also *be* and the part-whole operators (e.g., *consist of, have*), which carry the important semantic information in the pairing of subject and object. In addition, the relation SUBJ-OBJ was not useful in clustering and was ignored.

We also refined the algorithm to compare only operators of like argument number and type: arguments were distinguished according to whether or not

TABLE 12.5
Clusters generated at a threshold of .200

---

13 CLUSTERS OF 2 WORDS GENERATED

EVIDENCE	{*BAD CLASS: EVIDENCE SHOULD BE TRANSPARENT*}
FOR	{*FOR SHOULD NOT BE USED IN CLUSTERING*}
DISEASE LESION	{*INDIC(ator) CLASS*}
REVEAL SHOW	{*SHOW CLASS*}
FROM OVER	{*PREPTIME CLASS*}
LATERAL PA	{*TESTVIEW CLASS*}
LUMBAR LUMBODORSAL	{*ADJSPINE CLASS*}
EXAM EXAMINATION	{*VISIT CLASS*}

3 CLUSTERS OF 3 WORDS GENERATED
(not shown, subsumed in larger cluster)

2 CLUSTERS OF 4 WORDS GENERATED

X-RAY PELVIS SPINE CHEST	{*BODY-PART CLASS*} *with incorrect member X-RAY*
SPINE PELVIS X-RAY FILM	*BODY-PART* *TEST CLASSES:* *bad cluster*

0 CLUSTERS OF 5 WORDS GENERATED

---

they were themselves operators. This distinguished the lowest level operators of the language (verbs taking as subject and object only nouns) from the higher level operators (verb taking complex phrases as subject or object). No similarity coefficients were generated for operators of different argument number and/or type. Had we used full environments rather than pairs, this refinement would have been largely unnecessary.

The identification of phrasal attributes was perhaps the most important refinement to come out of these experiments. Certain phrases have a semantic class different from the class (or attribute) of the syntactic head of the phrase. The phrasal attribute depends on both the head and its modifiers. The distribution of the phrase will thus differ from the distribution of the head noun without its modifiers. Certain words are *transparent* with respect to their distribution. When a transparent word appears as the head of a noun phrase, the semantic class associated with the noun phrase is derived from the class associated with its left or right adjunct. That is, the semantic class of the phrase differs from the semantic class of the head. We can see this in the distribution of *evidence* in the radiology material in Table 12.1. *Evidence* should be treated as a transparent word, since the phrase *evidence of metastatic disease* shows the same distribution as its right adjunct, *metastatic disease*:

> *chest x-ray showed no metastatic disease;*
> *chest x-ray showed no evidence of metastatic disease.*

In the experiments described in the preceding section, *evidence* was not treated as transparent, giving rise to a bad cluster in Table 12.4 and 12.5. We did, however, recognize a number of transparent operators in generating the results shown in Tables 12.4 and 12.5: modal operators (*will, be capable of, need, seem*), aspectuals (*become, begin*), and operators of occurrence (*occur, take place, manifest, fact*). However, in work following the clustering experiments shown in Tables 12.4 and 12.5, the number of transparent classes increased to include dimension words (*dose, amount, period*), part words (*part, portion*), kind words (*kind, type, style*), repetition words (*repetition, history*), and evidential words (*evidence, indication*).

In addition to transparent classes, later work also revealed a number of other types of phrasal attributes, including *computed attribute* constructions. A computed attribute construction results from the interaction of a head and an adjunct, but is less regular than the transparent constructions described above. To take some examples from a medical sublanguage, expressions such as *stiff neck, fractured zygoma,* and *upset stomach* have the distribution of the class of abnormal findings (*stiffness, fracture*) and not that of parts of the body. In the medical sublanguage, we can find sentences such as *patient had a stiff neck,* but not *patient had a neck.* It is not clear how to 'discover' these patterns via distributional techniques, because one of their identifying characteristics is that they violate otherwise regular distributional patterns. The input that generated the clusters in Tables 12.4 and 12.5 did not take the computed attribute constructions into account. (The DIS in current use does take these constructions into account, as explained later).

The radiology material also presented problems with omitted (zeroed) material that were not present in the pharmacology. Due in part to the telegraphic style of the radiology reports, there were many more instances of omitted material. In fact, precisely those elements that could be uniquely reconstructed from context were omitted. For example, because the reports were *radiology* reports, the word *x-ray* was often omitted. This can be seen in the sample occurrences of the verb *show* in Table 12.1. The second sentence, *chest shows evidence of metastatic disease,* should be understood as *chest* **x-ray** *shows evidence of metastatic disease.*

Zeroing is the converse of transparency: an omitted word must be reinserted to restore the regularity of occurrence, whereas the transparent word should be ignored. Unfortunately, it is very difficult to distinguish whether we have a zeroing or a transparency on a strictly distributional basis. Perhaps the clearest distinction so far is that the transparent classes appear to be general classes of English, whereas the zeroing is highly sublanguage specific. The clustering program made no attempt to fill in any of the zeroed material, which resulted in some incorrect clusters. For example, in Table 12.5, *x-ray* appears in a cluster with body part words *pelvis, spine, chest,* as a result of zeroing. Initially, our hope was that the effect of these zeroings would be washed out statistically by occurrences without zeroing. To some extent this was true, but the effect was to make the clustering results highly dependent on the particular threshold chosen. By using a high threshold (as in Table 12.4), it was possible to get "good" word classes: *x-ray* and *film* in one class, *chest* and other parts of the body in a different class. However, a high threshold also meant that many words of medium frequency were missed (such as the SHOW class, including *show* and *reveal*). On the other hand, lowering the threshold caused *x-ray* to merge with the BODY-PART class, shown in Table 12.5.

CLASSIFYING INDIVIDUAL WORDS VIA PATTERN MATCHING

Because clustering is statistical, it cannot classify infrequently occurring words. Therefore, we need a different method to assign semantic classes to such words. To do this, we developed a two-pass method, which consisted of classifying the frequently occurring words, followed by a second pass to classify the remaining words on the basis of their distributional similarity to already classified words. This also provides an approach to classifying new words as they are encountered in a sublanguage.

Our approach was to match the environment of a new word to environments that characterize known words already assigned to a semantic class. For example, if we find the sentence containing the unclassified word *mammogram—Mammogram shows no metastic disease—*then *mammogram* belongs in the same TEST class as *x-ray, film, scan,* etc.

How did we identify characteristic environments? The most straightforward way was simply to collect the known patterns of semantic classes in the sublanguage, together with their frequencies of occurrence. Provided that the new word occurred in an environment that consisted partially or wholly of already subclassified words, we then compared this environment with known environments and picked the most likely one(s). To automate the process fully, we needed to generate the semantic patterns of the sublanguage (given, for example, by the tuples shown in Table 12.2). We also had to provide a syntactic analysis for the sentence containing the new word.

We performed an experiment to test the automatic generation of word class assignment based on matching the environments of known semantic word classes to a new word occurring in that environment. This experiment was done for a corpus of hospital discharge summaries (Sager et al., 1980). An initial set of 250 sentences (eight summaries) were processed, and the subclass patterns generated. Then an additional document, containing 66 sentences, was parsed. The dictionary contained word class information (e.g., noun or verb) for the "new" words, but no subclass (semantic) information. There was a total of 116 new words; 90 occurred only once, and only three occurred more than three times. Worse yet, many words occurred with little or no syntactic environment (they were single-word entries, e.g., *Medication: Percodan, cytozan.*). Of the original 116, only 57 produced some pattern of words/word classes; of these, only 42 occurred in environments containing an already known word. These 42 words were the only ones suitable for our experiment; they were passed to the MATCH program to find classes occurring in similar environments.

The MATCH program took as its inputs the data base of known patterns of classes and a set of environments containing the new word. It produced a listing of all matching environments (Table 12.6). For example, the word *dyspnea* (labored breathing) occurred once in the test sample, in the sentence *She had an episode of severe dyspnea.* This gave rise to the following patterns containing *dyspnea* (where *episode* belongs to class PERIOD, and *severe* to class AMOUNT):

HOST-ADJUNCT	AMOUNT	dyspnea
OF	PERIOD	dyspnea

Given the data from MATCH, the procedure was to choose as the best candidate the class that: (a) matched on the maximum number of patterns; (b) matched on the patterns with highest frequency. In the case of *dyspnea,* both INDIC and DIAG classes matched on both patterns, but INDIC had the greater frequency of occurrence (4 + 22 occurrences vs. 6 + 2 occurrences for DIAG). In this case, the INDIC class was the correct classification for *dyspnea.*

Overall, the results were inconclusive: using the methodology outlined above, 24 of the 42 words were correctly classified by one of the top three candidates generated by the MATCH program. The MATCH program included the correct class (though not necessarily as one of the top three candidates) in 74% of the cases (31 words). These results are summarized in Table 12.7.

Why were the results not as clean as we had hoped? There were several contributing factors. One was the sparseness of occurrences of the new

TABLE 12.6
Subclasses Occurring in the Same Environment as *Dyspnea*

NEW WORD: DYSPNEA

PATTERNS FOUND FOR NEW WORD: DYSPNEA

Operator	*Argument 1*	*Argument 2*
1. HOST-ADJUNCT	SUBCLASS AMOUNT	*
2. OF	SUBCLASS PERIOD	*

WORDS OCCURRING IN A SIMILAR ENVIRONMENT

SUBCLASS BODYMEAS	1	OCC. IN PATTERN NO. 1
SUBCLASS END	1	OCC. IN PATTERN NO. 1
SUBCLASS INDIC	4	OCC. IN PATTERN NO. 2
SUBCLASS DIAG	6	OCC. IN PATTERN NO. 2
SUBCLASS CHANGE	4	OCC. IN PATTERN NO. 1
SUBCLASS NORM	2	OCC. IN PATTERN NO. 1
SUBCLASS BODYFUNC	2	OCC. IN PATTERN NO. 1
SUBCLASS TEST	4	OCC. IN PATTERN NO. 1
SUBCLASS INDIC	22	OCC. IN PATTERN NO. 1
SUBCLASS DIAG	2	OCC. IN PATTERN NO. 1

Note: * marks location of the "new" word in the pattern

TABLE 12.7
Statistics for Experiment on Classifying New Words

Total new words	116	
No triples for word	59	
No matching environment found	15	
Matching environments found	42	
Words to which MATCH applied	42	100%
Correct class on list of candidates	31	74%
Correct class among top 3 candidates	24	52%

words. Clearly, the larger the number of environments for a given new word, the more possible it is to select a correct classification of that word. A second major source of error was the set of patterns we were working with. Because there was so little distributional data, we felt that we had to use it all, including environments that we had previously discarded as nondiscriminating, such as those generated by the operator *of*. Third, there was insufficient regularization. In the example, there should have been the additional pattern *HUMAN HAVE dyspnea,* because *episode* is a transparent word, which can be "looked through" to generate more discriminating patterns. It is possible that once we have refined the techniques of generating regularized patterns, this method may produce reasonable results on "new" words that appear in several environments. It may also be a way of focusing a query to the subject matter expert, who can pick the correct class out of a small list of possibilities.

A PORTABLE SEMANTIC SELECTION MECHANISM

As mentioned earlier, one of the major functions of the semantic component is to serve as a filter in producing reasonable meaning representations. This function is critical both in the disambiguation of syntactic constructions and in the choice of correct meaning for a word with multiple meanings. Both require domain-specific semantic information, as well as syntactic analysis.

The following example (taken from a medical sublanguage) illustrates how domain-specific semantic information is required to produce the correct analysis of a conjoined phrase interacting with a prepositional phrase:

N	P	N	and	N
Swelling	of	hands	and	feet
SIGN-SYMPT		BODY-PART		BODY-PART
Swelling	of	hands	and	fever
SIGN-SYMPT		BODY-PART		SIGN-SYMPT

In the first case, the correct reading has *hands* conjoined with *feet* inside the prepositional phrase. (The semantic class of each word is shown in capitals below the word). In the second case, the conjoining is between *swelling* and *fever,* so that the prepositional phrase does *not* include the conjunction (*swelling of hands and swelling of fever*). However, the choice of the correct meaning depends on applying the constraint that only nouns in "similar" classes can conjoin. Therefore, the BODY-PART noun *hand* can conjoin with the BODY-PART noun *feet,* but not with the SIGN-SYMPT noun *fever.* The proper analysis of these two phrases depends on a domain-independent constraint that draws on domain-specific knowledge (the semantic classes of the words) provided by the DIS (Hirschman, 1982).

The second example illustrates a different application of information from the Domain Information Schema. In these phrases, the set of allowable sublanguage patterns is used to disambiguate a sublanguage homograph, *discharge,* which can be either a medical action (MD-VERB) or a sign or symptom) SIGN-SYMPT).

hospital	*discharge*		
INST	MD-VERB	$\Longrightarrow$	INST MD-VERB
	SIGN-SYMPT	$\not\Longrightarrow$	INST SIGN-SYMPT
mucous	*discharge*		
BODY-PART	MD-VERB	$\not\Longrightarrow$	BODY-PART MD-VERB
	SIGN-SYMPT	$\Longrightarrow$	BODY-PART SIGN-SYMPT

In this case, the noun modifier disambiguates *discharge*: the noun-noun patterns INST MD-VERB and BODY-PART SIGN-SYMPT are allowed (are found in the noun-noun patterns of the medical Domain Information Schema), whereas the patterns INST SIGN-SYMPT (*? hospital fever*) and BODY-PART MD-VERB (*? mucous admission*) are not. The semantic mechanism requires that any modifier-host combination correspond to a pattern in the Domain Information Schema; it therefore rules out the incorrect meanings of *discharge* in these two examples.

The patterns that the selection mechanism draws on are contained in the DIS. They are displayed as lists of co-occurring semantic classes in a particular syntactic environment. For example, the list of semantic classes that can occur as arguments of the H-SHOW class (namely as subject, H-PT and as the object H-INDIC, H-RESULT, H-DIAG), would be represented in the Domain Information Schema as a member of the V-S-O list (the H- prefix indicates that the semantic classes come from the *hospital domain):*

LIST V-S-O =
H-SHOW:(H-PT:(H-INDIC, H-RESULT, H-DIAG)),

The semantic constraint mechanism uses the sublanguage patterns in the DIS to check the correctness of the syntactic analysis during parsing. The constraint mechanism takes as one input the DIS list of acceptable patterns for the sublanguage, and as its other input, the current parse tree. The mechanism works by comparing the pattern in the sentence being parsed to the data base of allowed patterns for the sublanguage. When a match occurs, the subclasses compatible with that known pattern are recorded for each sentence element participating in the pattern. This leaves a record in the output of the parser specifying how words have been disambiguated and how phrasal attributes have been assigned.

A selection mechanism drawing on the data in the DIS has proved very effective in eliminating incorrect parses. In an experiment performed on 216 sentences from a medical corpus, parsing with the selection mechanism reduced the number of incorrect analyses from 17% (37) without selection to 7% (15) with selection. Unfortunately the number of "no parse" results obtained increased, from 8% (17) without selection to 17% (36) with selection. The increase in "no parse" results was due largely to incomplete lists of sublanguage patterns; this caused certain correct combinations to be ruled out because they did not occur in the DIS. Nonetheless, this experiment demonstrated that the semantic constraint mechanism provides an important increase in the overall reliability of analysis.

GENERATION OF SUBLANGUAGE PATTERNS AND CIRCULARITY

The previous examples of disambiguation illustrate the role of regularized sublanguage semantic patterns in the semantic selection mechanism. Automatic generation of these patterns is an obvious way to provide an up-to-date list of patterns observed in the sublanguage and their associated frequencies. It is also a step towards automating generation of the Domain Information Schema.

Compared to the problems associated with automatic word classification, automatic pattern generation turned out to be relatively straightforward. By making a simple modification to the semantic constraint mechanism, it was possible to create a new component, the *pattern generator,* which operated on the completed syntactic analysis, including the information generated by the semantic mechanism. The semantic constraint mechanism locates the elements of a pattern in a sentence, and then checks these elements against the set of allowed patterns. The pattern generator uses the same procedure to locate the elements participating in the pattern, but just writes out the words and their associated classes onto a file. The pattern generation component operates on a complete parse, after the semantic component has finished its work of filtering out incorrect analyses, recording the correct reading for homographs, and marking phrasal attributes. This guarantees that the patterns generated by the pattern generator will correspond to allowable patterns for the domain.

The semantic component (and thus the pattern generator) also provides some regularization, because patterns are stated in terms of a limited set of canonical relations. For verbs, for example, there is only the V-S-O relation. This means that, when the semantic component encounters a passive construction, it automatically recognizes that the surface subject is the object of the active verb and applies the pattern accordingly. Thus, the record of semantic patterns produced by the pattern generator reflects a more regular set of relations than those found in the surface syntactic analysis.

For sublanguage homographs, if application of semantic constraints has disambiguated the word, this information will be recorded on the word. Therefore, when the pattern generator operates, it will record only the correct reading of the word.

The semantic component also computes phrasal attributes. When a word participating in a phrasal attribute construction is encountered by the semantic mechanism, the semantic class of the entire phrase is computed and attached to the head noun. Thus, when the pattern generation component applies, it uses this phrasal attribute for the semantic class, instead of the actual semantic class of the head word.

We have applied the pattern generator to a set of medical reports, as part of a joint SDC/NYU NSF research grant. Table 12.8 shows the form of output from the pattern generator. For each pattern generated, the first line gives the identifier of the sentence in which the pattern is found (e.g., 81A identifies the corpus, 1C.1.11 identifies the particular sentence). The second line gives the type of the pattern, in this case, a P-HOST-NSTGO pattern, consisting of a preposition, its host, and the prepositional argument. Following the pattern identifier (for debugging purposes) are the actual words occurring in the pattern (*OF EVIDENCE SYNOVITIS*). The pattern name is used to correlate the pattern information with the patterns in the Domain Information Schema. The remaining lines give the actual semantic pattern information. Each of these lines contains the word class (e.g., P for preposition), the actual word (*OF*) and its subclass. Where the word has no subclass, as in the case of *of,* the word itself appears. The pattern generator generates all patterns, whether or not they are used in the Domain Information Schema; another program takes the set of generated patterns and produces the corresponding Domain Information Schema.

In the second pattern in Table 12.8 (P-HOST-NSTGO IN SYNOVITIS REST), we see what happens with a pattern involving a transparent word such as *rest*. In the last line of the pattern, the word *REST* appears, but because *rest* is transparent, the associated class appears as H-AREA [H-PART], where H-AREA is the phrasal attribute (derived from the right adjunct, *joints*), and H-PART in brackets indicates the actual category of *rest*.

The automatic generation of sublanguage patterns is, of course, faced with a problem of circularity: in order to generate the patterns, the semantic component must have a correct parse; but in order to obtain the correct parse, the semantic mechanism needs the correct set of patterns. The present method relies on the correctness of the parse, which cannot be assured except by in-

TABLE 12.8
Automatically Generated Sublanguage Patterns

81A 1C. 1.11 NO EVIDENCE OF SYNOVITIS IN REST OF OTHER JOINTS EXAMINED.

* 81A 1C. 1.11			
P-HOST-NSTGO	OF	EVIDENCE	SYNOVITIS
P	OF	OF	
N	EVIDENCE	(H-EVID)	
N	SYNOVITIS	(H-INDIC)	
* 81A 1C. 1.11			
P-HOST-NSTGO	IN	SYNOVITIS	REST
P	IN	IN	
N	SYNOVITIS	(H-INDIC)	
N	REST	(H-AREA [H-PART])	
* 81A 1C. 1.11			
P-HOST-NSTGO	OF	REST	JOINTS
P	OF	OF	
N	REST	(H-PART)	
N	JOINTS	(H-AREA)	
*81A 1C. 1.11			
PRED-ARG1-ARG2	EXAMINED	()	JOINTS
VEN	EXAMINED	(H-VMD)	
N	()	(NIL)	
N	JOINTS	(H-AREA)	
*81A 1C. 1.11			
NVAR-APOS	JOINTS	OTHER	
N	JOINTS	(H-AREA)	
ADJ	OTHER	OTHER	
*81A 1C. 1.11			
NVAR-TPOS	EVIDENCE	NO	
N	EVIDENCE	(H-INDIC-[H-EVID])	
T	NO	NO	

spection. Nonetheless, our current work in automatic pattern generation will furnish us with valuable data concerning frequency of occurrence of identified sublanguage patterns.

   Boot-strapping is the obvious way to break out of the circularity described above. We can do this, for example, by choosing only those sentences that have a unique analysis and thus do not depend on semantic constraints to generate the correct analysis. If the sample corpus does not contain a sufficient number of such sentences, this may be a place where interaction with a subject matter expert could provide the necessary simple examples (perhaps by being asked to put together simple sentences using the most common nouns and verbs of the sublanguage). Alternatively, the subject matter expert might be asked to provide some very limited word classes for the sublanguage. If these classes contained the most frequently occurring words, this might be sufficient to identify the most common patterns, and this in turn could be used to parse more complex sentences. Another possibility is that for limited ambiguity, the subject matter expert could be queried, to disambiguate a set of sentences.

Given an initial corpus of correctly analyzed sentences, the emphasis then shifts to augmentation of existing classes and patterns. In this case, the technique of comparing new and existing patterns (outlined in the previous section) may provide an approach. Other possibilities include the use of a refined clustering algorithm based on predicate-subject-object relations (rather than taking these pair-wise, as originally done). Also clustering new words against occurrences of semantic classes (rather than just individual words) should improve the performance of the clustering. Again, it may be necessary to fall back on the subject matter expert, at least for the verification of the classification, or perhaps to choose between a few alternatives.

CONCLUSION

The preceding sections have sketched an approach to the automatic discovery of sublanguage structures. Over the past 10 years, we have developed a number of tools to help identify sublanguage word classes and patterns. These tools are useful in checking consistency of manually defined semantic classes and in maintaining Domain Information Schema used by the semantic selection component of the LSP English Grammar. However, there are major problems that must be overcome before these tools become useful in automating discovery of sublanguage structure.

One issue not raised so far is the identification of sublanguage "idioms" or frozen multiple-word expressions, such as, in medicine, *gram stain* or *acid fast bacteria*. These expressions should be treated as a single word for distributional purposes, rather than being analyzed into component parts. It is not clear how to detect these expressions automatically, although inclusion of such expressions as single entries in the lexicon can simplify and speed up processing significantly.

One of the major sources of "noise" in the statistical data gathered is the twin problems of transparency and zeroing. It is clear that this noise must be held to a minimum if the various statistical techniques are to work. If we could automatically identify zeroings and transparent constructions, then they could be regularized, to provide more reliable patterns.

If we could initially identify all transparent words independent of the sublanguage, we could first regularize these. We could then identify as *zeroing* all remaining patterns like those in lines 1–4 of Table 12.9. The zeroed material could then be filled in, at least in terms of the zeroed class, if

TABLE 12.9
Distribution of Zeroed and Transparent Elements

OPERATOR	ARGUMENT1	ARGUMENT 2
Zeroing		
1. show	film	metastasis
2. of	film	chest
3. show	chest	metastasis
regularize zeroing:		
4. show	[film]	metastasis
Transparency		
5. show	series	metastasis
6. of	series	films
7. show	films	metastasis
regularize transparency		
8. show	films	metastasis

not the actual word. If, however, we are not sure whether the patterns are due to zeroing or transparency, then we do not know how to regularize them: should we restore the missing element or "look through" the transparent element? Further research needs to be done to determine whether the transparent words are coherent classes of English belonging to the set of general semantic knowledge, or whether some transparent words are specific to particular sublanguages, in which case it may be necessary to query the subject matter expert to resolve the issue.

The problem of how to detect other phrasal attributes is even more difficult. What originally led to the discovery of these phrasal attributes was the fact that their distribution depended on the presence or absence of a particular set of modifiers. The techniques for distributional analysis that we have investigated to date have operated on a single syntactic relation. Description of phrasal attributes requires analysis of multiple syntactic relations (the pattern in which the phrase as a whole participates, together with the head-modifier pattern). This problem requires further exploration.

In general, this work on distributional analysis points towards a closer integration of syntactic and semantic processing. There is constant feedback between these two areas during determination of sublanguage structure. There should also be constant feedback between syntax and semantics during analysis of text. The two systems reinforce and constrain each other. This suggests a somewhat different approach than either strict syntax-directed processing (characteristic of the LSP system) or strict semantics-directed processing. This is an area of current research at SDC.

In conclusion, we are clearly still some years of research away from automatic (or even semiautomatic) discovery of sublanguage structures. Nonetheless, we are slowly closing in on solutions to these problems and, in the process, are enriching our understanding of the structure of sublanguages and our ability to process sublanguage discourse.

ACKNOWLEDGMENT

This research was supported in part by research grant MCS-8202397 from the National Science Foundation, Office of Mathematical and Computer Sciences.

REFERENCES

Chi, E. C., Sager, N., Tick, L. J., & Lyman, M. S. (1983). Relational data base modelling of free-text medical narrative. *Medical Informatics, 8,* 209–233.

Grishman, R., & Hirschman, L. (1978). Question-answering from natural language medical data bases. *Artificial Intelligence 11,* 25–43.

Grishman, R., Hirschman, L. & Friedman, C. (1982). Natural language interfaces using limited semantic information. *COLING-82 Abstracts: Proceedings of the Ninth International Conference on Computational Linguistics* (pp. 89–94), Amsterdam.

Grishman, R., Hirschman, L. & Friedman, C. (1983). *Isolating domain dependencies in natural language interfaces.* Conference on Applied Natural Language Processing. Santa Monica, CA.

Grishman, R., Nhan, N. T., Marsh, E., & Hirschman, L. (1984, July). Automated determination of sublanguage syntactic usage. *COLING-84 Abstracts: Proceedings of the Tenth International Conference on Computational Linguistics* (pp. 96–100), Stanford, CA.

Grosz, B. (1983). TEAM: A transportable natural-language interface system. *Proceedings of the Conference on Applied Natural Language Processing* (pp. 39–45), Santa Monica, CA.

Harris, L. R. (1978). The ROBOT system: Natural Language processing applied to data base query. *Proceedings of the 1978 Association for Computing Machinery Annual Conference* (pp. 165–172).

Harris, Z. S. (1947). *Structural linguistics.* Chicago: University of Chicago Press.

Harris, Z. S. (1968). *Mathematical structures of language.* New York: Wiley (Interscience).

Hirschman, L. (1982). Constraints on noun phrase conjunction: A domain-independent mechanism. In E. Hajicova (Ed.) *COLING-82 Abstracts: Proceedings of the Ninth International Conference on Computational Linguistics* (pp. 129–133). Prague.

Hirschman, L., Grishman, R., & Sager, N. (1975). Grammatically-based automatic word class formation. *Information Processing and Management, 11,* 39–57.

Hirschman, L., Grishman, R., & Sager, N. (1976). From text to structured information: Automatic processing of medical reports. *AFIPS Conference Proceedings* (pp. 267–275). Montvale, NJ: AFIPS Press.

Hirschman, L., & Sager, N. (1982). Automatic information formatting of a medical sublanguage. In R. Kittredge & J. Lehrberger (Eds.), *Sublanguage: Studies of language in restricted semantic domains.* Berlin: de Gruyter.

Marsh, E., & Sager, N. (1982). Analysis and processing of compact text. *COLING-82 Abstracts: Proceedings of the Ninth International Conference on Computational Linguistics* (pp. 201–208). Prague.

Sager, N. (1972). Syntactic formatting of scientific information. *AFIPS Conference Proceedings,* (pp. 791–800). Montvale, NJ: AFIPS Press.

Sager, N. (1978). Natural language information formatting: The automatic conversion of texts to a structured data base. In M. C. Yovits & M. Rubinoff (Eds.), *Advances in computers* (pp. 89–162). New York: Academic Press.

Sager, N. (1981). *Natural language information processing: A computer grammar of English and its applications.* Reading, MA: Addison-Wesley.

Sager, N., Hirschman, L., White, C., Foster, C., Wolff, S., Grad, R., & Fitzpatrick, E. (1980) *Research into methods for automatic classification and fact retrieval in science subfields.* String Program Report No. 13, Linguistic String Project, New York University.

Schank, R., & Abelson, R. (1977). *Scripts, plans, goals and understanding.* Hillsdale, NJ: Lawrence Erlbaum Associates.

Thompson, B., & Thompson, F. (1983). Introducing ASK, A simple knowledgeable system. *Proceedings of the Conference on Applied Natural Language Processing* (pp. 17–24), Santa Monica, CA.

Author Index

Numbers in *italics* denote pages with bibliographic information.

235

Subject Index

239